Marine Pollution

Marine Pollution

R. B. CLARK
Professor of Zoology
University of Newcastle upon Tyne

SECOND EDITION

CLARENDON PRESS · OXFORD
1989

Oxford University Press, Walton Street, Oxford OX2 6DP
Oxford New York Toronto
Delhi Bombay Calcutta Madras Karachi
Petaling Jaya Singapore Hong Kong Tokyo
Nairobi Dar es Salaam Cape Town
Melbourne Auckland
and associated companies in
Berlin Ibadan

Oxford is a trade mark of Oxford University Press

Published in the United States
by Oxford University Press, New York

© R. B. Clark 1986, 1989

First published 1986
Second edition 1989

British Library Cataloguing in Publication Data
Clark, R. B. (Robert Bernard), 1923–
Marine pollution.—2nd. ed.
1. Oceans Pollution
I. Title
363.7'394
ISBN 0–19–854263–1
ISBN 0–19–854265–8 (pbk)

Library of Congress Cataloging in Publication Data
Clark, R. B. (Robert Bernard). 1923–
Marine pollution/R. B. Clark.—2nd ed.
p.   cm.
Bibliography: p.   Includes index.
1. Marine pollution. I. Title.
GC1085.C5   1989   363.73'94—dc20
89–32125   CIP
ISBN 0–19–854263–1
ISBN 0–19–854265–8 (pbk)

Set by Cotswold Typesetting Ltd, Gloucester
Printed by Courier International Ltd, Tiptree, Essex

Preface to the second edition

It is now five years since the first edition of this book was written. Since then, there has been a great amount of investigation into the behaviour and impact of wastes discharged into the sea and a steady strengthening of controls over waste discharges. In spite of all this activity, there is now more uncertainty (or at least more dispute) among scientists and certainly more public concern about marine pollution.

The view that no wastes of any sort can safely be discharged into the sea—a few years ago regarded as an unreasonable and extreme position—is now much more widely accepted. There is certainly scope for reducing the volume and variety of wastes that are produced, but there will always be wastes to dispose of, and they have to be disposed of somewhere. If sea disposal is ruled out, the wastes will have to be disposed of on land. But disposal or treatment of wastes on land already attracts great opposition which would assuredly grow if all the waste at present reaching the sea was transferred to land.

A large volume of wastes, many of them noxious and all potentially damaging, will inevitably continue to be produced. Disposal or treatment of them will have an environmental cost, if not in the sea, then in fresh waters, on land, or in the atmosphere. There will also be a financial cost and experience has shown that if very high environmental standards are demanded, the financial cost can be very large indeed. Some balance will be struck, and present public attitudes suggest that it will be more towards protection of the marine environment than hitherto.

Since cleaning the seas will be expensive and will create unwelcome problems on land, it is important to have a clear view of what kinds of wastes reach the sea, what effect they have on the plants and animals living there, and, ultimately, what threats they pose, directly or indirectly, to human health and welfare. Priorities can be established and value judgements made only after the facts of each case have been dispassionately explored. Even then, it must be remembered that whatever conclusions are reached may later have to be revised in the light of new information or experience.

The second edition of this book illustrates the changes in knowledge and perspectives that have developed in the last five years. Estimates of the quantities of various kinds of wastes entering the sea have all been updated and in many cases the figures now accepted are encouragingly lower than those accepted a few years ago. This is partly because of a genuine reduction of discharges, but also is often because we now have more reliable estimates of inputs. However, for some materials the reverse is the case. There is now a better appreciation of the importance of inputs from the atmosphere. Estimates of their size are generally little better than informed guesses, but they are thought to be very large and may sometimes dwarf more obvious inputs.

There has also been a change of 'fashions' in marine pollution. What were seen as major problems a few years ago have now been superseded. Oil pollution, for some 20 years seen as the greatest threat in the marine environment, now has little prominence. Eutrophication, once a problem in some lakes but regarded as of minor importance in the sea, has recently become a major preoccupation in the North Sea and several other sea areas. Most other causes of pollution in the sea have advanced or receded in recent years, and no doubt there will be other changes in priorities in the next five years.

This book stemmed from an introductory course of lectures on marine pollution and deliberately tried to avoid making value judgements. The second edition follows the same plan and attempts to give the reader a clear view of current attitudes and controversies, the questions that have to be answered before any assessment can be made, and sufficient current factual information to allow the reader to form his or her own conclusions.

Newcastle upon Tyne   R.B.C.
December 1988

Acknowledgements

The author gratefully acknowledges the following sources of figures and data in this book.

Fig. 1.1. Meadows, D. H. *et al.*, *The limits to growth*, Earth Island Ltd, London (1972); **Fig. 2.4.** Royal Commission on Environmental Pollution, *Third Report*, HMSO, London (1972); **Fig. 2.5.** Royal Commission on Environmental Pollution, *Third Report*, HMSO, London (1972); **Fig. 2.7.** DSIR Wat. Pollut. Res. Pap., No. 11, *Effects of polluting discharges on the Thames estuary*, HMSO, London (1964); **Fig. 2.8.** Royal Commission on Environmental Pollution, *Third Report*, HMSO, London (1972); **Fig. 2.9.** (a), (c), (d) from: Mackay, D. W. *et al.*, *Mar. Pollut. Bull.*, 3, 7–10 (1972); (b) from: Steele, J. H. *et al.*, *Mar. Pollut. Bull.*, 4, 153–7 (1973); **Fig. 2.10.** Shelton, R. G. J., *Mar. Pollut. Bull.*, 2, 24–7 (1971); **Fig. 2.11.** (a), (c), (d) from: Pearce, J. B. *et al.*, *Mar. Pollut. Bull.*, 5, 132–3 (1974); (b) from: Pearce, J. B. and Young, J. S., *Mar. Pollut. Bull.*, 6, 101–5 (1975); **Fig. 2.12.** Steimle, F. W. and Sindermann, C. J., *Mar. Fish. Rev.*, 40, 17–26 (1978); **Fig. 2.13.** Gerlach, S. A., *Ber. Inst. Meeresk.*, 130, 1–87 (1984); **Fig. 2.14.** Justić, D., *Mar. Pollut. Bull.*, 18, 281–4 (1987); **Fig. 3.1.** *Shell Briefing Service*, No. 1, Shell Petroleum International, London, (1989); **Fig. 3.2.** Wardley-Smith, J., *The control of oil pollution on the sea and inland water*, Graham and Trotman, London (1976); **Fig. 3.3.** Sanders, P. F. and Tibbetts, P. J. C., *Phil. Trans. R. Soc. Lond.*, B316, 568 (1987); **Fig. 3.5.** Whittle, K. J. *et al.*, *Phil. Trans. R. Soc. Lond.*, B297, 193–218 (1982); **Fig. 3.6.** Wardley-Smith, J., *The control of oil pollution on the sea and inland waters*, Graham and Trotman, London (1976); **Fig. 3.7.** Wardley-Smith, J., *The control of oil pollution on the sea and inland waters*, Graham and Trotman, London (1976); **Fig. 3.8.** Wardley-Smith, J., *The control of oil pollution on the sea and inland water*, Graham and Trotman, London (1976); **Fig. 3.9.** North, W. J. *et al.*, *Symp. Pollut. mar. Micro-org. Prod. pétrol.*, 335–54, CIESMM, Monaco (1964) and Nelson-Smith, A., *Oil pollution and marine ecology*, Elek, London (1972); **Fig. 3.10.** Bourne, W. R. P., in *Marine pollution* (ed. R. Johnston), 403–502, Academic Press, London (1976); **Fig. 3.11.** Dicks, B. and Hartley, J. P., *Phil. Trans. R. Soc. Lond.*, B297, 285–307 (1982); **Fig. 3.12.** Dicks, B. and Hartley, J. P., *Phil. Trans. R. Soc. Lond.*, B297, 285–307 (1982); **Fig. 3.13.** Dicks, B. and Hartley, J. P., *Phil. Trans. R. Soc. Lond.*, B297, 285–307 (1982); **Fig. 3.14.** Kingston, P. F., *Phil. Trans. R. Soc. Lond.*, B316, 556 (1987); **Fig. 3.15.** Kingston, P. F., *Phil. Trans. R. Soc. Lond.*, B316, 549 (1987); **Fig. 4.1.** Brown, B. E., *Effects of heavy metals on the physiology of selected invertebrates*, unpublished thesis, University of London (1972); **Fig. 4.2.** Bryan, G. W., in *Marine pollution* (ed. R. Johnston), 185–302, Academic Press, London (1976); **Fig. 4.3.** Coombs, T. L. and George, S. G., in *Physiology and behaviour of marine organisms* (ed. D. S. McClusky and A. J. Berry), 179–87, Pergamon, Oxford (1977); **Fig. 4.4.** Bryan, G. W., in *Marine pollution* (ed. R. Johnston), 185–302, Academic Press, London (1976); **Fig. 4.5.** Sunila, I., *Ann. Zool. Fenn.*, 18, 213–23 (1981); **Fig. 4.6.** (a) from: Anderson, D. S., *Embryology and phylogeny in annelids and arthropods*, Pergamon, Oxford (1973); (b) from: Reish, D. J. *et al.*, *Mar. Pollut. Bull.*, 5, 125–6 (1974); **Fig. 5.1.** Cunningham, F. A. and

Tripp, M. R., *Mar. Biol.*, **31**, 311–19 (1975); **Fig. 5.2.** Ünlü, M. Y. *et al.*, in *Marine pollution and sea life* (ed. M. Ruivo), 292–5, Fishing News (Books) Ltd., London (1972); **Fig. 5.3.** Häkkinen, I. and Häsänen, E., *Ann. Zool. Fenn.*, **17**, 131–9 (1980); **Fig. 5.4.** Korringa, P., *Helgol. wiss. Meeresunters.*, **17**, 126–40 (1968); **Fig. 5.5.** Bryan, G. W. and Gibbs, P. E., *Occ. Pap. mar. biol. Ass. UK*, 2 (1983); **Fig. 5.6.** Bryan, G. W., in *Marine pollution* (ed. R. Johnston), 185–302, Academic Press, London (1976); **Fig. 5.7.** Murozumi, M. *et al.*, *Geochim. Cosmochim. Acta*, **33**, 1247–94 (1969); **Fig. 5.8.** Lee, J. A. and Tallis, J. H., *Nature, Lond.*, **245**, 216–8 (1973); **Fig. 5.9.** Gerlach, S. A., *Marine pollution: diagnosis and therapy*, Springer, Heidelburg (1981); **Fig. 6.2.** Smokler, P. E. *et al.*, *Mar. Pollut. Bull.*, **10**, 331–4 (1979); **Fig. 6.3.** Halcrow, W. *et al.*, *Mar. pollut. Bull.*, **5**, 134–6 (1974); **Fig. 6.4.** Goerke, H. *et al.*, *Mar. Pollut. Bull.*, **10**, 127–33 (1979); **Fig. 6.5.** Ernst, W. and Georke, H., *Mar. Biol.*, **24**, 287–304 (1974); **Fig. 6.6.** Mellanby, K., *Pesticides and pollution*, Collins, London (1967); **Fig. 6.7.** Patin, S. L., *Pollution and the biological resources of the oceans*, Butterworth, London (1982); **Fig. 6.8.** Ernst, W., *Helgol. Meeresunters.*, **33**, 301–12 (1980); **Fig. 6.9.** Bonner, W. N. and Hickling, G., *Trans. nat. Hist. Soc. Northumbria*, **42**, 65–84 (1974); **Fig. 7.2.** Hodge, V, F. *et al.*, *Proc. Symp. Radioactive Contamination of the Marine Environment*, 263–76, IAEA, Vienna (1973); **Fig. 7.3.** Kautsky, W., *Umschau*, **77**, 672–3 (1973); **Fig. 7.4.** Radioactive Waste Management Committee, *Fourth Annual Report*, HMSO, London (1983), with additional data from *MAFF Aquatic Environment Monitoring Report*, **16–19** (1985–8); **Fig. 7.5.** Hunt, G. J., *Aquatic Environment Monitoring Report*, **19**, Ministry of Agriculture, Fisheries and Food, Lowestoft (1988); **Fig. 7.6.** Fowler, S. W. and Gaury, J. C., *Nature, Lond.*, **266**, 827 (1977) and Pentreath, R. J., *Nuclear power: man and the environment*, Taylor and Francis, London (1980); **Fig. 7.7.** Woodhead, D. S., *Helgol. Meeresunters.*, **33**, 122–37 (1980); **Fig. 8.1.** Rosenberg, R., *Mar. Pollut. Bull.*, **8**, 102–4 (1977); **Fig. 8.2.** Anon., *Mar. Pollut. Bull.*, **1**, 115 (1970); **Fig. 8.3.** (a) from: Portmann, J. E., *J. mar. biol. Ass. UK*, **50**, 577–91 (1970); (b), (c) from: Howell, B. R. and Shelton, R. G. J., *J. mar biol. Ass. U.K.*, **50**, 593–607 (1970); **Fig. 8.4.** Dixon, T. R. and Dixon, T. J., *Mar. Pollut. Bull.*, **10**, 352–7 (1979); **Fig. 8.5.** Thorhaug, A., *Mar. Pollut. Bull.*, **9**, 191–7 (1978); **Fig. 8.6.** Langford, T. E., *Electricity generation and the ecology of natural waters*, University of Liverpool Press, Liverpool (1983); **Fig. 9.1.** Korringa, P., *Helgol. wiss. Meeresunters.*, **17**, 126–40 (1968); **Fig. 9.2.** (a) Royal Commission on Environmental Pollution, *Tenth Report*, HMSO, London (1984); ((b)–(e) based on data in *Quality Status of the North Sea*, Dept of Environment (1987); **Fig. 9.3.** Heimer, R., *Ambio*, **6**, 313–16 (1977); **Fig. 9.4.** Le Lourd, P., *Ambio*, **6**, 317–19 (1977); **Fig. 9.6.** Fonselius, S., *Mar. Pollut. Bull.*, **12**, 187–94 (1981); **Fig. 9.7.** Andersin, A. B., *Kieler Meeresforsch.*, Suppl. **4**, 23–52 (1978); **Fig. 9.8.** Thorhaug, A., *Ambio*, **10**, 295–8 (1981); **Fig. 9.9.** Beelhuis, J. V., *Ambio*, **10**, 325–31 (1981); **Fig. 9.10.** Adapted from: Zenkevich, L. A., *Treatise on marine ecology and paleoecology*, **1**, 891–916, Geol. Soc. Am., New York (1957); **Fig. 10.1.** Mann, K. H., *Helgol. wiss. Meeresunters.*, **30**, 445–67 (1977); **Fig. 10.2.** Lewis, J. R., *Phil. Trans. R. Soc. Lond.*, **B297**, 257–67 (1982); **Fig. 10.3.** Lewis, J. R., in *Marine pollution and sea life* (ed. M. Ruivo), 401–4, Fishing News (Books) Ltd., London (1972); **Fig. 10.4.** Bowman, R. S. and Lewis, J. R., *J. mar. biol. Ass. U.K.*, **57**, 793–815 (1977); **Fig. 10.5.** Buchanan, J. B. *et al.*, *J. mar. biol. Ass. UK*, **58**, 191–209 (1978); **Fig. 10.6.** Glover, R. S. *et al.*, in *Marine pollution and sea life* (ed. M. Ruivo), 439–45, Fishing News (Books) Ltd., London (1972); **Fig. 10.7.** Jones, R., *Phil. Trans. R. Soc. Lond.*, **B297**, 353–68 (1982); **Fig. 10.8.** Jones, R., *Phil. Trans. R. Soc. Lond.*, **B297**, 353–68 (1982); **Fig. 10.9.** Battaglia, B., *Helgol. Meeresunters.*, **33**, 587–95 (1980); **Fig. 10.10.** Mann, K. H., *Mar. Biol.*, **14**, 119–209 (1972).

Table 3.1. Steering Committee for the Petroleum in the Marine Environment Update, *Oil in the sea: inputs, fates and effects*, National Academy Press, Washington, DC (1985); **Table 3.2.** *Our industry petroleum*, BP Ltd., London (1977); **Table 3.3.** Dicks, B. and Hartley, J. P., *Phil. Trans. R. Soc. Lond.*, **B297**, 285–307 (1982); **Table 3.4.** Royal Commission on Environmental Pollution, *Eighth Report*, HMSO, London (1981); **Fig. 3.5.** Royal Commission on Environmental Pollution, *Eighth Report*, HMSO, London (1981); **Table 4.1.** Bryan, G. W., in *Marine Pollution* (ed. R. Johnston), 185–230, Academic Press, London (1976); **Table 4.2.** White, H. H. and Champ, M. A., in *Symp. Hazardous and Industrial Solid Waste Testing* (ed. R. A. Conway and W. P. Gulledge), 299–312, Amer. Soc. Testing and Materials, Philadelphia (1983); **Table 4.3.** Gray, J. S. and Ventilla, R. J., *Ambio*, **2**, 118–211 (1973); **Table 4.4.** Bryan, G. W., in *Marine Pollution* (ed. R. Johnston), 185–230, Academic Press, London (1976); **Table 5.1.** Scientific and Technical Working Group, *Quality status of the North Sea: summary*, Department of the Environment, London (1987); **Table 5.2.** Pacyna, J. M., in *Toxic metals in the atmosphere* (ed. J. O. Nriagu and C. I. Davidson), 33–52, Wiley Interscience, London (1986); **Table 5.3.** Buat-Ménard, P., in *The role of air–sea interchange in geochemical cycling* (ed. P. Buat-Ménard), 477–496, Reidel, Dordrecht (1986); **Table 5.4.** Keckes, S. and Miettinen, J. K., in *Marine pollution and sea life* (ed. M. Ruivo), 276–89, Fishing News (Books) Ltd., London (1972); **Table 5.5.** Keckes, S. and Miettinen, J. K., in *Marine pollution and sea life* (ed. M. Ruivo), 276–89, Fishing News (Books) Ltd., London (1972); **Table 5.6.** Boney, A. D. *et al.*, *Biochem. Pharmacol.*, **2**, 37–49 (1959); **Table 5.7.** Häkkinen, I. and Häsänen, E., *Ann. Zool. Fenn.*, **17**, 131–9 (1980); **Table 6.1.** Royal Commission on Environmental Pollution, *Tenth Report*, HMSO, London (1984); **Table 6.2.** House of Lords Select Committee on European Communities, *Session 1987–88, 17th Report*, HMSO, London (1988); **Table 6.3.** Atlas, E. L. and Giam, C. S., *Science*, **211**, 163–5 (1981); **Table 6.4.** Riseborough, R. W. *et al.*, *Mar. Pollut. Bull.*, **7**, 225–8 (1976); **Table 6.5.** Butler, P. A., in *Marine pollution and sea life* (ed. M. Ruivo), 262–6, Fishing News (Books) Ltd., London (1972); **Table 6.6.** Smokler, P. E. *et al.*, *Mar. Pollut. Bull.*, **10**, 331–4 (1979); **Table 7.1.** International Atomic Energy Authority, *Technical Reports Series*, **172**, IAEA, Vienna (1976) units adjusted; **Table 7.2.** Woodhead, D. S., *Proc. Symp. Radioactive Contamination in the Marine Environment*, 455–525, IAEA, Vienna (1976) units adjusted; **Table 7.3.** *Report of the Independent Review of Disposal of Radioactive Waste in the Northeast Atlantic*, HMSO, London (1984) units adjusted; **Table 7.4.** International Atomic Energy Authority, *Technical Report Series*, **172**, IAEA, Vienna (1976) units adjusted; **Table 7.5.** Woodhead, D. S., in *Marine Ecology* (ed. O. Kinne) **5**, 1112–287, Wiley, London (1984) units adjusted; **Table 8.1.** Water Research Centre, *Technical Report*, **TR 20** (1984) from Oslo Commission *Eighth Annual Report* (1984); **Table 8.2.** Dixon, T. R. and Dixon, T. J., *Mar. Pollut. Bull.*, **10**, 352–7 (1979); **Table 9.1.** Scientific and Technical Working Group, *Quality status of the North Sea: summary*, Department of the Environment, London (1987); **Table 9.2.** Kullenberg, G., in *The role of the oceans as a waste disposal option* (ed. G. Kullenberg), 388, Riedel, Dordrecht (1986); **Table 9.3.** Brigmann, L., *Mar. Pollut. Bull.*, **12**, 214–18 (1981); **Table 9.4.** Thorhaug, A., *Ambio*, **10**, 295–8 (1981).

Contents

1
What is pollution?

Some questions

Everyone knows what pollution is and that it is a Bad Thing, but for a scientific examination of marine, or any other sort of pollution, value judgements of this kind have to be quantified. In what way bad? How bad? Bad for whom?

To answer these questions, we must consider:

(1) what kind of materials are discharged into seas or estuaries, or otherwise get there as a result of human activities;

(2) what effect these additions to the sea have on the marine or estuarine environment and the plants and animals living there;

(3) what implications these effects have for human health, food resources, commercial interests, amenities, wildlife conservation, or ecosystems in general;

(4) what is being done, can be done, or should be done to reduce or remove the damaging or undesirable effects of these additions to the marine environment;

(5) what would be the consequences of not releasing these materials to the sea and would such consequences be better or worse than the existing situation.

A quantitative, step-by-step approach to this subject is clearly required, and the rest of this book is concerned with answering these questions in quantitative terms and with assessing the importance of various kinds of pollution impact. Before embarking on that, it is necessary to look at what types of materials enter the sea as a result of human activities.

Categories of additions

Degradable wastes

By far the greatest volume of discharge into coastal waters and estuaries is composed of organic material which is subject to bacterial attack. Essentially, this is an oxidative process and ultimately reduces organic compounds to stable inorganic compounds such as CO_2 (carbon dioxide), H_2O (water), and NH_3 (ammonia).

Wastes included under this heading are:

- a large part of urban sewage;
- agricultural wastes (now in substantial quantities where factory farming is practised);
- food processing wastes from slaughter houses, freezer plants, pulp from sugar beet factories, etc.;
- brewing and distillery wastes;
- paper pulp mill wastes which include much wood fibre;
- chemical industry wastes, including a great variety of large molecules which are relatively unstable and readily broken down;
- oil spillages.

In principle, such degradable wastes are no different from plant and animal remains which are subject to bacterial decay. Since bacteria are an important base of many food chains in the sea, the addition of organic matter represents an enrichment of the ecosystem, comparable to adding stable manure as a fertilizer in the garden.

If the rate of input exceeds the rate of bacterial degradation, organic materials **accumulate**. The rate of bacterial action depends on temperature, oxygen availability, and other factors; if these become limiting, the rate of bacterial action falls and the capacity of the waters to receive organic wastes without accumulation is much reduced. If the input is large, there is intense bacterial activity until the oxidative processes of degradation outrun the supply of oxygen dissolved in the water, leading to **deoxygenation**. In these circumstances, further degradation depends on the activity of **anaerobic** bacteria, which is slow and yields end-products such as hydrogen sulphide and methane.

Accumulation of organic materials and deoxygenation of the water both have a strong impact on the flora and fauna, and at very low oxygen levels most plants and animals are excluded. Thus, if the input of organic wastes is within the capacity of the receiving waters—which is related to temperature, oxygen availability, water currents, etc.—it will result in enrichment, of benefit chiefly to plants in the first instance. If the capacity of the receiving waters is exceeded, the accumulation of organic material and the development of anoxic conditions results in impoverishment of the fauna and flora.

Fertilizers

Agricultural fertilizers may have a similar effect to organic wastes. Nitrates and phosphates are leached from arable land and carried to the sea by rivers. In the sea, the fertilizers enhance phytoplankton production, sometimes to the extent that the accumulation of dead plant-remains on the seabed produces anoxic conditions.

Dissipating wastes

A number of industrial discharges into the sea and estuaries rapidly lose their damaging properties after they enter the water. Any effects they may have are therefore confined to the area immediately around the point of discharge, though the extent of that area depends on the rate of the discharge, water currents, etc.

- *Heat.* This comes principally from the cooling water from coastal power stations and factories, although some other industrial effluents may be heated. Commonly the discharge is about 10 °C above the temperature of the receiving water. Dissipation of the heat depends chiefly on mixing of the hot with cold water. In temperate seas, heated discharges are generally of little consequence, but in tropical seas where summer temperatures are already near the thermal death point of many organisms, the increase in temperature can cause substantial losses.
- *Acids and alkalis.* Seawater has a large buffering capacity and the effect of such discharges is extremely localized.
- *Cyanide.* This comes principally from metallurgical industries. Cyanide rapidly dissociates in seawater and has little effect except in the immediate neighbourhood of the outfall.

Particulates

Inert particulate matter may clog the feeding and respiratory structures of animals, may reduce plant photosynthesis by reducing light penetration, and when it settles on the bottom, may smother animals and change the nature of the seabed. Such materials include;

- dredging spoil;
- powdered ash (fly ash) from coal-fired power stations;
- china clay waste;
- colliery waste;
- clay from gravel extraction. Gravel dredged from the seabed contains a proportion of clay and silt which is washed out in the course of extraction and settles back on the seabed.

A variety of man-made plastics which are also inert, reach the sea. These include polystyrene spherules, polythene containers, plastic sheeting, nylon ropes, nets, and other fishing gear.

Conservative wastes

Some materials are not subject to bacterial attack and are not dissipated, but are reactive in various ways with plants and animals, sometimes with harmful effects. The principal categories of such wastes are:

- heavy metals (mercury, lead, copper, zinc, etc.);

- halogenated hydrocarbons (DDT and other chlorinated hydrocarbon pesticides, polychlorinated biphenyls (PCBs) etc.);
- radioactivity.

Nature of inputs

Although it is convenient to consider materials added to the sea as being in the above categories because of their shared properties and the similarity of the effects they have, it must be remembered that actual inputs to the sea are rarely so simple in their constitution.

- Power station effluent is chiefly hot water, but also contains some chlorine injected into the water at the intake to discourage marine organisms settling in the cooling system and reducing its efficiency or blocking it. Also, small amounts of metals are leached from the cooling system and turbines.
- Urban sewage is principally organic but also contains considerable amounts of metals, oils and greases, detergents, and industrial wastes (since most industrial plants use the same sewers as domestic users).

Similar complexity may exist in particular geographical sites. An industrialized estuary has a multiplicity of inputs from surrounding industry, often in great variety, as well as from the urban population. In addition the estuary receives whatever is carried by the river flowing into it and this may include pesticides and other products of agricultural activity in the entire drainage system.

Sources of inputs

Direct outfalls

The most obvious inputs of material to the sea are through pipes discharging directly into it.

Estuaries.   Historically, most ports grew up on estuaries and became centres of population and industry. The urban and industrial wastes were discharged directly into the estuary without treatment. With the growth of population and industry, the major industrial estuaries (Thames, Tees, Tyne, Mersey, Clyde) became foul, stinking, and lifeless towards the end of the last century.

Coastal towns.   Most coastal towns have little industry but in the past, untreated municipal waste and sewage was discharged directly into the sea by numerous outfalls, sometimes at the high-water mark and rarely far below low water. This resulted in the fouling of local beaches, and many holiday resorts have extended the outfalls further offshore to reduce this or have introduced sewage treatment.

Coastal industry. With increasing pressure to conserve rivers and lakes for drinking water supplies, new industry with demands for large volumes of water for cooling or effluent disposal have tended to be sited on the coast. Nuclear power stations in Britain are nearly all sited on the coast.

River inputs

Rivers flow via their estuaries to the sea and potential pollutants reach rivers over the entire drainage area.

- Organic wastes are subject to bacterial attack in transit and, depending on the distance of major inputs from the river mouth, the organic load entering the sea from upstream is correspondingly reduced and may be negligible.
- Pesticides and fertilizers from agriculture and forestry are washed off the land by rain, enter water courses, and eventually reach the sea.
- Petroleum and oils washed from roads by rain enter the sewage system as a rule, but storm water overflows carry these materials into rivers and to the sea.

All land-based materials washed off by rainfall and entering rivers and streams contribute inputs to the sea, and in aggregate they may form a very large contribution.

Shipping

Ships carry many toxic substances on the course of trade: oil, liquified natural gas, pesticides, industrial chemicals, etc. Shipwrecks and other accidents at sea may release these substances, and the very large size of some vessels—crude oil carriers of up to 350 000 tons, for instance—means that when accidents do occur, the consequences may be very damaging. Spectacular oil tanker wrecks are an obvious example.

Other shipping is responsible for less dramatic inputs of materials to the sea, both as a result of accidents and in the course of routine operations. A ship does not have to be wrecked and become a total loss for this to happen. In all but the worst accidents much of the cargo is salvaged, but particularly noxious or dangerous materials are frequently carried as deck cargo as a safety precaution for the ship, and these may be lost overboard in severe storms.

In the course of routine operations, ships discharge oily ballast water and bilge water (not always legally), and cargo tank washings; they also discard much litter, of which plastics probably constitute the worst nuisance.

Offshore inputs

A variety of material is dumped at sea in designated dumping grounds.

- *Dredging spoil*. Shipping channels in estuaries and at the entrance to ports may require frequent dredging to keep them open and the dredged material is barged out to sea and dumped. This dredging spoil, particularly from industrialized estuaries, may contain appreciable quantities of heavy metals and other contaminants which are then transferred to the dumping grounds.
- *Sewage sludge*. Sludge from sewage treatment plants is dumped at sea in considerable quantities by Britain; less so by other countries. It has a high organic content but is contaminated with heavy metals, oils and greases, and many other substances.
- *Other wastes*. Fly ash from power stations and colliery waste are dumped at sea, as are various dangerous materials such as radioactive waste and ammunition.
- *Offshore industrial activities*. These result in a variety of inputs or disturbances in the sea: offshore oil exploration and extraction; gravel extraction; and in the future, manganese nodule extraction.

Atmospheric inputs

Discharges to the atmosphere are returned to land or the sea in rain or, if particulate, as fall-out. Gaseous wastes dissolve directly in the sea at the sea surface. Such inputs are, of course, on a regional or even global scale rather than local. There are too many unknown factors for atmospheric inputs to the sea to be estimated precisely, but they are generally supposed to be very large and to represent major contributions.

The total global input of lead to the sea from natural and man-made sources is estimated to be about 400 000 t yr^{-1}. Of this about half is derived from vehicle exhausts containing leaded-petrol additives which reach the atmospheric and are then rained out.

The total global input of mercury to the sea from volcanic activity and weathering of mercury-bearing ores is at least 5000 t yr^{-1} but may be as high as 25 000 t. A further 5000 t yr^{-1} are added from the use of mercury and mercurial compounds in industry and agriculture. An additional 3000 t are derived from burning fossil fuels, principally coal. This contains only minute amounts of mercury but is burned in such quantity that, in total, it makes a major contribution to mercury in the sea.

Such global figures are estimates only and cannot be regarded as accurate measurements, but it is clear that materials discharged to the atmosphere can make unexpectedly large contributions to the budget of these contaminants in the sea.

These two examples also reveal that there is often a substantial natural input of materials which in some circumstances prove to be pollutants.

Defining pollution

Some of the substances reaching the sea (e.g. halogenated hydrocarbons or plastics) are man-made and do not occur in nature, but most of the substances discussed so far exist naturally in the sea:

- organic material subject to bacterial degradation;
- metals in the run-off from metalliferous deposits;
- oil from oil deposits seeps into the sea in the Gulf of Mexico, on the Californian coast, and at Kimmeridge on the Dorset coast;
- particulate material from coastal erosion, including on the north-east coast of England, coal from seams exposed in coastal cliffs;
- hot water from geothermal springs around Iceland, in the Galapagos trench, and elsewhere;
- radioactivity on the coast of Brazil and south-west India.

Are all inputs, both natural and man-made, to be regarded as polluting? Or are only man-made inputs polluting, even though natural inputs of the same substances may be much greater? What, in fact, constitutes pollution?

The view taken by most pollution scientists, and that recommended by such international advisory bodies as the United Nations Group of Experts on the Scientific Aspects of Marine Pollution (GESAMP) or the International Council for the Exploration of the Sea (ICES), is that a distinction must be made between contamination and pollution.

Contamination is the presence of elevated concentrations of substances in the water, sediments or organisms, i.e. concentrations that are above the natural background level for the area and for the organism.

Pollution is the introduction by man, directly or indirectly, of substances or energy to the marine environment resulting in deleterious effects such as harm to living resources; hazards to human health; hindrance of marine activities including fishing; impairment of the quality for use of seawater; and reduction of amenities.

In other words, contamination may provide a warning signal, but it does not constitute pollution unless, first, it is caused by human activities and, second, it has some damaging effect. It should be noted, too, that even if laboratory studies show that a contaminant is toxic to particular marine organisms, this may provide another—possibly stronger—warning signal but does not necessarily prove that the contaminant has harmful effects in the natural environment.

From a strictly biological point of view, even if toxic contaminants do cause the death of some plants and animals in the natural environment, this is usually of little consequence unless the deaths result in a change in the population as a whole. Most marine animals reproduce on a colossal scale and the overwhelming majority of offspring die prematurely in the natural course of events. Mortality from toxic contaminants may be totally insignificant beside these natural losses and may have no effect on the population. Where this is the case, it can hardly be claimed that the contamination has a deleterious or harmful effect.

It follows from these considerations that whereas there is no doubt about the existence of pollution when the damage is severe, there is often considerable difficulty in identifying the damage caused by low levels of contamination. Pollution is by no means as clear cut as might appear at first sight.

Priorities

It will be noticed that in the definition of pollution, the examples quoted of its deleterious effects all relate to human interests in the sea. Pollution is, in practical terms, an example of one set of human interests:

- the use of leaded petrol in cars,
- burning coal,
- transporting oil,
- generating electricity,
- disposing of waste products,

coming into conflict with other human interests:

- human health,
- commercial fisheries,
- amenities, tourism, recreation, aesthetic values,
- scientific interest.

Generally, we would consider transport, the provision of electricity, and many vital industrial processes to be as important as preserving a fish supply or providing tourist facilities. So we are really concerned with striking the most favourable balance (for humans) between these conflicting interests. In other words, we are concerned with priorities.

As a rule, a threat to human health is given the highest priority for abatement or control. There are too many examples to the contrary to claim that it is given overriding priority over all other considerations, but it is certainly an issue which is given the greatest importance.

When only two interests conflict and both are commercial, it is fairly easy to decide the priorities. When the oil tanker *Torrey Canyon* was wrecked off the Cornish coast in 1967 and deposited a large amount of oil on the beaches, a decision had to be taken whether or not to treat the spilled oil with chemical dispersants which at that time were very toxic to marine organisms. If the oil was cleaned up by this means there was a serious risk of great damage to the local fishing industry, but to leave the oil untreated would have been to the great detriment of the tourist industry. The fishing industry was then worth £6 million per year, but the tourist industry £60 million per year, and on that basis the decision was taken to clean the beaches. In the event, fears about damage to the fishing industry happily proved to be unfounded and it was not noticeably affected.

Generally the issues are not so clear cut and the decisions are more difficult. A more sophisticated approach is needed and, for this, a great deal of information is required:

- What is the level of contamination in the area we are interested in?
- What form does it take?
- Where does it come from?
- What happens to it?
- What does it do to the plants and animals there?
- If plants and animals are affected, does it matter?
- To whom does it matter? What other interest is affected?
- How much does it matter to them?
- If it does matter, what can we do about it?
- What do we do with the polluting material if it is not put in the sea?
- Would the alternative be better or worse than putting it in the sea?
- How much would it cost?

Cost of pollution abatement

A number of these questions introduce matters which are economic or political and are outside the realm of pure science. But while it is unusual for scientists to have to consider such vulgar matters as cash, this is crucial to pollution abatement, for the costs escalate rapidly.

The cost of designing a new coal-fired power station to remove particulates from the smoke emitted is as follows:

90% extraction of particulates adds 10% to the capital cost;
95% extraction adds 20–30%;
99% extraction doubles the capital cost of the power station.

A sugar beet processing plant handling 2700 tons per day discharges an effluent high in organic wastes. The organic load is measured in BOD (Biochemical Oxygen Demand, see p. 12) and can be reduced by treating the waste before discharge, but at a cost (see Fig. 1.1):

30% reduction costs less than $1 per lb of BOD;
65% reduction costs $20 per lb of BOD;
95% reduction costs over $60 per lb of BOD.

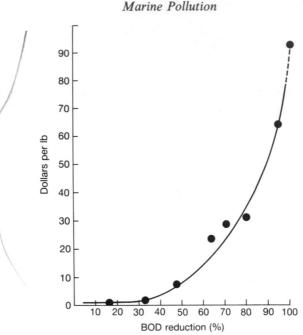

Fig. 1.1. Cost of reducing the organic content (as measured by BOD) of the wastes from a sugar beet factory.

Pollution abatement can clearly become extremely expensive, so the questions to be answered are:

- How clean do you want to be?
- How clean can you *afford* to be?

Or in more practical terms, what is the relationship between the cost of reducing the pollution and the benefit that would come from it.

Many of the questions that have been posed cannot be answered with great precision, but they do point to the practical problems and the sort of information which needs to be provided by scientific investigations and which will give a firmer basis for the practical decisions that have to be made.

2

Oxygen-demanding wastes

The amount of oxygen dissolved in the water has a profound effect on the plants and animals living in it. Wastes which directly or indirectly affect the oxygen concentration are therefore of great importance.

Oxygen demand

By far the greatest volume of waste discharged to watercourses, estuaries and the sea is sewage which is primarily organic in nature and subject to bacterial decay. Bacterial degradation results in the oxidation of organic molecules to stable inorganic compounds. Aerobic bacteria make use of oxygen dissolved in the water to achieve this.

$$C_6H_{12}O_6 + 6O_2 \rightarrow 6H_2O + 6CO_2$$
(glucose) (oxygen) (water) (carbon dioxide)

As a result of this bacterial activity, the oxygen concentration in the water is reduced and this is made good by the uptake of atmospheric oxygen. However, oxygen diffuses only slowly through water and there is a time-lag before the oxygen used by bacterial activity is replenished. When the oxygen concentration falls below about 1.5 mg l^{-1}, the rate of aerobic oxidation is reduced. Anaerobic bacteria can oxidize organic molecules without the use of oxygen, but the end-products include compounds such as H_2S (hydrogen sulphide), NH_3 (ammonia) and CH_4 (methane) which are foul-smelling and toxic to many organisms, and the process is much slower than aerobic degradation. There is therefore the likelihood of an accumulation of wastes in addition to the production of noxious end-products.

Some inorganic wastes become oxidized in water without the intervention of bacteria, and these, too, deplete the water of oxygen.

When planning the discharge of any waste to water, it is important to know its total oxygen demand to avoid undesirable environmental consequences. The chemical composition of nearly all organic wastes is extremely complicated and different constituents require different amounts of oxygen to achieve complete oxidation. It is impracticable to analyse a waste to discover its exact mix and indirect methods are used to measure the effluent load it represents by measuring the overall oxygen demand for complete degradation.

Chemical Oxygen Demand (COD)

This is measured by adding an oxidant such as potassium permanganate ($KMNO_4$) or potassium dichromate ($K_2Cr_2O_7$) with sulphuric acid (H_2SO_4) to a sample of the effluent. The sample is then titrated after a standard interval to determine the amount of oxidant remaining. From this, the total amount of oxidizable material can be calculated.

Biochemical Oxygen Demand (BOD)

For organic wastes, it is more usual to measure the oxygen concentration in a sample before and after bacterial digestion for a standard time (e.g. 3 days, 5 days), recorded as BOD_3 or BOD_5. It may be necessary to add bacteria and nitrate if these are deficient in the initial sample. This gives a direct measure of the oxygen utilization in bacterial degradation of the sample.

The dilution factor

If water is saturated with oxygen, there is sufficient to oxidize a BOD of about 8.0–8.5 mg l^{-1}, but the BOD of organic effluents is usually much greater than this. Urban sewage commonly has a BOD of 500 mg l^{-1}; spilled beer has a BOD of 70 000 mg l^{-1}. It is therefore necessary to find some way of diluting the effluent to achieve a BOD of about 8 mg l^{-1}; hence the old adage of sanitary engineers: 'The solution to pollution is dilution'.

The common practice is to discharge the effluent into a large volume of water, preferably a river or the sea, where water movement produces mixing and achieves the necessary dilution. If the effluent is discharged into a river (Fig. 2.1), it is swept downstream and mixes with the river water in a **mixing zone**. The concentration of effluent is high near the outfall but progressively reduced downstream. The dilution achieved depends upon the rate of flow of the river, its organic load, and the rate of input of the effluent and its oxygen demand.

$$\text{River flow} \quad 8 \text{ m}^3 \text{ s}^{-1} \text{ with BOD } 2 \text{ mg l}^{-1}$$
$$\text{Effluent input} \quad 1 \text{ m}^3 \text{ s}^{-1} \text{ with BOD } 20 \text{ mg l}^{-1}$$

$$\text{BOD after mixing} = \frac{\text{total BOD}}{\text{total volume}} = \frac{(8 \times 2) + (1 \times 20)}{8 + 1} = 4$$

This achieves the necessary dilution.

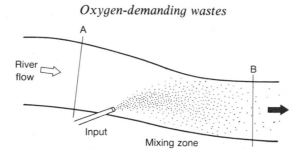

Fig. 2.1. Discharge of an organic effluent into a river and its mixing zone. Position A upstream of the input and position B downstream of the mixing zone are explained in the text.

Oxygen budget

Bacterial activity consumes oxygen. Figure 2.2 shows the effect of an organic input on the dissolved oxygen in the water, either with time following a single input to a static body of water, or with distance downstream from a continuous input to flowing water.

As the bacteria multiply, oxygen consumption increases to a peak and then declines as the organic matter is oxidized. This extracts oxygen from the water column and when the dissolved oxygen falls below saturation, oxygen is taken up from the atmosphere; the greater the oxygen depletion of the water, the greater the rate of oxygen uptake. Uptake lags behind utilization because of the time taken for oxygen diffusion through the water. At a **critical point**, the rate of re-aeration overtakes the rate of oxygen utilization and this corresponds with the minimum concentration of dissolved oxygen in the water.

Thus, the effect of an organic input is to produce an **oxygen sag**, corresponding to the dissolved oxygen in the receiving water, less bacterial respiration, plus re-aeration. The oxygen sag may be trivial, but if the receiving waters are seriously overloaded with organic material it may be sufficient to produce anoxic conditions.

Fluctuations in dissolved oxygen

In practice, the situation is more complicated than this, because the organic input leads to enrichment and the growth of phytoplankton which, because of its photosynthetic activity, provides a supplementary source of oxygen. This shows a **diurnal fluctuation** in response to the diurnal light regime. Thus if dissolved oxygen is measured upstream and downstream of an organic input (as shown in

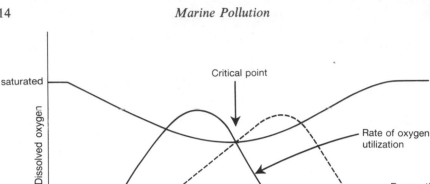

Fig. 2.2. Oxygen budget for a river or body of water receiving organic wastes. The horizontal axis represents time for a single input of waste to a static body of water, or distance downstream from a continuous input to a river.

Fig. 2.1), with a correction for the flow rate so that measurements are made in the same body of water, greater fluctuations are detected downstream than upstream (see Fig. 2.3). This is because the dissolved oxygen downstream consists of the:

incoming dissolved oxygen (at A)   + photosynthesis by phytoplankton
                                   + photosynthesis by fixed plants
                                   − respiration of plankton
                                   − respiration of benthos
                                   − oxygen used by bacteria in oxidizing
                                      organic matter
                                   ± oxygen exchange at the water sur-
                                      face.

Upstream of the outfall, there is a diurnal fluctuation of dissolved oxygen in the water because of the photosynthetic activity of the plants. The discrepancy between this and the dissolved oxygen downstream of the outfall is the result of the increased plant biomass and its photosynthetic activity.

There is also a **seasonal variation** in dissolved oxygen, to which a number of factors contribute. Because of the greater day-length and light intensity, diurnal fluctuations in photosynthetic activity are greater in summer than in winter, but in summer the higher water temperature results in greater bacterial activity and a higher oxygen demand. Furthermore, river flow—and hence dilution—is least in summer and greatest in winter and spring. The high water temperature combined

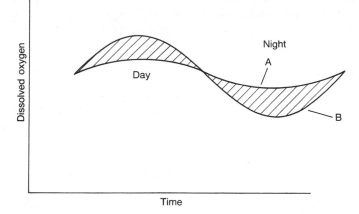

Fig. 2.3. Diurnal fluctuations of dissolved oxygen in a river: A, upstream or an input of organic waste; B, downstream of the mixing zone.

with low flow rate in summer is most likely to cause problems by increasing the oxygen sag.

Estuaries

The situation in tidal waters is much more complicated than in rivers.

Settlement

The previous calculations (p. 12) assume that all the discharge is in solution or in suspension, but in practice the effluent often contains solids which settle to the bottom, and it is important to know the settlement characteristics of the discharge if the dilution factor is to be properly calculated. The rate of settlement of particles in water depends on their size and density, and the viscosity and speed of the water; it is governed by Stokes' Law and Newton's Law. However, particles tend to flocculate into larger aggregations and Stokes' and Newton's Laws do not apply in these circumstances.

In estuaries, the change of pH and redox potential as freshwater encounters the sea causes intense flocculation of clay and other particles with increased adsorption of metals and other materials on the flocculates. While sedimentation takes place in all but the swiftest rivers, estuaries are subject to particularly heavy sedimentation, leading to the development of extensive mud-flats containing much of the organic material, metals, pesticides, etc. from the water column.

No two situations are the same and a detailed study of the settlement characteristics of an effluent in the receiving waters is needed before it can be calculated how much waste can be discharged, where, and at what rate, to reduce the BOD to within the capacity of the receiving waters.

Residence time

Whereas rivers flow in one direction, there is a tidal ebb and flow in estuaries and the net seaward flow over the complete tidal cycle may be small. Mean figures for the Thames at London are

> high water to low water: downstream flow 15 km
> low water to high water: upstream flow 13 km

giving a net seaward flow of only 2 km per tidal cycle, and towards the seaward end of the estuary, the seaward flow becomes very slow indeed (Fig. 2.4).

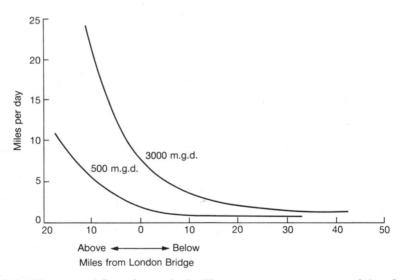

Fig. 2.4.   Net seaward flow of water in the Thames estuary at two rates of river flow in million gallons per day. (*Published with the permission of the Controller of Her Majesty's Stationery Office.*)

   Thus, a body of water (or effluent) entering an estuary moves only slowly through it and had a long **residence time** in it. It follows that the dilution capacity of the estuary is correspondingly reduced. The oxygen sag is more pronounced and may create an **anoxic zone** from which most life disappears, except for anaerobic bacteria, fungi and yeasts, and some Protozoa. It becomes foul-smelling from the products of anaerobic oxidation, and migratory fish such as salmon—or more particularly their young which require a minimum oxygen concentration of 4 mg l^{-1}—cannot pass through this block.

Stratification

Depending on their shape, some estuaries, such as the Tees, show **stratification** with the denser seawater flowing upstream in a wedge and the river water flowing out over it (Fig. 2.5). Other estuaries, such as the Thames, are not stratified. If an

Fig. 2.5. Vertical distribution of salinity at high water of spring tides in the Tees (*upper*) and Thames (*lower*) estuaries. (*Published with the permission of the Controller of Her Majesty's Stationery Office.*)

effluent is discharged into the bottom water layer of a stratified estuary and has neutral buoyancy, it may actually move upstream until it reaches the end of the wedge and comes under the influence of the seaward moving upper layers of water. If it has negative buoyancy, it may never travel seaward at all.

Mixing zone

In rivers, there is a defined mixing zone downstream of the point of discharge of an effluent (Fig. 2.1). In estuaries, the mixing zone is downstream of the point of discharge during an ebbing tide, but on a rising tide the mixing zone may swing upstream from the point of discharge and a considerable stretch of the estuary comes under the influence of the effluent because of this. Particularly in stratified estuaries where different effluents behave differently, the whole estuary constitutes the mixing zone.

Sewage treatment

River water with a BOD of less than 2 mg l^{-1} is regarded as unpolluted; with a BOD of more than 10 mg l^{-1} it is grossly polluted. A borderline acceptability is a BOD of about 4 mg l^{-1}. A common dilution factor in rivers is 8:1 and to achieve the standard of acceptability, the BOD of the effluent should not exceed about 20 mg l^{-1} (see example on p. 12).

If more waste has to be disposed of than the receiving waters can accept, and it is impossible to get the necessary dilution, it is necessary to introduce sewage treatment in which favourable conditions are provided for accelerated bacterial degradation of part of the organic material. This will reduce the BOD of the final product before it is discharged to the receiving waters. Various stages of treatment may be used, depending on the quality of effluent that is required (Fig. 2.6).

Primary treatment

The sewage is screened to remove large solids, comminuted or macerated to reduce it to a slurry, grit is extracted, and the remainder placed in settlement tanks. The supernatant liquid which still has a high BOD and a certain proportion of suspended solids is discharged to the receiving waters, and the sludge which has settled out is disposed of elsewhere.

Secondary treatment

If a greater reduction of BOD is required, the liquid is subjected to biological treatment. It may be filtered through beds of 4–15 cm rocks or coke providing a large surface area for bacteria which degrade organic matter in the water as it percolates through the bed. Material settled from the outflow may be disposed of and the supernatent liquid discharged to the receiving waters.

The sludge from the first stages of digestion gains a very high bacterial count (activated sludge). This may be retained and air blown through a suspension of the effluent and activated sludge; very high rates of bacterial activity can be achieved by this method.

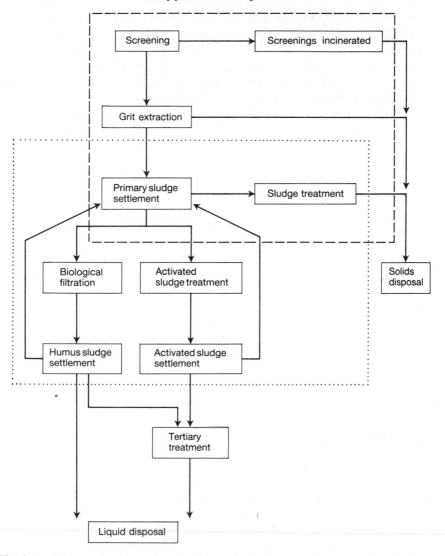

Fig. 2.6. Scheme of primary (Enclosed by a *dashed line*) and secondary (enclosed by a *dotted line*) treatment of sewage.

Tertiary treatment

If a high quality of effluent is required, it may be necessary to give it further treatment. The liquid derived from secondary treatment may be retained in sedimentation ponds or passed through sand or earth filters to remove suspended solids. Nitrates may be removed by algal growth in retaining ponds and phosphates can be removed by electrolytic methods.

The provision of sewage treatment plants is costly: a modern treatment plant giving secondary treatment to sewage for a population of 200 000 people costs about £20 million to build; providing the sewers, etc. costs 2–3 times as much again; and the running costs are about 5 per cent of the capital costs per year. In view of this, no more sewage is treated than is necessary, and advantage is taken of the natural capacity of receiving waters to degrade wastes, so far as this can be done safely.

Disposal of sewage sludge

Sewage treatment produces large quantities of settled solids which are not discharged with the effluent but are disposed of in some other way. In some respects this may be regarded as transferring pollution from one place to another, but the objective is to distribute the organic load in such a way that it does least harm and possibly some good.

Ideally, organic wastes should be returned to the land to fertilize crops. Some crude sewage is sprayed on to crops as a fertilizer, or sludges in various forms are applied to crops or ploughed in as a fertilizer and soil conditioner. Nearly half the sewage sludge in Britain is used in this way. There is too much for it all to be returned to the land (1000 people produce on average 25 t of solid waste per year) and urban sewage contains industrial waste and is contaminated with metals, pesticides, detergents and other toxic material which make it unsuitable for agricultural use. There is also a small public health risk associated with its use as fertilizer (see p. 30). Sewage sludge is therefore disposed of on land tips, incinerated, or, for cities with reasonable access, is dumped at sea.

Sewage sludge has a high water content and most of it has a very objectionable smell. To reduce transportation costs, it is therefore **dewatered** and commonly subjected to further treatment to produce a more acceptable material for tipping. For dewatering, the sludge is retained in shallow drying beds where, by drainage and evaporation, the water content is reduced from 90 per cent or more to 45–60 per cent. The sludge may be exposed to further bacterial action under heat and this treatment results in the production of combustable gases which can be used as a fuel source in the sewage treatment works. The sludge, if properly treated, acquires a tarry or peaty rather than a septic smell, and is then more acceptable for dumping on tips.

Consequences of organic discharges to estuaries

The most serious problems are encountered in industrialized and urbanized estuaries. Two case histories illustrate contrasting difficulties and the measures adopted to reduce them.

Thames estuary

The Thames was a major salmon river until about 1820. Sewage from London was either carried to fields in the surrounding countryside and used as fertilizer, or simply left to rot in cess pits or the streets. The population was largely dependent on wells for its drinking water; these were frequently contaminated and typhoid was common and cholera epidemics occurred at intervals. Then came an improved piped water supply, the water closet was introduced and construction of the main system of sewers was begun, discharging the wastes into the Thames. As a result of these public health measures, disease was reduced, but the river was progressively overloaded and by the 1850s had become foul smelling and fish had disappeared from it.

A reduction in the number of separate outfalls and increased sewage treatment around the turn of the century greatly improved the condition of the river, but the growth of London's population outran the capacity of the sewage treatment system and by the 1950s about 20 miles of the Thames through London was anoxic in dry weather (Fig. 2.7). Improvements and expansion of sewage treatment works around 1960 resulted, within 10 years, in a dramatic increase in the numbers and variety of benthic invertebrates, of both marine and estuarine fish and of shore birds and waders feeding on the mud-flats in winter.

Mersey estuary

The Mersey is probably the most heavily polluted estuary in Britain and cleaning it up presents an intractible problem.

The river Mersey and its tributaries pass through Greater Manchester, Oldham, Bolton, Rochdale, Stockport, and other heavily industrialized areas with a total population of 3–4 million. Although sewage and industrial wastes are treated before they are discharged into the rivers, the sewage treatment capacity is limited and sewage overflows into rivers at numerous points in wet weather. Thus, unlike the industrial estuaries of the Tyne and Tees, and to a degree the Thames, which have unpolluted rivers entering them, the Mersey receives a very heavy effluent load upstream.

In addition, the Manchester Ship Canal, constructed in 1893, carries much of the river water, bypassing the upper and middle parts of the estuary and entering it at Eastham. The canal gates to the lower estuary are opened only intermittently

Fig. 2.7. Oxygen sag in the tidal river Thames at various times since 1893. (*Published with the permission of the Controller of Her Majesty's Stationery Office.*)

to maintain the water level, and there is therefore a very small freshwater input to the estuary.

From Warrington, at the head of the estuary, downstream, the numerous inputs of sewage and industrial wastes are mostly untreated (Fig. 2.8). They discharge into the estuary or the ship canal. Liverpool alone has 26 separate outfalls into the lower estuary. There is thus a heavy effluent load in the estuary which depends on tidal flushing for its removal. At high tide, seawater tends to push back water in the ship canal which overflows, with its effluent load, into the middle estuary.

The effects, predictably, are a low dissolved oxygen level in the upper estuary which becomes anoxic in summer, and heavy metal contamination of the mud-banks throughout most of the estuary. The main problem in the lower estuary is the presence of visible solid wastes, much of which come ashore on amenity beaches at New Brighton, Crosby, and Formby, outside the mouth of the estuary.

It would obviously be a long and costly task to bring the Mersey estuary to the healthy condition of the Thames, but some improvement has been made in recent years. The first priority is to improve the water quality of the rivers entering the estuary and to reduce visible pollution in the lower estuary and on amenity beaches. Increased sewage treatment capacity has already reduced the incidence of anoxic conditions in the upper estuary downstream of Warrington.

There has also been a substantial reduction of industrial effluent discharge directly into the estuary, from a five-day BOD of 104.5 t day^{-1} in 1972, to

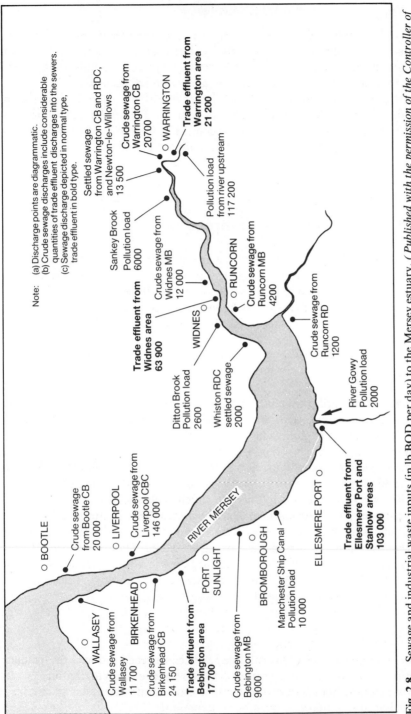

Fig. 2.8. Sewage and industrial waste inputs (in lb BOD per day) to the Mersey estuary. (*Published with the permission of the Controller of Her Majesty's Stationery Office.*)

Note: (a) Discharge points are diagrammatic.
(b) Crude sewage discharges include considerable quantities of trade effluent discharges into the sewers.
(c) Sewage discharge depicted in normal type, trade effluent in bold type.

Settled sewage from Warrington CB and RDC, and Newton-le-Willows 13 500

Crude sewage from Warrington CB 20700

WARRINGTON

Trade effluent from Warrington area 21 200

Pollution load from river upstream 117 200

Sankey Brook Pollution load 6000

Crude sewage from Widnes MB 12 000

RUNCORN

Crude sewage from Runcorn MB 4200

Trade effluent from Widnes area 63 900

WIDNES

Crude sewage from Runcorn RD 1200

Ditton Brook Pollution load 2600

Whiston RDC settled sewage 2000

River Gowy Pollution load 2000

BOOTLE

Crude sewage from Bootle CB 20 000

LIVERPOOL

Crude sewage from Liverpool CBC 146 000

Trade effluent from Ellesmere Port and Stanlow areas 103 000

ELLESMERE PORT

RIVER MERSEY

WALLASEY

Crude sewage from Wallasey 11 700

BIRKENHEAD

Crude sewage from Birkenhead CB 24 150

Trade effluent from Bebington area 17 700

PORT SUNLIGHT

BROMBOROUGH

Crude sewage from Bebington MB 9000

Manchester Ship Canal Pollution load 10 000

71.6 t day^{-1} in 1979 and 33.6 t day^{-1} in 1986. Some of the improvement has been due to a decline in industrial activity, but much is due to the remedial measures that have been taken. A new sewer is under construction to intercept the 26 separate outfalls from Liverpool and conduct the sewage to a new treatment plant before discharge to the lower estuary. This will do much to remove the visible pollution of neighbouring beaches. These measures attack the most conspicuous problems, but very much more would need to be done to restore the Mersey and its estuary to an unpolluted condition.

Consequences of sludge dumping at sea

Major sludge dumping grounds in the sea around Britain are Liverpool Bay for sewage sludge from Manchester and Liverpool, off the Thames estuary for London and in the Firth of Clyde for Glasgow and Clydeside. Since 1924 New York has dumped about twice as much sewage sludge as London, in New York Bight. It is instructive to compare the different experiences at some of these dumping grounds.

Firth of Clyde

The Clyde River Purification Board dumps about 1 million t yr^{-1} of sewage sludge in the Firth of Clyde off Garroch Head at the south end of Bute (Fig. 2.9(a)). The dumping ground is in an area with weak bottom currents and the wastes tend to accumulate. The nutrient enrichment produces phytoplankton populations as represented by the chlorophyll concentration, 10 times the normal level for inshore waters, to the south-east of the dumping ground (Fig. 2.9(b)). The polychaete *Capitella capitata* which is characteristically associated with organically enriched sediments, dominates in the dumping area to the exclusion of other species, and there is a transition from *Capitella* domination to a normal benthic fauna away from the most affected area. There are elevated levels of heavy metals in sediments and the benthic fauna in and around the dumping ground (Fig. 2.9(c) and (d)). This is a 'sacrificial' dumping ground and is comparable to a waste tip on land.

Thames estuary

About 5 million t yr^{-1} of sewage sludge has been dumped in the outer Thames estuary from London for the last century (Fig. 2.10). The dumping grounds are in an area with fast bottom current which disperse and dilute the wastes and prevent a localized accumulation of damaging contaminants. The dumping area is used

Fig. 2.9. Sewage sludge dumping in the Firth of Clyde: (a) organic carbon content of sediments, (b) summer chlorophyll level, representing phytoplankton production, (c) copper and (d) lead in sediments. *(Pergamon Press.)*

to its full capacity, however, because recent surveys have shown the first signs of metal accumulation in one small area of the site.

New York Bight

Sewage sludge from New York's 20 sewage treatment plants was dumped at a site in New York Bight since 1924. Until recently about 10 million t yr^{-1} were disposed of in this way. The impact is intermediate between that in the sacrificial dumping ground in the Firth of Clyde and that in the dispersing ground in the Thames estuary. There is organic enrichment and an accumulation of metals, with faunistic impoverishment in the centre of the dumping area, but despite the

Fig. 2.10. Sewage sludge dumping in the outer Thames estuary: (a) location of dumping ground, (b) organic carbon content of sediments. *(Pergamon Press.)*

very much greater volume of waste dumping, the concentrations reached are only half those in the Clyde. There is some evidence of a spread of the contaminated area, and contaminated sediments are carried by slumping into the Hudson Trench (Fig. 2.11). Use of this site has now ceased.

Enrichment and eutrophication

Many of the wastes entering the sea act as plant nutrients. Decaying organic matter, and nitrates and phosphates in sewage enhance plant growth. Another important source of plant nutrients is agricultural fertilizers in run-off from areas of intensive farming. Inputs of plant nutrients promote the growth of phytoplankton and fixed plants and this **enrichment** benefits a number of food chains, as does the increase in bacterial populations stimulated by an organic input.

If the input of plant nutrients is too great, **eutrophication** results. The great abundance of phytoplankton excludes animals either by clogging gills and other structures or because of the toxic properties of some phytoplankton organisms. Surface waters acquire a very high oxygen concentration because of increased photosynthesis. The abundance of decaying plant material falling to the seabed severely reduces the oxygen concentration in bottom waters and most benthic animals are killed or excluded from the area.

Eutrophication is a familiar problem in freshwaters: tropical and subtropical rivers and lakes become choked with water hyacinth; eutrophication of parts of the Great Lakes of North America caused population changes in commercial fish

Fig. 2.11. Sewage sludge dumping in New York Bight: (a) location of dumping ground, (b) organic carbon content of sediments, (c) copper and (d) lead in sediments. (*Pergamon Press.*)

stocks. In the sea, a common sign of sewage pollution on a beach is the growth of the green algae *Enteromorpha* and *Ulva*, but until recently, more widespread eutrophication was not regarded as a particularly serious problem in the sea except in one or two areas of restricted water exchange.

Enrichment

Increased concentrations of plant nutrients have been noted in recent years in the Baltic, Kattegat, Skagerrak, and off the German North Sea coast. To counter this, a number of cities have introduced tertiary sewage treatment (see p. 19), but an important source of nutrients is agricultural fertilizers entering the sea by rivers and land run-off. Germany and Denmark have introduced measures to reduce the use of fertilizers on farm land in sensitive areas.

Many enclosed sea areas that receive a discharge of sewage also show enhanced plant nutrient levels, but none are on the scale of that in the Baltic and eastern North Sea.

Red tides

A large input of nutrients is commonly, though not always, associated with the development of **red tides**. These are phytoplankton blooms of such intensity that the sea is discoloured (not always red, the blooms may be yellow or brown). Many animals, most importantly commercial fish species, are excluded from the area.

A particularly damaging form of red tide is when the bloom is composed of the dinoflagellates *Gonyaulax* or *Gymnodinium*, some species of which contain a dangerous neurotoxin. These toxins may be accumulated by bivalve molluscs at no risk to themselves, but present a serious hazard to those that eat them. Fatalities among sea birds and fish have been recorded, as well as illness and sometimes death among humans. Areas regularly affected by toxic dinoflagellate blooms in summer include the coasts of California and Florida, the Bay of Fundy in Nova Scotia and, in Britain, on the north-east coast of England. While adequate nutrients are necessary to support these toxic blooms, their location does not appear to be particularly related to high levels of organic inputs.

In May 1988, an exceptionally large and persistent bloom of *Chrysochromulina* in the Skagerrak and North Sea caused serious damage to coastal fish farms in Sweden and southern Norway. This alga had not previously been known to form blooms and does not appear to be toxic; the damage seems to have been caused by the sheer density of phytoplankton. Nutrient levels in the Skagerrak have increased in recent years, but on this occasion physical and climatic conditions appear to have been a more important influence.

Oxygen depletion

In prolonged, warm, calm weather, a **thermocline** may develop separating cold, dense bottom water from the warm surface layer and from atmospheric oxygen. Bacterial degradation of organic matter on the seabed is likely to reduce oxygen levels in bottom water under these circumstances. Dangerously low oxygen concentrations are more likely if the area is the site of a phytoplankton bloom, with dead phytoplankton raining down on the bottom, or if the area receives an input of organic wastes.

Oxygen depletion of bottom waters is a normal feature of parts of the Baltic and Caspian Seas (see Chapter 9) and summer thermoclines often develop in the central and eastern North Sea and in the New York Bight. These are not usually damaging, but sometimes lead to widespread mortality of fish and the benthic fauna.

In spring and summer 1976, a strong thermocline developed over a large part of the middle Atlantic Bight (Fig. 2.12) accompanied by an intense phytoplankton bloom. Bottom oxygen concentrations were reduced over an area of 1200 km². It is estimated that 143 000 t of the clam *Spisula* were killed.

In summer 1981, a similar phenomenon was detected in a wide area of the German Bight and eastern North Sea (Fig. 2.13). In the worst affected areas almost no live fish were caught, most having left, but numerous dead flatfish (*Pleuronectes* and *Limanda*) were observed on the seabed by underwater television. Brittle stars *Ophiura albida*, clams *Venus striatula*, and no doubt other burrowing fauna, were also killed. Similar events were observed in this area in 1983 and 1986. The sewage sludge dumping grounds of the city of Hamburg were in this area, but this practice ceased in 1981 and the main source of plant nutrients in the area is the river inputs from the Elbe and Rhine.

River inputs and coastal discharges are probably responsible for the increasing eutrophication of the upper Adriatic (Fig. 2.14). Records of oxygen concentra-

Fig. 2.12. Maximum extension of the area of reduced dissolved oxygen in bottom water of the Middle Atlantic Bight in summer 1976. The sludge dumping ground is in the north-west corner of the area. (*US Government Printing Office, Washington, DC.*)

Fig. 2.13. Areas of the German Bight that experienced dissolved oxygen concentrations in bottom waters below 20% saturation (equivalent to about 1.5 mg l^{-1}) during the summers of 1981–3.

tions in surface and bottom waters since 1911 show that episodes of oxygen depletion in bottom waters first appeared in the mid-1950s off the delta of the river Po and this area was extended eastwards in subsequent years. Increased oxygen saturation of surface waters in the same areas is associated with high rates of primary production.

Public health risks

All human sewage contains enteric bacteria, pathogens and viruses, and the eggs of intestinal parasites. Contamination of food or drinking water may therefore pose a public health hazard. Generally, faecal contamination is measured by a count of the bacterium *Escherichia coli* ('**coliform count**'). *Escherichia coli* is not a pathogen but is always present in the human intestine and appears in the faeces. The coliform count does not reflect the level of contamination by pathogens directly, merely the level of faecal contamination, but that in itself is a good

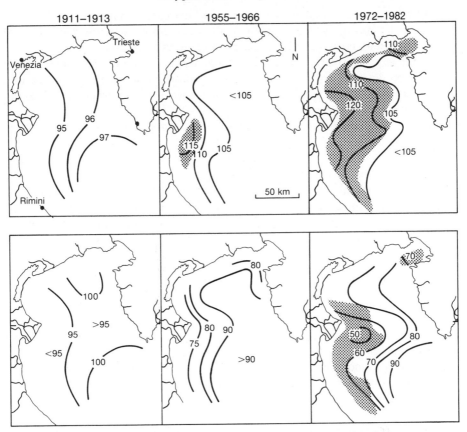

Fig. 2.14. Oxygen saturation (%) of surface waters (*upper*) and bottom waters (*lower*) in the upper Adriatic during the periods 1911–13, 1955–66, and 1972–82. Hatched areas experienced oxygen saturation above 120% in surface water and below 20% in bottom water.

measure of the risk to which the human population is exposed, depending on the general incidence of diseases which can be communicated in this way.

Parasite eggs, including those of the nematodes *Ascaris* and *Ancylostoma* (hookworm) and of tapeworms such as *Taenia*, are resistant to drying and may persist in both crude sewage and sewage sludge. The use of either for agricultural use therefore presents some health risk, though more particularly for salad crops because the eggs are destroyed in the course of cooking vegetables. The problem is greatest in tropical countries and where the incidence of intestinal parasites in the human population is high.

Since humans do not drink seawater, it is generally assumed that there is no danger to sea bathers from faecal contamination of coastal waters unless the pollution is so gross that is is visible, in which case conditions would be so offensive that no-one would bathe there. ('If you cannot see it, it is safe.') This an optimistic view. Pathogenic bacteria are not necessarily killed by exposure to seawater, as was formerly supposed, but may enter a dormant phase so that they cannot be detected by normal methods ('**non-platable bacteria**'). They are, however, still capable of causing illness if ingested. Furthermore, sea-bathing certainly occurs in some extraordinary places close to sewer outfalls, swimmers often swallow some seawater, and there have been some instances of hepatic or enteric disease being contracted through bathing in contaminated waters. EEC regulations have set bacteriological standards for bathing beaches and a serious effort is being made in most European countries to reach these standards by introducing sewage treatment in coastal resorts or by extending submarine outfalls so that the discharge does not return to the beaches.

The chief health risk from sewage discharges to sea is undoubtedly through the ingestion of contaminated seafood. Filter-feeders, most conspicuously bivalve molluscs, flourish in waters enriched by a neighbouring input of organic wastes, but they accumulate the human pathogens on their gills and these may be transmitted to the consumer. The risk is obviously greatest if the bivalves are freshly harvested and eaten uncooked. Most bivalves in commerce which are collected from waters known to be contaminated by sewage effluents are, in fact, usually transferred to uncontaminated water for a few weeks before marketing (i.e. **depurated**), and during this time they lose their burden of pathogens and are safe to eat. Seafood organisms that are not filter-feeders, such as most crustaceans and fish, do not accumulate pathogens from sewage-contaminated water and do not represent a health risk from this source.

Blooms of toxic dinoflagellates *Gonyaulax* or *Gymnodinium* in red tides (see p. 28) render contaminated shellfish very dangerous to eat. Humans that do so are at risk of suffering **paralytic shellfish poisoning** from the toxin, with the symptoms of nausea, loss of balance, defective vision, and, in severe cases, convulsions and death. Shellfish beds in areas subject to toxic dinoflagellate blooms have to be closed during the summer months. While there must be adequate nutrients to support the blooms, their location and occurrence do not appear to be closely related to waste inputs to the sea.

3
Oil pollution

Oil pollution of the sea attracts great public attention because it is visible and most people encounter it, either at first hand on bathing beaches, or from pictures on television and in the press whenever there is a spectacular oil spill. Petroleum hydrocarbons reach the sea by many routes, however, and tanker accidents are by no means the only source of oil pollution.

Inputs

It is difficult to calculate the total quantity of petroleum hydrocarbons entering the sea. Recent estimates vary between 1.7 and 8.8 million t yr^{-1}. The best estimate is a little over 3 million t yr^{-1} and the contributory sources are shown in Table 3.1.

Tanker operations

The world production of crude oil is about 3 billion t yr^{-1} and half of it is transported by sea (Fig. 3.1). After a tanker has unloaded its cargo of oil it has to take on seawater as ballast for the return journey to the oil fields. The ballast water is usually stored in the cargo compartments which previously contained the oil. During unloading of the cargo, a certain amount of oil remains clinging to the walls of the compartments; this may amount to as much as 800 t in a 200 000 t tanker. The ballast water inevitably becomes contaminated with this 'clingage' which in any case has to be cleaned from all the compartments before they can be filled with a fresh cargo of oil. Formerly this dirty ballast and clingage were discharged to sea during the return journey and were responsible for much of the casual oil pollution of the world's oceans. Two techniques have substantially reduced this: 'load-on-top' and 'crude oil washing'.

In the **load-on-top** system (Fig. 3.2), cargo compartments are cleaned by high pressure jets of water. The oily water is retained in the compartment until the oil floats to the top; the water underneath, containing only little oil, is then discharged to the sea and the oil is transferred to a slop tank. This process is continued until all the compartments have been cleaned and the tanker carries only clean ballast water. At the loading terminal, fresh cargo is loaded on top of the oil in the slop tank, hence the name of the technique.

Table 3.1. Estimated world input of petroleum hydrocarbons to the sea (million t yr^{-1})

Source		Total
Transportation		
Tanker operations	0.70	
Tanker accidents	0.40	
Bilge and fuel oils	0.30	
Dry docking	0.03	
Non-tanker accidents	0.02	
		1.45
Fixed installations		
Coastal refineries	0.10	
Offshore production	0.05	
Marine terminals	0.02	
		0.17
Other sources		
Municipal wastes	0.70	
Industrial waste	0.20	
Urban run-off	0.12	
River run-off	0.04	
Atmospheric fall-out	0.30	
Ocean dumping	0.02	
		1.38
Natural inputs		0.25
Total		3.25
Biosynthesis of hydrocarbons		
Production by marine phytoplankton	26 000	
Atmospheric fall-out	100–4000	

The load-on-top method reduces but does not totally eliminate the discharge of oil to the sea and such is the quantity of oil transported by tanker that the total input remains high. Furthermore, it is not very effective in areas such as the Mediterranean where journeys are short and there is insufficient time for adequate separation of the oil from the water after cleaning of the compartments.

Some modern tankers have **segregated ballast**, i.e. the ballast water is carried in separate compartments and does not come in contact with oil. The clingage is removed by jets of crude oil (**crude oil washing**). To avoid the danger of explosion of the petrol vapour generated by this process, the compartments have to be flooded with inert gas which is supplied by the engine exhaust gases. No oil or oily water is discharged to sea.

Fig. 3.1. Major oil movements at sea (million barrels per day) in 1987.

Fig. 3.2. Load on top: (a) empty tanks are cleaned by water jet and the washings transferred to the slop tanks, (b) oil floats to the top in tanks containing dirty ballast; the water is discharged to sea and oil transferred to the slop tank, (c) eventually the ship carries only clean ballast, and oil in the slop tanks floats to the surface, (d) underlying water is pumped out and (e) new cargo is loaded on top of the oil remaining in the slop tank.

Dry docking

All ships, including oil tankers, require periodic dry docking for servicing, repairs, cleaning the hull, etc. It is essential for all oil to be removed from the cargo compartments of tankers and from the empty fuel tanks of all shipping, to avoid the risk of explosion from petroleum gases. Unless the ship repair yards have slop reception facilities and can accept the oily washings, and many still do not, there is no alternative but to clean the tanks and discharge the oil water to sea during the short journey from the final port of call to the shipyard.

Marine terminals

Accidents through human error and pipeline failure are an inevitable accompaniment to loading oil on to tankers and discharging it at oil terminals. The small size of this input reflects the care taken to reduce such accidents to a minimum.

Bilge and fuel oils

All shipping may need to take on ballast water when travelling unladen or in bad weather. Ballast tanks take up valuable cargo space and are limited in size, so additional ballast may be carried in empty fuel tanks. When the ballast water is pumped overboard it carries oil into the sea. In addition, all shipping needs to pump out bilge water which invariably contains oil from the ship's engines. Individually the quantity of oil released may be small, but since all shipping contributes, the total amount entering the sea is considerable.

Tanker accidents

As with other shipping, a large number of accidents involving oil tankers happen every year. Most result in no, or quite trivial spillages of oil; the accident may not rupture the cargo compartments, a damaged vessel may be salvaged, or its cargo may be off-loaded into other tankers. Major shipping disasters involving oil tankers are a different matter. In March 1978, the *Amoco Cadiz*, carrying 223 000 t of Arabian and Kuwait crude oil, was wrecked on the coast of Brittany and lost its entire cargo, causing immense damage over a wide area. Fortunately such catastrophes are rare events.

Because shipping hazards are greatest close to shore and in narrow straits, such as the Straits of Dover, or near the entrances to ports where the density of shipping is high, most tanker accidents occur close to shore and if oil is spilled, coastal pollution almost invariably results.

Non-tanker accidents

When a ship is in an accident, its fuel oil may be lost to the sea. Some cargo ships, particularly bulk carriers, are now very large and carry as much fuel oil as a 1960 oil tanker carried crude oil, so this source of oil contamination is not negligible.

Offshore oil production

The oil that is extracted from the seabed invariably contains some water (**production water**) which must be extrated before the oil is transported to the refinery. This is done by oil separators on the platform and the oil concentration in the water that is discharged is usually less than 40 parts per million (p.p.m.), but in aggregate this amounts to a considerable quantity.

When an oil well is being drilled, **drilling muds** are pumped down the well. These maintain a head of pressure and prevent a blow-out when oil is struck, lubricate the drill bit, and carry the cuttings back to the surface (Fig. 3.3). The

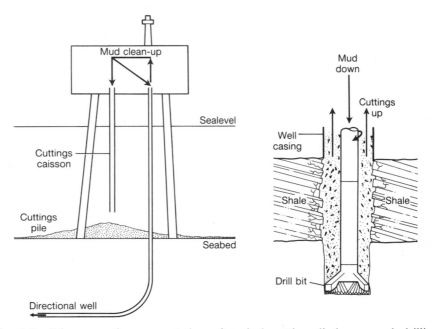

Fig. 3.3. Diagrammatic representation of typical cutting discharges and drilling operations in the North Sea.

drill muds contain water or, if the nature of the strata demands it, 70–80 per cent oil; formerly the oil was diesel, but increasingly low-toxicity oils are used. While there is some attempt to separate the drill cuttings from the **oil-based muds** before they are dumped on the seabed beneath the platform, they are inevitably still heavily contaminated and 90 per cent of petroleum hydrocarbons entering the North Sea as a result of offshore oil extraction is from this source.

Blow-outs, the uncontrolled release of oil from the well, are catastrophes and great precautions are taken to prevent them. Nevertheless, accidents happen occasionally and great quantities of oil may be released to the sea before the blow-out is brought under control. In April 1977, a well in the Ekofisk field in the Norwegian sector of the North Sea blew out and discharged 20 000–30 000 t of oil. In June 1979, a well in the Ixtoc field off the Mexican coast blew out and was on fire. It took nine months to bring it under control and in that time it is estimated to have discharged 350 000 t of crude oil into the Gulf of Mexico. Gas blow-outs, as in the Piper field in the North Sea in 1988, are less likely to result in oil pollution.

Atmosphere

The incomplete combustion of petrol or diesel in motor vehicles results in petroleum hydrocarbons being released into the atmosphere. They are washed out in rain either directly into the sea or indirectly by contributing to river run-off.

Municipal and industrial wastes

Domestic wastes and sewage contains a quantity of oils and greases and, depending on the nature of the industry, its wastes may also contain a considerable quantity of petroleum hydrocarbons. In coastal areas, these wastes are often discharged into the sea and even if subjected to treatment, the sewage sludges may retain petroleum hydrocarbons which are then discharged to sea.

Coastal oil refineries

Older refineries use a steam-cracking process (see p. 54) and the water recovered, which is discharged in the effluent, contains up to 100 p.p.m. of oil in the water. In more modern refineries, the oil does not come in contact with the water and it is possible to reduce the quantity of oil in the effluent to 25 p.p.m. Refineries require a large volume of water and the total discharge of oil is not negligible, the more so as it is continuously discharged into the same body of water.

Urban and river run-off

Every time it rains, irridescence caused by oil and petrol can be seen on the roads. This is washed down drains and into water courses and eventually reaches the sea. Garage forecourts sustain a large amount of spilled oil which is washed into the drains.

Remarkably little engine oil purchased for use in motor vehicles is recovered and, with motorists increasingly making their own oil changes, it is suspected that a considerable amount of this oil finds its way into drains or on land, from which it is carried into rivers.

Licenced dumping at sea

Shipping channels in estuaries and ports commonly need regular dredging. The dredging spoil, which is usually dumped at sea, is contaminated with oil. Various kinds of solid municipal and industrial wastes that are dumped at sea may also contain petroleum hydrocarbons.

Natural sources

Oil deposits close to the earth's surface seep out and have done so for millennia. The pitch lakes of Trinidad are the product of natural seeps, and coastal oil seeps occur in many parts of the world.

Biosynthesis

Oil deposits are produced by plant remains that have become fossilized under marine conditions (coal results under freshwater conditions). Living plants produce hydrocarbons; the aromatic scent of pinewoods is caused by them. Estimates of the annual production of hydrocarbons by marine phytoplankton and by land plants from which the products are rained out into the sea are inevitably vague, but at the least, the figures dwarf the input of fossil hydrocarbons by several orders of magnitude. Recent and fossil hydrocarbons have different constitutions and may well have different effects on marine ecosystems, but the dominating input of hydrocarbons from plants needs to be borne in mind when assessing the effect of petroleum hydrocarbons.

What is oil?

Crude oil is a complex mixture of hydrocarbons with 4 to 26 or more carbon atoms in the molecule (Fig. 3.4). Arrangements include straight chains, branched chains or cyclic chains including aromatic compounds (with benzene rings). Some polycyclic aromatic hydrocarbons (PAH) are known to be potent carcinogens. Sulphur and vanadium compounds are also included in crude oil and non-hydrocarbons may represent up to 25 per cent of the oil. The exact composition of crude oil varies from one oilfield to another: much of the North Sea oil is light, with little sulphur and low in tars and waxes; oil from the Beatrice field in the Moray Firth and that to the west of Shetland is a very heavy waxy oil which needs to be heated in order to pump it through pipelines. The composition of the crude oil also varies during the life of a single oilfield.

   Crude oil must be refined before it can be used. Refining is essentially a distillation process with different fractions or **cuts** taken at different boiling ranges (Table 3.2). Light gasolene is the basis for petrol used in motor vehicles; naphtha provides feedstock for the petrochemical industry; the residue is used as bunker fuel in ships and power stations, and the higher fractions are used as tars, etc. Many of the commercial products are further refined, made into particular

(a) Methane (CH₄), the
simplest hydrocarbon

(b) A straight-chain alkane (or
paraffin): heptane (C₇H₁₆)

(c) A branched-chain alkane

(d) A cyclo-alkane
(naphthene)

(e) An unsaturated hydrocarbon

(f) Benzene, the simplest
aromatic hydrocarbon

(g) Benzo[a] pyrene, a
polycyclic aromatic
hydrocarbon (PAH)

Fig. 3.4. The structure of some hydrocarbons.

formulations and receive additives of other materials to suit them for their
various purposes.

All components of crude oil are degradable by bacteria, though at varying
rates, and a variety of yeasts and fungi can also metabolize petroleum
hydrocarbons. Small, straight- and branched-chain compounds degrade most
rapidly, cyclic compounds the slowest. High-molecular-weight compounds, the
tars, degrade extremely slowly.

Table 3.2.   Refinery 'cuts' of crude oil

	Boiling range (°C)	Molecular size (Number of carbon atoms)
Petroleum gases	30	3–4
Light gasoline, benzine	30–140	4–6
Naphtha	120–175	7–10
Kerosene	165–200	10–14
Gas oil (diesel)	175–365	15–20
Fuel oil and residues	350	20+

Fate of spilled oil

When liquid oil is spilled on the sea, it spreads over the surface of the water to form a thin film—an **oil slick**. The rate of the spreading and the thickness of the film depend on the sea temperature and the nature of the oil; a light oil spreads faster and to a thinner film than a heavy waxy oil.

The composition of the oil changes from the time it is spilled (Fig. 3.5). Light

Fig. 3.5.   Time-course of factors affecting oil spilled on the sea.

(low-molecular-weight) fractions evaporate, water-soluble components dissolve in the water column, and immiscible components become emulsified and dispersed as small droplets. The rate of emulsification of the oil in water depends on the agitation provided by waves and water turbulence. In some sea conditions, a water-in-oil emulsion is produced; this may contain 70–80 per cent of water and forms a viscid mass, known from its appearance as '**chocolate mousse**'. This forms thick pancakes on the water and intractable sticky masses if it comes ashore. The heavy residues of crude oil form **tar balls**, ranging in size from less than 1 mm to 10–20 cm in diameter.

Emulsified oil is in microscopic drops and therefore presents a large surface area at which bacterial attack can take place. Tar balls and mousse present a small surface area compared to their volume, and degrade extremely slowly for this reason. Tar balls of various sizes occur in the surface waters of all oceans, though they predominate in major shipping routes and in major ocean currents such as the Gulf Stream. They are mostly derived from tanker washings and routine shipping operations.

An oil slick does not remain in one place but travels downwind at 3–4 per cent of the wind speed (Fig. 3.6) except in enclosed waters and estuaries where tides and water currents have a greater influence on movements of the slick. When a slick encounters land it is stranded on the shore with well-known consequences.

Treatment of oil at sea

Cleaning oil from beaches is difficult, time-consuming, labour-intensive, and costly. There are obvious advantages if an oil slick that threatens the coast can be removed or otherwise dealt with while it is still at sea. A variety of techniques to do this has been developed, but only three have proved effective and even these can rarely prevent beach pollution if a large amount of oil is spilled close to shore.

The natural process of emulsification of oil in the water can be speeded up by spraying chemical **dispersants** on the oil slick from ships or aircraft. Dispersants are not effective against heavy oils or oil that has been on the sea for some time ('weathered oil'). The first dispersants to come into use were highly toxic and there was some reluctance to use them, but low-toxicity dispersants have now replaced them. While dispersants are useful for treating small quantities of fresh oil, in any large spill their chief limitation is the difficulty of deploying sufficient ships or aircraft to spray more than a small proportion of the oil.

Seawater intakes, mariculture installations or other important sites can be protected by the use of floating **booms**, with a 'sail' above the water-line and a 'skirt' below (Fig. 3.7), to deflect the floating oil to less sensitive areas. Large 'V'-shaped booms may also be used to corral the oil which can then be pumped out where it accumulates at the point of the 'V'.

A variety of **slick-lickers** (Fig. 3.8) has been developed in which a continuous belt of absorbent material dips through the oil slick and is passed through rollers to extract the oil. Slick lickers can deal with only small quantities of oil and are useful in harbours and sheltered waters rather than the open sea.

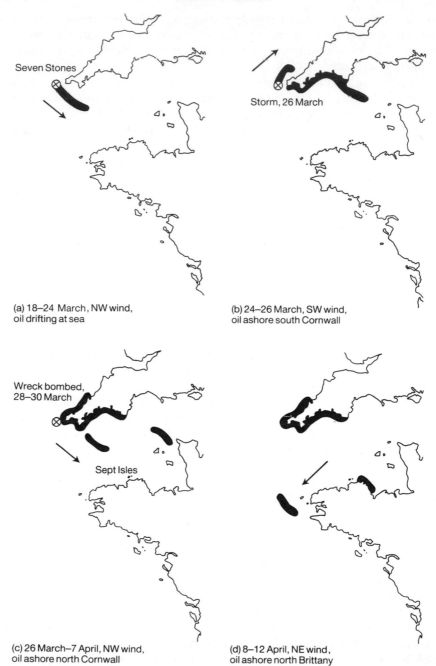

(a) 18–24 March, NW wind,
oil drifting at sea

(b) 24–26 March, SW wind,
oil ashore south Cornwall

(c) 26 March–7 April, NW wind,
oil ashore north Cornwall

(d) 8–12 April, NE wind,
oil ashore north Brittany

Fig. 3.6. Movement of oil from the wrecked tanker *Torrey Canyon* in response to changing wind direction.

Fig. 3.7. Design of one type of floating boom.

Beach cleaning

If a large quantity of oil is stranded and the shore is accessible, much of the oil can be pumped into road tankers and removed, thus reducing the chance of the oil being removed on a succeeding tide and redeposited elsewhere, thereby extending the area that is contaminated. Even when it is possible to recover some of the oil from the beach, a considerable amount remains on and between rocks and drained into the substratum. The techniques to remove this depend on the nature of the shore and since the treatment is often more damaging to the fauna and flora than the oil itself, it is often preferable not to attempt to clean up an oiled beach. The decision to clean or not to clean depends on the value placed on the beach. A tourist amenity beach has a high priority for cleaning because the fauna and flora is of far less interest than the preservation of oil-free conditions.

Rocks, harbour walls, and similar surfaces may be cleaned by high-pressure hoses, high-pressure steam or dispersants. If chemical agents are used, they must be accompanied by a large volume of water in which the oil can be dispersed. To achieve this, rocks are sprayed with dispersant ahead of a rising tide when breaking waves provide the agitation and water volume to remove the oil. Alternatively, the rocks must be hosed down after the dispersant has been applied.

Dispersants are useless on pebble or sandy beaches because the dispersed oil merely drains into the beach; it disappears from the surface only to reappear at

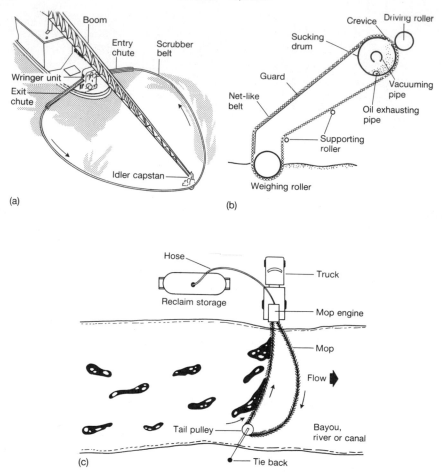

Fig. 3.8. Devices for mopping up floating oil.

some later date. The only means of cleaning such beaches is to remove the oiled surface layers of the substratum, either manually or by bulldozer.

These are drastic treatments and the damaging effects on the fauna and flora can be reduced by using straw or cut vegetation as an absorbent to mop up much of the oil. On sheltered rocky shores with a good algal growth, a large amount of oil is trapped in the seaweeds which can be cut and gathered. Physical removal of the oil by these methods results in only partial cleaning and much oil remains.

Unless beach oil can be dispersed into the sea, any beach cleaning operation produces a large volume of oil-contaminated debris. A few tonnes of oil can easily result in hundreds of tonnes of oily sand, pebbles, and other debris, and disposal of this material presents a serious problem. It cannot be incinerated unless the oil content is very high; it is usually unsuitable for dumping on waste tips because of the risk of the oil leaching out and contaminating water courses; and oil refineries cannot deal with it. It is possible to plough oily material into land where bacterial degradation eventually disposes of it, but this is unlikely to be an effective way of dealing with large quantities of oil material. At present tipping on waste dumps where the oil can be contained appears to be the only practicable, if unsatisfactory, solution.

Toxicity of petroleum hydrocarbons

Water-soluble components of crude oils and refined products include a variety of compounds that are toxic to a wide spectrum of marine plants and animals. Aromatic compounds are more toxic than aliphatics, and middle-molecular-weight constituents are more toxic than high-molecular-weight tars. Low-molecular-weight compounds are generally unimportant because they are volatile and rapidly lost to the atmosphere. A spillage of diesel fuel, with a high aromatic content, is therefore much more damaging than bunker fuel and weathered oil, which have a low aromatic content. A spillage of petrol or other 'white spirit' may present a serious fire hazard, but has little impact on marine organisms in the water.

Ecological impact of oil pollution

Rocky substrata

Spectacular changes on some rocky beaches in south-west England following the wreck of the tanker *Torrey Canyon* off Land's End in March 1967, drew public attention to the great impact a very large oil spill could have. It caused concern about the effect of pollution in general on the health of the oceans, and it stimulated a large research effort in marine pollution in the following years.

Rocky shores are high-energy beaches and stranded oil is quickly removed from the intertidal region by wave action and water movement. This is not necessarily an advantage if fresh oil is then redeposited on other beaches, repeating the damage elsewhere. Oil is removed most slowly from extreme high- and low-water levels and sheltered crannies where wave energy is least. Depending on the nature and age of the oil, a considerable variety of animals and the more sensitive red and green algae are killed; but much of the oil reaching the beaches is crude oil or bunker fuel which has been at sea for some days and lost most of its toxic constituents and it poisons few organisms on the beach. Limpets, *Patella*, have even been observed to graze dried oil from the rocks without coming to harm. But even if relatively non-toxic, weathered oil may cause damage through its physical properties. Many seaweeds secrete mucins which prevent oil adhering to them, but if it does adhere to the fronds, seaweeds can then be torn from their stipes during storms because of their increased weight. Large amounts of stranded oil may kill animals by smothering them. On shores that received oil from the Santa Barbara blow-out in California, large *Balanus perforatus* projected above the oil and survived, but smaller species of barnacles were killed by smothering.

The conspicuous damage on some Cornish beaches following the wreck of the *Torrey Canyon* was, ironically, not due to the stranded oil but to the very toxic oil-spill dispersants then in use which had, in the confusion, been poured neat over a few beaches. The dispersant or the mixture of oil and dispersant proved far more lethal than the oil alone and most organisms on the affected beaches were killed. Most critically, the limpets *Patella* were eliminated. In the absence of these herbivores, diatoms and algae colonized the rocks and an algal succession continued unchecked during the summer, culminating in a dense stand of *Fucus*. The presence of *Fucus* inhibited a settlement of *Patella* or barnacles the following season and the change from a community dominated by *Balanus* and *Patella* to one dominated by algae appeared to be long standing. Some four to five years later, *Patella* became re-established and, surprisingly, was able to graze down the *Fucus* by rasping at the stipe which became weakened and the fronds were then torn off. More than ten years after the spill, although barnacle domination of the rocky shore community had been restored, the associated fauna still appeared to be less rich and varied than before.

A similar consequence of the loss of dominant herbivores has been recorded in a sub-littoral rocky community. In March 1957, a small tanker, the *Tampico Maru* was wrecked and lost its cargo of diesel fuel at the mouth of a small bay on the Mexican Pacific coast of Baja California. The dominant sub-littoral herbivores were the abalone *Haliotis* and two species of the sea urchin *Strongylocentrotus*, and these were either killed or left the affected area. A dense growth of giant kelp *Macrocystis* followed and persisted in the bay for five years before the herbivores were re-established and brought it under control (Fig. 3.9).

In both the Cornish and Mexican examples, restoration of the original community was delayed because of the elimination of the dominant herbivores, the establishment of an algal cover during the period when there were no colonizing larvae of the herbivores, and then the presence of a dense stand of algae inhibiting recolonization by herbivores in the following season. In both cases, such algal domination persisted for several years and, at least on the Cornish beaches, evidence of this disturbance could still be detected a decade after the original oil spill. Similar consequences of the loss of herbivores, and a similar time-course of recovery have been confirmed on many occasions subsequently. Less critical damage, or damage at such a time that the herbivores can be re-established before there has been too dense a growth of algae, is made

Fig. 3.9. Growth of the giant kelp *Macrocystis* (shown in black) following pollution by diesel fuel from a wrecked tanker on the Mexican Pacific coast.

good much more rapidly. Even Cornish beaches affected by oil from the *Torrey Canyon* were, in many cases, essentially in a normal condition again within two years.

Soft substrata

Stranded oil is not readily removed from low-energy sedimentary beaches, and if still liquid, it drains down into the substratum. Here the low oxygen concentration does not favour bacterial degradation of the oil which may therefore retain its toxic properties for some time. When the *Amoco Cadiz* was wrecked on the Brittany coast in March 1978, releasing 223 000 t of crude oil, a considerable amount of it was carried into estuaries and inlets where it became incorporated in sediments. In addition to the immediate damage to the fauna, the persistance of toxicity prevented the start of recovery processes, and oil leaching from the sediments a year later caused renewed contamination.

In September 1969, the barge *Florida* ran aground during a storm in Buzzard's Bay, Massachusetts, near West Falmouth and spilled 10 000 gallons (nearly 40 000 l) of diesel fuel. Although this was a relatively small oil spill, the toxic nature of the oil (containing 41 per cent aromatics) and the circumstances of the spillage made it unusually damaging. Winds and strong surf drove the oil into Wild Harbor, on to beaches, and churned up bottom sediments with which the oil became incorporated and was carried down to the bottom. Subsequent sediment transport extended the contaminated area. There was an immediate kill of fish, particularly in shallow creeks and bays which shelter juveniles of commercial species such as flounders and blue fish, and the adults of a variety of bait fish. Lobsters, crabs, shrimps, and bivalves were killed in large numbers. Scallops were particularly badly affected; oysters and soft-shell clams less so. Commercial shellfish beds had to be closed because of tainting on a long-term basis due to the continued risk of contamination by oil released from the shifting sediments. Detailed studies of the sub-tidal benthic community revealed instability persisting for more than five years in the most polluted parts of Wild Harbor; less contaminated areas began to show a successional recovery two years after the spillage.

Plankton

Plankton, and especially the neuston living in the top few centimetres of the sea, might be supposed to be particularly at risk because it is exposed to highest concentration of water-soluble constituents leaching from floating oil.

Oil and oil fractions are toxic to a wide range of planktonic organisms, aromatic compounds more so than aliphatic ones. Weathered oil, after loss of volatile and water-soluble components is not very toxic and, indeed copepods have been observed to ingest oil particles and pass them through the gut without harm. Very low concentrations of petroleum hydrocarbons, below 50 ng g^{-1} enhance photosynthesis, presumably because they have a nutritive effect. Above 50 ng g^{-1} there is a progressive depression of photosynthesis in algal cultures. At concentrations above 250 ng g^{-1}, feeding in the copepod *Acartia* is depressed and food selection is altered.

Studies of the response of whole plankton communities in the natural environment following oil spills yield conflicting results, but do not support the gloomy predictions from the laboratory studies. Following an oil spill from the tanker *Tsesis* in Swedish waters in 1977, zooplankton biomass fell dramatically for about five days by the death of the animals or their avoidance of the area. In the absence of the grazing zooplankton, there was a marked increase in phytoplankton biomass and productivity; it is not clear if the oil had any nutritional effect. Following the wreck of the *Amoco Cadiz* in 1978, and the massive oil pollution of the Brittany coast, whatever initial impact there may have been on plankton, there was no sign of abnormality two to three weeks later, although there is a suggestion that the spring plankton outburst was depressed for a period.

Although it cannot be doubted that oil pollution, if sufficiently severe, kills planktonic organisms, it has not been possible to detect more than very transient effects and sometimes not even those. Whatever losses are incurred are evidently rapidly made good, either by renewed growth or immigration from unaffected areas. Since petroleum hydrocarbons are subject to degradation by yeasts and bacteria, their main effect is to enhance primary production and act as a nutritive source.

Fixed vegetation

Salt marshes and, in the tropics, mangrove swamps are, like intertidal mud-banks, low-energy areas likely to trap oil, and the plants which form the basis for these ecosystems suffer accordingly. Both are important ecosystems at the boundary between land and sea. They control coastal erosion, are a source of organic production which is transferred to the sea, and they provide shelter for the young stages of marine organisms, some of commercial value.

The effect of oil pollution on annual plants living in a salt marsh depends on the season: if the plants are in bud, flowering is inhibited; if the flowers are oiled they rarely produce seeds; if the seeds are oiled, germination is impaired. Generally it may be expected that annuals will be killed by oiling and be dependent on reseeding from outside the area; recovery of annual populations may therefore require two or three seasons. Perennials show a range of reactions. Shallow-rooted plants with no or small food reserves, such as *Sueda maritima* or *Salicornia* are readily killed. Others will generally survive at least a single exposure to oil and perennials with large food reserves, e.g. with taproots, survive repeated oilings. Generally the foliage is cut back, but decomposing oil has a nutrient effect and there is rapid and luxuriant renewed growth (a 'flush'). Experience of isolated oil spills suggests that oil pollution of this kind is less damaging to salt marshes than efforts to clean up the oil.

Mangroves present a rather different problem. They live in anoxic muds and have extensive air spaces carrying oxygen to the submerged part of the tree. Lenticels, by which the air is taken up, occur on the aerial roots of *Avicennia* or proproots of *Rhizophora*, and if the lenticels are clogged with oil, the oxygen level in the root air spaces fall to 1–2 per cent of normal within two days. Although mangroves have certainly suffered damage by oil spills, there are a number of cases where heavy oilings have not killed the plants. Too few studies of these tropical ecosystems have been made to allow a proper assessment to be made of their vulnerability to oil pollution.

Sea birds

Whatever other effects oil pollution may have, the loss of sea birds attracts the greatest public concern. It is difficult to give a precise estimate, but it is quite possible that tens or even hundreds of thousands of sea birds are oiled in the north-east Atlantic every year. This sort of toll has continued ever since shipping converted from coal to oil-fired boilers around the time of the First World War and motor cars became numerous in the 1920s. It is feared that sea birds might show a population decrease as a result of this heavy and persistent mortality.

Unlike most other organisms in the sea, sea birds are harmed through the physical properties of floating oil, and the toxicity of its constituents is of minor importance. If liquid oil (or any other surface-active substance) contaminates a bird's plumage, its water-repellent properties are lost. If the bird remains on the sea, water penetrates the plumage and displaces the air trapped between the feathers and the skin. This air layer provides buoyancy and thermal insulation. With its loss, the plumage becomes waterlogged and the birds may sink and drown. Even if this does not happen, the loss of thermal insulation results in a rapid exhaustion of food reserves in an attempt to maintain body temperature, followed by hypothermia and, commonly, death. Birds attempt to free their plumage of contaminating oil by preening and they swallow quantities of it. Depending on its toxicity, the oil may then cause intestinal disorders and renal or liver failure. Quite small quantities of oil ingested by birds during the breeding season depress egg-laying, and of the eggs that are laid the proportion that hatch successfully is reduced. If oil is transferred from the plumage of an incubating bird to the eggs, the embryos may be killed.

Indirect effects of oil pollution on reproduction appears to be much less important than the direct mortality of adult birds, and most attention has been directed towards the latter problem. The species most commonly affected are auks: guillemots (murre), razorbills and puffins; and some diving sea-ducks: scoters, velvet scoters, long-tailed ducks (old squaw), and eiders. These birds spend most of their time on the surface of the water and so are particularly likely to encounter floating oil, and because they dive rather than fly up when disturbed, they are as likely as not to resurface through the oil slick, so becoming completely coated with oil Furthermore, these ducks are extremely gregarious except when ashore for breeding, and the auks are gregarious at all times of the year. Thus, if there are casualties they are likely to be numerous. Indeed quite small oil slicks drifting through concentrations of birds resting on the sea may inflict very heavy casualties quite disproportionate to the quantity of oil. Thus, when 230 000 t of crude oil was lost from the *Amoco Cadiz* on the Brittany coast, the known sea bird casualties numbered 4572; but the largest known kill of sea birds from oil pollution was in the Skagerrak in January 1981 when 30 000 oiled birds appeared on the beaches, and this appears to have been caused by small amounts of oil discharged by two vessels. Indeed, the estimated loss of 12 000 birds on the north-east coast of England in January and February 1970 from oil slicks that were never even identified, equals the estimated loss following the wreck of the *Torrey Canyon*.

Other species besides auks and sea-ducks are also regularly affected, though usually in much smaller numbers because of their habits and because they do not occur in such dense flocks. These include grebes and divers (loons), shags and cormorants, mergansers, gannets, and pelicans. The flightless penguins in the southern hemisphere occupy much the same ecological niche as guillemots in the northern hemisphere, but except for the jackass penguin around the coast of

South Africa, the centre of population of most penguins is well to the south of heavily trafficked sea lanes or other sources of oil pollution and they rarely encounter oil slicks.

It is usually impossible to estimate more than crudely the number of birds killed by oil pollution. The only reliable figures are of the number of oiled birds or carcasses found on the shore, although an unknown proportion of the carcasses may have become oiled after death from other causes. An unknown number of oiled birds never reach the shore and, depending on wind speed and direction, sea conditions, distance from shore of the bird flocks, and accessibility of the coast to observers, it is likely that counts of oiled birds coming ashore underestimate actual casualties by anything up to 90 per cent. Fig. 3.10 shows winter sea bird

Fig. 3.10. Average number of dead birds per kilometre found in beach surveys in late February, 1967–73, and the percentage of them that had been oiled.

casualties around North Sea and English Channel coasts, and the values reflect the interaction of these factors. The high proportion of birds stranded on the coast of Holland that are found oiled, for example, reflects the prevalence of westerly winds in winter, drifting both the bird flocks and any floating oil to the eastern side of the North Sea. The exceptionally heavy loss of sea birds in the Skagerrak in January 1981 followed a period of westerlies which had funnelled large numbers of wintering birds into those narrow waters.

The auks not only include species which suffer most heavily from oil pollution, but they also have a reproductive pattern which does not favour rapid recovery from heavy adult losses. Guillemots, for example, do not start to breed until they are 3–4 years old and thereafter do not breed every year; they produce only a single egg and the risk of losing eggs or chicks from predators or simply from rolling off precarious cliff ledges is such that only about 0.2 chicks per year are successfully reared for each breeding bird. The decline in guillemot and puffin colonies in south-western Britain, Brittany, and on the New England coast that had continued for much of this century, appeared to confirm that steady losses from oil pollution could not be made good by natural reproduction. Similar fears were expressed for the population of those species of sea-duck particularly exposed to oil pollution, but since these produce numerous young there is less justification for concern.

Contrary to what had been predicted, while southerly colonies of puffins, guillemots, and razorbills were declining, more northern colonies of these and other sea birds have shown a dramatic increase in the last one or two decades, despite continuing oil pollution. The decline of southern colonies appears to have been the result of climatic changes in the north Atlantic in the period 1850–1950. The reasons for the growth of more northerly colonies is uncertain but appears to be a consequence of young birds starting to breed at an earlier age than before. It may be noted that occasional catastrophic mortality is not unusual for arctic and subarctic sea birds—a long period of severe weather which prevents feeding can cause as great a mortality as the worst oil spill—and despite their low reproductive potential, it would be surprising if a biological mechanism did not exist to maintain the population in the face of erratic losses of this kind.

Marine mammals

Although there have been occasional reports of seal pups being severely oiled and possibly killed by crude or bunker oil, there is no evidence that cetaceans or other marine mammals are particularly at risk from oil pollution.

Impact of refinery waste water

Oil refineries discharge waste water containing some petroleum hydrocarbons. The receiving waters are therefore subject to low-level, chronic pollution.

The refinery at Fawley in Southampton Water uses a steam-cracking process in which water comes in contact with oil and the effluent inevitably has a high oil content. From 1953, two effluent streams were discharged into creeks running across a salt marsh system. As well as oil and chemicals normally present in refinery effluent, oil from accidental spillages in the refinery and at the unloading jetty entered the stream from time to time. Between 1953 and 1970, these discharges caused the loss of vegetation from a considerable area of the marsh. In

Fig. 3.11. Fawley salt marsh: (a) distribution of vegetation (black) in 1970, (b) distribution of *Salicornia* in 1980.

Fig. 3.12. Fawley salt marsh: (a) hydrocarbons and (b) oligochaetes in the substratum in 1980.

Fig. 3.13. Milford Haven, Pembrokeshire: (a) location of oil terminals and refineries, (b) hydrocarbons in sediments.

1970, a programme of effluent improvement was instituted and by 1975, the oil content of the effluent had been reduced from 31 p.p.m. to 10 p.p.m. and the quantity of the discharge from 28 000 m^3 h^{-1} to 21 000 m^3 h^{-1} (Table 3.3). The salt marsh was monitored from 1970 onwards and by 1980 vegetation had become re-established over a considerable part of the area (Fig. 3.11). The sediments, however, remained contaminated and in 1980 their content of

Table 3.3.   Quality of effluent from Fawley refinery

	Average oil content (p.p.m.)	Discharge rate ($m^3 h^{-1}$)
1963–70	31	28 000
1972	25	28 000
1974	14	23 000
1979	10	21 000

aliphatic hydrocarbons ranged from 340 to 17 750 p.p.m. The fauna of the area previously denuded of vegetation remains impoverished and consists mainly of enchytraeid and tubificid oligochaetes. They are found in large numbers in soil containing up to 4750 p.p.m. aliphatic hydrocarbons, but in small numbers in the heavily contaminated areas (Fig. 3.12). Inshore sediments are also contaminated and contain reduced numbers of the polychaete *Nereis diversicolor*.

Experience at Milford Haven is in marked contrast to that at Fawley. It is the site of the largest deep-water oil terminal in Europe and five refineries have been constructed around it, all discharging waste water into the Haven. It has an exceptionally rich marine fauna and flora and is part of the Pembrokeshire Coast National Park; because of this, unusual care is taken to minimize damage. There are, nevertheless, accidental spillages of oil at the terminal and refinery effluents contain oil, though because of the refining process used, less than at Fawley. All spilled oil is treated with chemical dispersants to reduce if not eliminate the amount coming ashore. Hydrocarbons have become incorporated in sediments (Fig. 3.13) but their distribution is related to the proportion of mud in the substratum rather than the sources of industry input. The sub-tidal benthic fauna remains rich throughout the area and is not obviously affected by this level of contamination.

Impact of offshore operations

An offshore platform may suffer a blow-out, resulting in an uncontrolled discharge of oil, but this is fortunately a rare event. Routine inputs of oil to the sea are from production water (see p. 37) and from small amounts of spilled oil washed off the platform by rain. Where oil-based drill muds (see p. 38) are used, bottom sediments receive a considerable amount of oil from contaminated cuttings.

No effect has been detected from oil discharged in production water or washed off platforms, and even the Ekofisk blow-out (see p. 38) had no detectable environmental impact.

Fig. 3.14. Three types of abundance variation of benthic annelid worms influenced by disturbance at North Sea oil platforms.

Drill cuttings dumped on the seabed, however, have a profound effect on the benthic fauna. The drill cuttings blanket the seabed, creating anoxic conditions and the production of toxic sulphides in the bottom sediment with the almost total elimination of the benthic fauna. Surrounding this area, there is a recovery zone showing a succession of, first, opportunistic species such as *Capitella capitata*, then of species able to tolerate stressful conditions and to out-compete the less tolerant species which gradually reappear further from the centre of disturbance (Fig. 3.14). This disruption of the biological system extends for about 500 m around the drilling platform in the North Sea oilfields (Fig. 3.15). In regions where bottom currents are stronger, it is likely that the discarded drill cuttings are more widely dispersed and there is less blanketing of the seabed.

It is difficult to separate the toxic effects of oil-based drill muds from those of
sulphate-reducing bacteria which produce sulphides in areas where the seabed is
blanketed with drill cuttings and organically enriched by the oil-based muds.
Diesel degrades faster than the low-toxicity formulations, and platforms that
have used diesel-based muds show greater enhancement of the opportunistic
fauna than platforms that have used low-toxicity oil-based muds.

Public health risk from oil pollution

Some petroleum hydrocarbons are toxic to human beings and there are a few
cases on record of children being made seriously ill or even dying after
inadvertently swallowing kerosene (paraffin). But humans have an extremely low
taste threshold for petroleum hydrocarbons and the taste is particularly
repulsive. There is therefore little risk of humans unknowingly receiving
measurable doses of these toxins from contaminated food or drinking water.

Oil includes polycyclic aromatic hydrocarbons (PAH) some of which are
known carcinogens. In the early 1970s there was a fear that PAH behaved in
much the same way as chlorinated hydrocarbons like DDT, that is they were
resistant to bacterial attack and were excreted only slowly, if at all, by animals. As
a result, it was concluded that these compounds might concentrate in the tissues
of marine organisms with the concentrations increasing up the food chain to
reach the highest levels in carnivorous fish. Human consumers of these fish might
therefore be exposed to relatively large amounts of these carcinogens even in the
absence of overt oil pollution. Fortunately these fears have proved to be
groundless. There is little evidence that petroleum hydrocarbons accumulate in
marine organisms, and seafood contains small concentrations of PAH (as
measured by benzo[a]pyrene, a potent carcinogen) (Table 3.4) compared with
those occurring naturally in some other foodstuffs which are eaten in far greater
quantity (Table 3.5). Consumption of seafood is unlikely to contribute more than
2–3 per cent of the normal dietary intake of PAH.

Commercial damage from oil pollution

Fisheries

Fixed installations where fish or shellfish are held in intensive mariculture are
particularly vulnerable to damage from accidental oil pollution because the
animals cannot escape. A slick of oil drifting through such an installation may
inflict commercial damage quite incommensurate with the size of the spillage.
Japan, where mariculture is more varied and more advanced than in most other
countries, has had many such unfortunate experiences.

Fig. 3.15. Diversity of the benthic fauna (measured by the Shannon–Wiener index) in relation to distance from North Sea oil production platforms. Broken lines indicate the maximum and minimum values obtained in studies made before operations began.

Table 3.4. Concentration of benzol[*a*]pyrene (in µg kg^{-1}) in seafood from unpolluted and relatively polluted water

	Unpolluted	Polluted
Clam (*Mercenaria*)	0.38–1.1	8.2–16.0*
Shrimps	ND–0.5	ND–90.0
Crabs	ND–5.0	ND–30.0
Plaice	ND	0.05*
Herring	ND–0.1	0.4–13.0
Cod	ND–3.0	ND

ND = none detected
* Evidence of tainting

In the open sea, and as a rule in inshore waters, adult fish of commercial importance appear to be able to avoid areas affected by floating oil and are rarely killed. During the period when oil from a blow-out in the offshore oilfield at Santa Barbara, California, contaminated coastal waters, spotter planes used by the local fishing fleets to detect fish shoals, found them in normal abundance in areas of clear water between the streamers of oil.

Since fish eggs and larvae are more sensitive than adults to toxins and are commonly in surface waters where they are likely to encounter high concentrations of petroleum hydrocarbons, they are expected to be particularly vulnerable to damage by oil pollution. In the laboratory, it has been found that Ekofisk

Table 3.5. Concentration of benzo[*a*]pyrene (in µg kg⁻¹) in various foodstuffs

	Benzo[*a*]pyrene content
Cooked meats and sausage	0.17–0.63
Cooked bacon	1.6–4.2
Smoked ham	0.02–14.6
Cooked fish	0.0
Smoked fish	0.3–60.0
Flour and bread	0.1–4.1
Vegetable oils and fats	0.4–36.0
Cabbage	12.8–24.5
Spinach	7.4

crude oil reduced the hatching success of fertilized capelin eggs at concentrations of 10–25 nl l⁻¹. Concentrations of 250 µl l⁻¹ cause developmental abnormalities in several species, which at best reduce their efficiency and in all probability result in their early death. Indeed, exposure of cod eggs to water-soluble extracts of Iranian crude oil for 100 hours caused immediate casualties, and these continued even after the larvae were transferred to uncontaminated water.

Many commercial species of fish and shellfish produce enormous quantities of eggs, and even massive additional juvenile mortality may have no influence on the stock of adults which form the basis of the fishery.

Following the wreck of the *Torrey Canyon*, considerable areas of sea were sprayed with the very toxic dispersants then in use. A 90 per cent kill of pilchard (*Sarda pilchardus*) eggs was observed in the areas of spraying and a 50 per cent kill over a much wider area. Cornish pilchards form a small, isolated population but no shortfall could be detected two to three years later when the affected year-class were old enough to start appearing in the commercial catch.

One case is known in which an oil spill appears to have had a perceptible impact on fish stocks and that was following the wreck of *Amoco Cadiz* on the Brittany coast in 1977 and the devastating pollution that resulted. The one-year class of flatfish is, in this instance, thought to have been reduced.

On theoretical grounds, it has been calculated that a major oil spill at the time and in the place of the main fish spawning in the North Sea would at worst cause a slight reduction in the overall catch for one year. In all probability the effect would never be detected.

There have been reports of tumours and fin erosion in fish from areas chronically polluted by oil, and tumours and pre-cancerous conditions in bivalves collected in such areas. Such pathological states occur naturally, but their incidence is increased in any polluted waters. They do not appear to be particularly related to petroleum hydrocarbons.

Most of the harmful effects of oil on fisheries refer to shellfisheries, either intertidally or in shallow water, and the damage may persist for years. A spillage of 700 t of diesel fuel (No. 2 fuel oil) in Buzzard's Bay, West Falmouth, Massachusetts in 1969, contaminated shellfish beds, salt marshes, and beaches, and the oil became incorporated in the sub-littoral sediment. Some eight months after the accident, an area of 20 km^2 was polluted. Effects on crab populations were still obvious seven years later. Also, following the grounding of the *Arrow* in Chedabucto Bay, Nova Scotia in 1970, 8000 t of Bunker C contaminated 240 km of shoreline. Populations of the clam *Mya arenaria* were still adversely affected six years later.

Not all shellfish beds suffer in this way. A sudden decline in production of the Louisiana oyster fishery in 1932–3 coincided with the beginning of coastal oil extraction and gave rise to fears that the subsequent intensive development of inshore and offshore oilfields would be inimicable to the oyster industry. In fact, this did not happen: the oyster fishery has had fluctuating success; occasional declines are not related to the activities of the oil industry but to other factors, such as incursions of freshwater into oyster lagoons. In fact, offshore oil platforms represent the only hard substrata in these waters and have attracted an exotic encrusting and sessile fauna; accompanying these are exotic fish species and oil plaforms have proved to be greatly favoured by sports fishermen in the area.

Tainting

As serious as losses are resulting from deaths of fish and shellfish, the most important commercial damage is from tainting. Light oils and the middle-boiling range of crude oil distillates are the most potent source of taint, but all crude oils, refined products, refinery effluents, wastes from petrochemical complexes, the exhaust from outboard motors burning oil–petrol mixture, and a host of other sources can impart an unpleasant flavour to fish and seafood which is detectable at extremely low levels of contamination. 'Oily' or 'petroleum' flavours are generally repulsive to humans and fish tainted in this way is unmarketable. Low levels of contamination may produce indefinite, but certainly detectable 'off-flavours' which are at least damaging to the market.

The concentrations of oil in water necessary to cause tainting in finfish vary widely with the oil and the fish: fatty fish like salmon contract a taint much more readily than non-fatty species. In the natural environment, finfish rarely become tainted from floating oil because they avoid contaminated areas. The chief risk to commercial fishermen comes from fouling of fishing gear and this may result in tainting of the whole catch. In chronically polluted waters, fish are either excluded or, generally, are not fished. Some chronically contaminated waters, such as Hong Kong harbour, are fished and the fish are tainted. The market in this case accepts tainted fish.

Shellfish may be affected in a variety of ways. Stranded oil contaminates the shells of molluscs without damaging them, but even a small quantity of oil on a few shells of mussels, cockles, or winkles can taint the whole catch if, as if commonly the case, they are boiled before eating. Since oil can be retained on shells for a considerable time, this source of tainting is very persistent.

A commoner form of shellfish taining that affects all filter-feeders results from the uptake of fine droplets of emulsified oil in the course of normal feeding processes, and their subsequent incorporation into the tissues. Tainting in this way is common and bivalves are the principal subjects. The oily taste is lost within three to four weeks if the source of contamination is removed and the shellfish are transferred to uncontaminated waters.

The fishing industry is vulnerable to irrational moves in a way that few others are, and even the suspicion that fish may be tainted or contaminated is sufficient to depress the market. During the period when the wreck of the *Torrey Canyon* was in the news, fish sales on the Paris market fell by half even though no fish from any area affected by oil was ever on sale.

Tourism

Tourists prefers their bathing beaches free from oil and most coastal resorts put a good deal of effort into removing tar and oily residues from their amenity beaches. This oil pollution, mostly resulting from casual discharges, is a nuisance but not necessarily a heavy financial burden on the resort because the beaches are cleared of litter, plastics, and other debris regularly in the course of preserving the local amenities, and removing odd patches of tar adds little to the cost of beach cleaning.

Severe pollution resulting from a major accident in the vicinity of a resort is a different matter. It may well be beyond the means of the local community to deal with it and is generally treated as a national emergency calling for a national response. Tanker wrecks, like those of the *Torrey Canyon, Betelgeuse, Arrow,* and *Amoco Cadiz*, are in this category.

It is commonly said that oil pollution of beaches is harmful to the tourist industry, but although tourists may grumble there is little evidence that they actually stay away from beaches and resorts subject to minor oil pollution. Even large-scale pollution as from a tanker wreck does not apparently deter tourists who have been known to flock to view a disaster or potential disaster.

4

Conservative pollutants

Organic wastes considered in previous chapters are subject to bacterial degradation, and environmental damage is caused by them when, by overloading the receiving waters, the intensity of bacterial action reduces the dissolved oxygen concentration, excluding fish and, at very low oxygen concentrations, other animals and plants as well. The sea, lake bottom, or riverbed may become blanketed with fine material and undecayed organic matter leading to changes in, or even the elimination of, the benthic fauna. There may be a human health risk through the transmission of pathogens in untreated domestic sewage, but the chief hazard of organic wastes is the possibility of damage to natural resources.

Conservative pollutants present a different problem. They are not subject to bacterial attack or other breakdown, or if they are it is on such a long time-scale that for practical purposes they are permanent additions to the marine environment. Substances included in this category are:

(1) heavy metals such as mercury, cadmium, copper, zinc, and lead (considered in Chapter 5); and
(2) halogenated hydrocarbons (considered in Chapter 6) which include such insecticides as DDT and dieldrin, and industrial chemicals in the group of polychlorinated biphenyls (PCBs).

Plants and animals vary widely in their ability to regulate their metal content; most can do so only over a limited range. Both metals and halogenated hydrocarbons which cannot be excreted remain in the body in an unchanged state and are continually added to during the life of the organism.

This is known as **bioaccumulation** and its dangers are illustrated by the following example. DDT has about the same toxicity to man as aspirin. A lethal dose of aspirin is about 100 tablets; the same quantity of DDT is also lethal. But it is possible to take 0.5–1.0 g of aspirin a day indefinitely without ill effect because it is excreted. DDT is not excreted, so lethal doses can be acquired after repeated exposure.

Animals feeding on bioaccumulators have a diet enriched in these conservative materials and if, as is commonly the case, they too are unable to excrete them or do so only slowly, they, in turn, acquire an even greater body-burden of the substance. This is **biomagnification**. Its chief significance is that top predators, which in the sea include man, may be exposed to very large concentrations of a conservative substance in their food. If the substances are toxic, they may cause damage at any level in the food chain, but the risks are obviously greatest for top predators. Conservative materials subject to bioaccumulation and bio-magnification are therefore a potential human health risk as well as a threat to natural resources, and they have been responsible for human deaths. For this reason, conservative pollutants are regarded very seriously.

Measures of contamination

Concentrations of contaminants in organisms are expressed as:

$$\mu g\ g^{-1}\quad \text{(parts per million, p.p.m.)}$$
$$\mu g\ kg^{-1}\quad \text{(parts per billion, p.p.b.)}$$

(note that billion used in this context is 1000 million)

The concentrations may be calculated on the basis of the **wet weight** or **dry weight** of the tissue. The former is the weight of a sample of whole tissue removed from the body and often drained of free water; the latter is the weight after drying at 105 °C to remove unbound water. If 80 per cent of the total weight of a fish represents water, the dry weight concentration will appear as five times greater than the wet weight concentration. Tissues vary widely in their water content: feathers and hair contain practically none, lobster (*Homarus*) shell 25 per cent, but the muscle tissue of scallops (*Pecten*) is 75 per cent water; body fluids contain little solid matter and may be 90 per cent, or more, water. Dry weight concentrations provide the best basis for comparing the concentration of a substance in different tissues or different organisms, but many determinations are given only on a wet weight basis. Unfortunately, it is not always made clear whether a concentration is based on wet or dry weight of the tissue and much confusion can result from this oversight.

Concentrations of contaminants in sediments are always based on dry weight.

Toxicity

Toxicity is a measure of how poisonous a substance is, or how large a dose is required to kill or damage an organism; the more toxic the substance, the smaller the lethal dose. Although the concept of toxicity appears straightforward, measuring it is subject to many complicating factors.

Measurement of toxicity

Organisms vary widely in the route by which toxins enter the body—via the mouth and digestive tract, at the gill surface, or across the integument—and toxins vary widely in the way they cause damage to the organism. Toxicity tests on aquatic animals generally avoid the problems of administering a known dose, or determining how much toxin an animal receives, by measuring the concentration of toxin dissolved in the water in which the organism is placed. In these circumstances, an organism is not given a single dose of toxin, but is exposed to it continuously.

In conducting toxicity tests, it is customary to expose a sample of test organisms to a particular concentration of toxin and measure how long it takes them to die. It may be difficult to detect with precision the moment of death and commonly some arbitrary criterion of lethal damage, such as immobility or loss of a defensive reflex, is used. Whatever criterion is used, because of variation in sensitivity to the toxin, the test organisms in the sample do not all die at the same time. Instead, mortality shows a sigmoid relationship to the period of exposure (Fig. 4.1). It is impractical and probably unrealistic to prolong an experiment

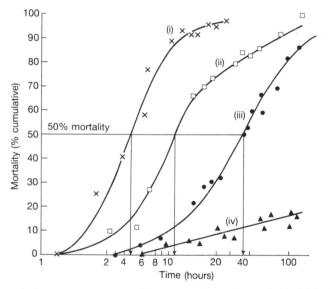

Fig. 4.1. Cumulative percentage mortality of mussels *Mytilus* in (i) 10^{-2} M, (ii) 10^{-3} M, (iii) 10^{-4} M, (iv) 10^{-5} M solution of zinc sulphate.

until all the test organisms are dead, and the statistic used is the time for the death of 50 per cent of the test organisms, or the **median lethal time**, and is written as:

$$LT_{50} \text{ or } LT_m.$$

The lethal time depends on the concentration of toxin to which an organism is exposed—the higher the concentration the shorter the time—and there may be a lower threshold concentration below which the material is not toxic. The LT_{50}, in itself, is therefore not a very useful statistic and it is usual to determine instead, the

concentration of toxin at which 50 per cent of the test organisms are killed within
a specified time. This time is commonly 48 hours or 96 hours, though for tests on
certain organisms, such as invertebrate larvae, it may be as short as 2 hours. The
toxicity is then recorded as the **median lethal concentration**:

$$96 \text{ h } LC_{50} \text{ or } 96 \text{ h } LC_m,$$

or with some other appropriate time indicated.

The median lethal concentration is measured by determining the median lethal
time at several different concentrations, the latter usually being at logarithmic
intervals, and reading the LC_{50} from a plot of the results (Fig. 4.2). More crudely,

Fig. 4.2. The 96 h LC_{50} of copper determined from the relationship between copper
concentration (as citrate) in 50 per cent seawater and the median lethal time for copper-
tolerant (from Restronguet Creek) and copper-intolerant (from the Avon estuary) *Nereis
diversicolor*.

the mortality after 96 hours exposure to different concentrations may be
recorded; the LC_{50} then lies between the concentrations which cause more and
less than 50 per cent mortality.

When the test animals are subject to a single dose of the toxin, by injection or
oral administration, the corresponding statistic is the size of dose that causes
50 per cent or median mortality:

$$LD_{50} \text{ or } LD_m.$$

When a response other than death (or some arbitrary criterion of death) is used,

EC, the effective concentration, or ED, effective dose, are used instead of LC or LD.

Some technical problems

The toxicity of metals depends on the form in which they are presented to the animal. Valency may change in seawater or complexes be formed between the metal and organic substances. Table 4.1 shows the form ('species') in which some heavy metals are believed to exist in the sea. Figure 4.3 shows the uptake of lead by the mussel *Mytilus edulis* when the metal is added as the nitrate, citrate, or complexed with organic molecules. Metal citrates are commonly used in toxicity tests because of the ready solubility of this salt, but lead citrate has three or four times the rate of uptake and final tissue concentration of the nitrate. Complexes with organic molecules double the rate of uptake. Organic complexes of heavy metals also tend to be more toxic than inorganic compounds: organo-mercurials and organo-tins are 10–100 times more toxic. Organic arsenic on the other hand is less toxic than inorganic arsenical compounds.

Other toxins present different problems for designing realistic experiments.

Oil, for example, is immiscible with water and toxicity is usually measured as that of the water-soluble components, although the concentrations and identity of these are not known in detail, and in any case, in the natural environment the organisms are likely to ingest emulsified droplets of whole oil. Furthermore, volatile components evaporate so that the nature of the material to which the organism is exposed changes throughout the course of an experiment.

As another example, chlorinated hydrocarbons have very low solubility in water and, in nature, animals are usually exposed to these compounds when they are adsorbed on to particles which the animal ingests. This is impossible to simulate accurately in the laboratory because of sedimentation of particles to the bottom of the container and adsorption of the chlorinated hydrocarbons on to the walls of the test chamber, which progressively reduces the availability of the material to the test organisms.

Organisms vary widely in their sensitivity to a toxin. Different species, of course, differ in their sensitivity, but even within a single species, sensitivity to a toxin depends on age, size, sex, reproductive condition, exposure to other stresses, nutritional state, and previous history, as well as the genetic constitution of the test organisms. The wide range of variation that may be due to these factors is illustrated in Table 4.2: young forms, for example, may be 100 times less sensitive or 1000 times more sensitive than adults of the same species.

Antagonism and synergy

In the natural environment, toxins are rarely present in isolation and they may interact with other substances. The combined effect of several toxins may be:

Table 4.1. Average concentration and total quantities of metals in ocean water, and the form in which they probably exist

Metal	Formula	Average concentration in ocean water (p.p.b.)	Probable dissolved species	Total in oceans (million t)
Silver	Ag	0.1	$AgCl_4^{3-}$, $AgCl_3^{2-}$, $AgCl_2^-$	137
Aluminium	Al	5	$Al(OH)_4^-$	6 850
Arsenic	As	2.3	$HAsO_4^{2-}$	3 150
Cadmium	Cd	0.05	$CdCl_2$, $CdCl^+$, $CdCl_3^-$	68
Cobalt	Co	0.02	Co^{2+}, $CoCl^+$	27
Chromium	Cr	0.6	(OH)?	822
Copper	Cu	3	$CuCO_3$, Cu^{2+}, $CuOH^+$	4 110
Iron	Fe	3	$Fe(OH)_3$?	4 110
Mercury	Hg	0.05	$HgCl_4^{-2}$, $HgCl_3Br^{2-}$, $HgCl_3^-$	68
Manganese	Mn	2	$Mn(OH)_{3+4}$?	2 740
Molybdenum	Mo	10	MoO_4^{2-}	13 700
Nickel	Ni	2	Ni^{2+}, $NiCl^+$	2 740
Lead	Pb	0.03	$PbCl_2$, $PbCl^+$, $PbOH^+$	41
Antimony	Sb	0.2	$Sb(OH)_6^-$	274
Selenium	Se	0.45	SeO_4^{2-}	616
Tin	Sn	0.01	(OH)?	14
Vanadium	V	1.5	$(H_2V_4O_{13})^{4-}$, HVO_4^{2-}, VO_3^-?	2 060
Zinc	Zn	5	Zn^{2+}, $ZnCl^+$	6 850

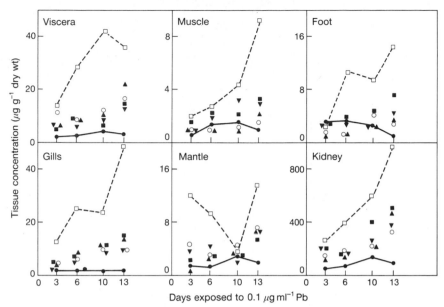

Fig. 4.3. Uptake of lead by various tissues of the mussel *Mytilus edulis*, with lead added as nitrate (○), citrate (□), humate (▲), alginate (▼), and pectinate (■), with seawater control (●).

Table 4.2. Sources of variation in bioassays

Source of variation	Ratio for comparing responses	Ratio range
Age of test organism	Old:young	0.01 to 1000
Sex of test organism	Male:female	0.5 to 5 or wider range
Genotypic difference	More resistant genotype:less resistant genotype	1 to 100 or wider range
Acclimation regime	Acclimated:non-acclimated	1 to 10 or wider range
Duration of exposure	Short bioassay test:long bioassay test	1 to 100

- the addition of one mortality to another;
- or the containment of one within another;
- or one may increase the mortality caused by the other (**synergy**);
- or reduce it (**antagonism**).

Table 4.3 shows the result of an experiment in which the ciliate protozoan

Table 4.3. Percentage reduction of growth of *Cristigera* caused by different concentrations and combinations of metal salts

	ZnSO$_4$								
	0			0.125 p.p.m.			0.25 p.p.m.		
		Pb(NO$_3$)$_2$			Pb(NO$_3$)$_2$			Pb(NO$_3$)$_2$	
	0	0.15 p.p.m.	0.3 p.p.m.	0	0.15 p.p.m.	0.3 p.p.m.	0	0.15 p.p.m.	0.3 p.p.m.
HgCl$_2$ (0)	0	8.5	11.8	8.3	14.4	18.8	14.2	18.3	25.9
HgCl$_2$ (0.0025 p.p.m.)	9.5	10.7	14.5	13.9	16.2	22.6	18.8	29.0	51.3
HgCl$_2$ (0.005 p.p.m.)	12.1	18.7	21.8	18.9	21.3	23.2	35.5	36.5	67.8

Cristigera was exposed to zinc, mercury, and lead salts in various concentrations and combinations of all three. The average percentage reduction in the growth of the culture was recorded in each case.

If the toxic effects are additive, the sum of the growth reduction for each of the metals acting alone should be the same as the reduction caused by all three acting together. In this example, 0.005 p.p.m. mercuric chloride causes 12.1 per cent reduction, 0.3 p.p.m. lead nitrate reduces growth by 11.8 per cent and 0.25 p.p.m. zinc sulphate reduces it by 14.2 per cent. The sum, $12.1 + 11.8 + 14.2 = 38.1$ per cent, should be the same as the effect of these concentrations of the salts in a mixture. In fact, as shown in the bottom right-hand figure in the table, it is 67.8 per cent.

In contrast to this synergistic effect, a mixture of 0.0025 p.p.m. mercuric chloride (causing 9.5 per cent reduction in growth if used alone) and 0.15 p.p.m. lead nitrate (causing 8.5 per cent reduction) produces only a 10.7 p.p.m. reduction in the growth of the population, instead of $9.5 + 8.5 = 18.0$ per cent reduction if the effects were additive.

A variety of non-additive effects of multiple contaminants has come to light. Well-known examples are the antagonistic effects of selenium and mercury, and of zinc and cadmium, the former often reducing the effect of the latter in each case. Molybdenum in association with sulphate reduces the toxicity of copper to sheep; whether it confers the same benefit to marine animals is less certain.

Influence of other stresses

In the natural environment, organisms are exposed to a wide variety of stresses that either demand the expenditure of energy to counter them, or impair the organism's performance in some other way. Often, the responses to natural stresses may be regarded simply as part of the normal maintenance activities of the organism, as in osmotic or ionic regulation or any other physiological response to changes in the environment. Excretion of contaminants is also a demand on the energy resources of the organism, and its ability to make this defensive reponse to a toxin depends on what other calls there are on its energy resources. If demands are considerable, the organisms will be the less able to survive exposure to the toxin.

Fig. 4.4 shows how the resistance of the fiddler crab *Uca* to cadmium is affected by increased temperature and reduced salinity. The 240 h LC_{50} is about 48 p.p.m. when the crabs are under approximately normal conditions of temperature (10 °C) and salinity (30 per mille), but falls rapidly if the salinity is below 20 per mille. A combination of low salinity (10 per mille) and high temperature (30 °C) reduces the LC_{50} to only 2–3 p.p.m.

Fig. 4.4. Influence of temperature and salinity on the 240 h LC_{50} for cadmium to the fiddler crab *Uca pugilator*.

Delayed impact of toxins

Standardized toxicity tests measure only the mortality that takes place during a test. It is recognized, of course, that the longer the test goes on, the greater the number of test organisms that will die, but the test takes no account of mortality that may take place after organisms that have been exposed to a toxin are removed to uncontaminated water. A toxin that has a delayed effect of this kind may well have a deceptively low toxicity rating in short-term tests.

Figure 4.5 shows the survival of mussels, *Mytilus edulis*, living in uncontaminated seawater for a period of three weeks following 24 hours exposure to copper sulphate in various concentrations. Concentrations up to 0.3 p.p.m. have little impact. Higher concentrations cause deaths, but these do not appear until after a time-lag of five or six days.

Sub-lethal effects

It is often possible to detect damage to organisms by toxins at far lower concentrations than those that kill them. These sub-lethal responses range from little more than physiological adjustment to changed circumstances, to major physiological stress or developmental abnormalities which, in the natural environment, would be likely to result in early death.

Erosion of fins and the development of pre-cancerous growths (papillomas) on

Fig. 4.5. Survival of mussels, *Mytilus edulis*, during three weeks following exposure to various concentrations (in p.p.m.) of copper sulphate.

the ventral surface are commonly observed in a proportion of flatfish living on very contaminated sediments. Since the same effect has been observed whether the contaminant is sewage sludge, oil, or titanium dioxide waste, the response is not a specific one to a particular pollutant.

The ingestion of crude oil by herring gulls (*Larus argentatus*) and some other sea birds causes damage to the intestine and liver, and impairs the functioning of the nasal salt glands.

Skeletal deformities are relatively common in fish, particularly from polluted waters: as much as 8.4 per cent of herring caught in the southern North Sea in a single year are afflicted in this way, and 6 per cent of caregonid white fish caught in the German Bodensee have spinal deformities. To some extent this condition is due to hereditary factors, parasitic infection, developmental errors, or other natural causes, but a variety of toxins, including chlorinated hydrocarbons and organophosphorus pesticides, dispersed oil, and heavy metals, can also cause it.

Sub-lethal concentrations of 0.05–0.10 p.p.m. copper sulphate and zinc sulphate cause the production of abnormal larvae in the polychaete *Capitella capitata*. These larvae are bifurcated (Fig. 4.6) and fail to survive beyond the eight-segment stage. A similar abnormality occurs in 10–16 per cent of larvae of this species in the second generation reared in water contaminated with a detergent.

Physiological stress is not necessarily harmful. Commercial fish hatcheries often subject fry to as many as possible of the stresses they are likely to encounter in nature in order to increase their survival rate after release. In theory such

Fig. 4.6. (a) Normal polychaete larva; (b) abnormal larva of *Capitella capitata* living in sub-lethal concentrations of copper or zinc sulphate. (*Pergamon Press.*)

adaptive physiological responses are distinguished from harmful ones if they contribute to the survival, growth, and reproduction of the species, but the distinction is not always easy to make.

Interpretation of toxicity data

Toxicity, as measured in the laboratory, has limited relevance to events in a natural situation (though it is very significant within those limits), and the results of toxicity tests must be interpreted with caution. A variety of factors relating to the toxin, the test organism, and the design of the toxicity test may all influence the results. Even when these factors can be adequately controlled, a different range of factors relating to the population dynamics and ecological role of the species have to be taken into account before the results of laboratory tests can be translated into terms applicable to the natural environment.

   Table 4.4 summarizes the factors influencing the toxicity of heavy metals in solution. It may be possible to standardize the organisms used in tests and, by suitable control of experimental conditions, to control the form in which a metal is presented to the organisms. The use of continuous-flow rather than static systems avoids depletion of oxygen and accumulation of excretory products, or loss of the toxin in the course of a prolonged toxicity test. Even with such refinements, however, the test situation is far removed from that in the natural

Table 4.4.   Factors influencing the toxicity of heavy metals in solution

Form of metal in water	Inorganic / Organic	Soluble	Ion / Complex ion / Chelate ion / Molecule
		Particulate	Colloidal / Precipitated / Adsorbed
Presence of other metals or poisons	Synergy / No interaction / Antagonism		More-than-additive / Additive / Less-than-additive
Factors influencing physiology of organisms and possible form of metal in water	Temperature / pH / Dissolved oxygen / Light / Salinity		
Condition of organism	Stage in life history (egg, larva, etc.) / Changes in life cycle (e.g. moulting, reproduction) / Age and size / Sex / Starvation / Activity / Additional protection (e.g. shell) / Adaptation to metals		
Behavioural response	Altered behaviour		

environment where the behaviour of the toxin may be modified by the physico-chemical environment or because it interacts with other substances that are also present.

Further to these complications, the ecological consequences of mortality caused by a toxin, which are a principal reason for measuring toxicity, introduce many more questions. Whether or not a local mortality affects the local population depends upon the population dynamics of the species (the survivors may flourish through reduced competition), the mobility of the species (adjacent populations may fill gaps caused by the mortality), and the persistence of the toxin. Each species is a member of a community and interacts with other members all of which are exposed to the toxin. Population changes among them may secondarily effect the first species. These factors are considered in Chapter 10.

Toxicity tests have been conducted on few species and are focused particularly on those that are hardy, readily available, and lend themselves to laboratory investigation. At least these tests are useful in ranking substances in order of toxicity to a spectrum of test organisms. There will undoubtedly prove to be organisms unusually sensitive or unexpectedly more resistant to the toxin than the standard tests reveal, but they provide a method of screening new products and giving early warning of more obvious hazards. With suitably refined techniques, it may be possible to identify which of several contaminants is primarily responsible for known damage or to identify which contaminants in combination are causing ecosystem damage. But in general, these tests are not useful in predicting the ecological impact of a toxin.

Acute and chronic exposure

It is important to distinguish between two ways in which an organism may be exposed to a poisonous substance. **Acute** exposure is a single event, **chronic** exposure continues over a long time. The wreck of an oil tanker on the coast is an acute incident: a single, damaging event from which, once the oil is removed, recovery can begin. A refinery effluent containing petroleum hydrocarbons is chronic: the initial damage may be much less than from an acute oil spill, but since the discharge continues, recovery cannot begin and, indeed, the damage is progressive.

In the same way, the **acute toxicity** of a substance is the lethal amount when it is administered in a single dose. The **chronic toxicity** is the lethal amount when the substance is administered continuously over a long period. It generally follows that the LD_m for acute poisoning is much higher than that for chronic poisoning.

Detoxication

Extraordinarily high concentrations of heavy metals have been found in some animals in the sea: 2000 p.p.m. (dry weight) of cadmium in the digestive gland of some scallops and 57 000 p.p.m. (dry weight) of zinc in some oysters. If such concentrations were circulating freely in the animal they would be lethal, but in at least some animals methods have been developed for storing metals in the body in an innocuous form. Two methods of such **detoxication** are known.

One method involves the formation of **metallothioneins**. Exposure of the animal to a low concentration of metal induces the synthesis of low-molecular-weight proteins which form a complex with the metal. The metal is then unable to become involved in chemical processes, interference with which is the source of its toxicity. This phenomenon was first discovered in mammals but very similar metal-binding proteins have been found in a variety of other animals and they are probably widespread. Cadmium-binding proteins have been identified in seals, rockfish (*Sebastodes*), and molluscs. Both copper and cadmium are bound by a thionein in crabs, where the primary storage site of the metallothionein is the hepatopancreas. Metallothioneins incorporating zinc, copper, and cadmium have been found in the sea urchin *Strongylocentrotus purpureus*. Metallothioneins binding gold, silver, and mercury have been found in the rat liver and it is possible that these and perhaps others will prove to occur in a variety of marine animals.

A second method of detoxicating metals has now been detected in nearly all animal groups. The metal is stored in granular form; the granules are bounded by a membrane and are therefore isolated from chemical activity in the cell. The membrane may be derived from endoplasmic reticulum, the Golgi apparatus, or the cell membrane of the storage cell. So far, three types of granule have been found:

(1) copper-containing granules which generally also contain sulphur and perhaps traces of calcium;
(2) calcium-containing granules either of high purity, or in which, in addition to calcium, there is also manganese, magnesium, and phosphorus, and sometimes other metals such as zinc, cadmium, lead, and iron;
(3) iron-containing granules.

The calcium-containing granules of high purity are commonly involved in some essential activity in the animal and are not concerned with heavy-metal detoxication. Examples of such granules occur in the calciferous glands of earthworms, and they are stored and used for calcification of the shell in bivalves and barnacles.

Impure calcium-containing granules appear to be a system for incorporating and detoxifying metals, though the mechanisms of this are not yet fully understood.

Iron appears to be accumulated through life by the heart urchin *Bryssopsis*, but in many organisms the metal granules can be excreted, though this may involve a special process which is not yet understood. Reduction of the amount of copper and zinc in the commercial shrimp *Penaeus semiculcatus* during pre- and post-moult periods suggests that the granules are eliminated from the hepatopancreas at these times.

Some of these detoxicating mechanisms have only a limited capacity, though little study has been made of this feature of them. When the maximum capacity of the detoxicating mechanism is reached, the animal is then exposed to the toxic effects of the heavy metal.

5

Metals

Input routes

Metals are natural constituents of seawater and assessing the effect of inputs resulting from human activities is complicated by the very large natural inputs from the erosion of ore-bearing rocks, wind-blown dust, volcanic activity, forest fires, and vegetation.

Most rivers make a major contribution of metals to the sea, the nature of the input depending on the occurrence of metal and ore-bearing deposits in the drainage area. Where the river passes through urban or industrialized centres, the metal burden is augmented by human wastes and discharges.

The intense sedimentation in estuaries (see p. 15) traps a large quantity of metals which become adsorbed on to sediment particles and carried to the bottom. Sediments in industrialized estuaries with major ports contain the legacy of a century or more of waste discharges. Regular dredging of shipping channels in such areas produces large quantities of dredging spoil which is heavily contaminated with metals and is usually dumped at sea.

A third major input of metals to the sea, particularly near the coasts of industrialized countries, is from the atmosphere (see below). Atmospheric processes are still poorly understood and estimates of inputs of metals to the sea by this route vary quite widely, but all estimates suggest that this input is considerable.

Much smaller quantities of metals are added to the sea by direct discharges of industrial and other wastes by pipeline, and in sewage sludge and industrial wastes that are dumped at sea. Ocean incineration (see p. 110) makes a very small contribution. Although these inputs are relatively small, they may be locally significant if they are added to areas of sea where there is limited water circulation.

Table 5.1 shows the estimated inputs of four metals to the North Sea by various routes. The atmosphere is a more significant route for lead than it is for other metals, but apart from this, the relative importance of the various routes is much the same for all metals. The North Sea is a relatively enclosed body of water, surrounded by industrialized countries, with the rivers entering it draining much of the most heavily industrialized parts of central

Table 5.1. Input of four metals to the North Sea (t yr^{-1})

Source	Copper	Mercury	Lead	Zinc
Rivers	1290–1330	20–21	920–980	7360–7370
Dredgings	1000	17	170	8000
Atmosphere	400–1600	10–30	2600–7400	4900–11 000
Direct discharge	315	5	170	1170
Industrial dumping	160	0.2	200	450
Sewage sludge	100	0.6	100	220
Incineration	3	—	2	12

and western Europe. The figures in the table therefore reflect an extreme situation.

Atmospheric inputs

An important route by which some metals enter the sea is via the atmosphere. There are large natural inputs of some metals, such as aluminium in wind-blown dust derived from rocks and shales, and mercury from volcanic activity and degassing of the earth's crust, but for some metals, inputs to the atmosphere as a result of human activities are greater, sometimes much greater, than natural inputs (Table 5.2).

Table 5.2. World-wide emissions of trace metals to the atmosphere (in thousand t yr^{-1})

Metal	Natural sources	Anthropogenic sources
Arsenic	7.8	24
Cadmium	0.96	7.3
Copper	19	56
Nickel	26	47
Lead	19	449
Selenium	0.4	1.1
Zinc	4	314

These atmospheric contaminants may exist as gases (mercury, selenium, and boron) or aerosols (most other metals). They are deposited by **gas exchange** at the sea surface or the fallout of particles (**dry deposition**) or scavenged from much of the air column by precipitation within clouds (**wet deposition**). Sometimes the particles provide the nuclei about which water drops form. The length of time a

Marine Pollution

contaminant remains in the atmosphere, and so the distance it travels in an air mass, depends on its reactivity if it is a gas or its density if a particle. Lead has a residence time of about 5 days; gaseous organic compounds, tens or hundreds of days.

It is difficult to estimate atmospheric inputs to the sea; rates of precipitation over the sea, crucial for estimating wet deposition for example, are very poorly known. Table 5.3 shows current estimates of metal inputs from the atmosphere to

Table 5.3. Transfer of metals from the atmosphere to the sea surface (in $ng\ cm^{-2}\ yr^{-1}$)

Element	North Sea	Western Mediterranean	South Atlantic Bight	Tropical North Atlantic	Tropical North Pacific
Aluminium	30 000	5000	2900	5000	1200
Manganese	920	—	60	70	9
Iron	25 500	5100	5900	3200	560
Nickel	260	—	390	20	—
Copper	1 300	96	220	25	8.9
Zinc	8 950	1080	750	130	67
Arsenic	280	54	45	—	—
Cadmium	43	13	9	5	0.35
Mercury	—	5	24	2.1	—
Lead	2 650	1050	660	310	7.0

various sea areas, but these figures may need revision as more information becomes available.

Air–sea interactions are not a one-way process. Bubbles bursting at the sea surface release sea salt particles to the atmosphere and there is evidence that these particles become enriched with other contaminants during their formation. The sea is therefore a **source** of contaminants to the atmosphere as well as a **sink** for atmospheric contaminants. Too little is understood about these processes to make very firm estimates of the relative importance of inputs to and outputs from the sea surface. Some idea of the possible scale of natural contributions from the sea to the atmosphere can be gained from the discovery that dimethyl sulphide synthesized by phytoplankton blooms of coccolithophores in the North Sea and released to the atmosphere, may be responsible for half the acid rain falling on coastal areas in summer.

Uptake of metals

Many metals are essential for living organisms:

- the respiratory pigment haemoglobin found in vertebrates and many invertebrates contains iron;
- the respiratory pigment of many molluscs and higher crustaceans, haemocyanin, contains copper;
- the respiratory pigment of tunicates contains vanadium;
- many enzymes contain zinc;
- vitamin B_{12} enzymes contain cobalt.

Metals of biological concern may be divided into three groups:

(1) light metals (sodium, potassium, calcium, etc.) normally transported as mobile cations in aqueous solutions;
(2) transitional metals (e.g. iron, copper, cobalt, and manganese) which are essential in low concentrations but may be toxic in high concentrations;
(3) heavy metals or metalloids (e.g. mercury, lead, tin, selenium, and arsenic) which are generally not required for metabolic activity and are toxic to the cell at quite low concentrations.

Particularly among polychaete worms, metals are accumulated for unexpected reasons. High concentrations of zinc in the jaws of nereids and copper in the jaws of *Glycera* have a structural role, strengthening the tips of the jaws. *Nereis* also accumulates manganese in its jaws. Copper accumulated in the gills of the ampharetid *Melinna palmata* has the defensive function of reducing the palatability of the worm to predators. The cirratulid *Tharyx marioni* has a high and constant level of arsenic in its feeding palps; its function is unknown.

Absorption of heavy metals from solutions is dependent on active transport systems in some micro-organisms and sea urchin larvae, but generally in plants and animals it is by passive diffusion across gradients created by adsorption at the surface, and by binding by constituents of the surface cells, body fluids, etc. An alternative and important pathway for animals is when metals are adsorbed on to or are present in food, and by the collection of particulate or colloidal metal by a food-collecting mechanism such as the bivalve gill. There is considerable variation in the extent to which plants and animals can regulate the concentrations of metals in the body. Plants and bivalve molluscs are poor regulators of heavy metals. Decapod crustaceans and fish are generally able to regulate essential metals such as zinc and copper, but non-essentials such as mercury and cadmium are less well regulated.

Mercury

Sources and inputs to the marine environment

The annual world production of mercury reached a peak of 10 600 t in 1971, falling to a little over 6000 t in 1987. A typical pattern of the use of mercury in an industrialized country is shown in Table 5.4.

A substantial proportion of this annual production eventually reaches the

Table 5.4.   Consumption (in t) of mercury in the United States

	1968	1974–5
Agriculture	118.3	91.4
Amalgams	9.8	8.6
Catalysts	59.0	81.8
Dental applications	120.7	131.1
Electrical apparatus	593.4	783.2
Electrolytic preparation of chlorine and caustic soda	601.1	788.8
General laboratory use	71.6	71.6
Industrial and control instruments	307.1	319.1
Paints	364.5	370.0
Paper and pulp	12.9	8.6
Pharmaceuticals	20.7	22.4
Other*	269.6	205.6
Total	2548.7	2882.2

* Including start-up of new chlorine cells

natural environment. Table 5.5 shows estimated losses for different years in Finland and Sweden. About half the mercury lost is from the chlor-alkali industry. Chlorine and caustic soda are produced electrolytically using mercury electrodes and it has been common with this process for 150–200 g of mercury to be lost to the atmosphere and in waste waters for each tonne of product. Most of the remaining half of the lost mercury comes from uses which inevitably disperse mercurial compounds into the environment: 'slimicides' used in the lumber and paper pulp industries to prevent fungal growth, anti-fouling paints for ship hulls, pesticides and seed dressings in agriculture, and in pharmaceuticals.

These inputs are estimated to amount to about 5000 t yr^{-1} world-wide, but a further 3000 t yr^{-1} is derived from burning fossil fuels. Crude oil and coal contain only traces of mercury, varying widely but perhaps averaging 1 µg g^{-1} (p.p.m.). They are, however, burned in such large quantities that their input to the atmosphere is considerable.

Following the discovery in the early 1960s of the dangers to human health of mercury in the sea, there has been a marked reduction in inputs from some major sources in some areas. Direct inputs of mercury in waste water from new chlor-alkali plants are now usually small, though older factories have difficulty in reducing the mercury content in their effluent below 8 µg g^{-1}. Mercury losses to the atmosphere from this source can be reduced by cooling the exhaust gases.

Sweden banned the use of mercurial slimicides in the wood and paper pulp industries in 1967 and several other countries followed suit. This has not been without its problems, however, because pentachlorophenol which replaced the mercurial slimicides proves to be damaging to macrofauna at concentrations of

Table 5.5. Consumption of mercury (in t yr^{-1}) in Finland and Sweden, and estimated losses to rivers, lakes, and the sea

	Consumption (t yr^{-1})	
	Finland 1954–66	Sweden 1967
Chlorine industry, increase of capacity	22	?
Chlorine production, replacement for losses	10	25–38
Paper and pulp industry, as slimicides and fungicides	10	14*
Agriculture, as pesticides	4	5
Other uses	4	~30
Total	50	74–87
	Losses into waters (t yr^{-1})	
	Finland 1954–66	Sweden 1967
Chlorine industry	4	8
Paper and pulp industry		
as slimicides	3.6	3.2†
as caustic soda	0.5	1.0
Agriculture, as pesticides	0.3	0.3
Other industries	0.2	1.5
	8.6	14.0

* Now discontinued
† 1941–68

75 µg l^{-1} and has been found to accumulate in at least one marine organism, the polychaete *Lanice*.

Natural inputs of mercury are from two sources. About 3500 t yr^{-1} is derived from the weathering of mercury-bearing rocks, but anything from 25 000–150 000 t yr^{-1} is released to the atmosphere as gases from volcanic areas, geothermal vents, and other sites of degassing of the Earth's crust.

Although it cannot be estimated reliably, atmospheric input is important in the open oceans where mercury concentrations vary between 0.001 and 0.05 µg l^{-1} (p.p.b.). Major sources of mercury in coastal waters are rivers, marine outfalls, and wastes dumped directly into the sea. The existence of such localized inputs is reflected in the raised mercury content of local plankton and mussels.

Dissolved mercury in the sea is in the form of $Hg(OH)_2$ or $HgCl_2$ with chloride predominating, but to a considerable extent, mercury is adsorbed on to particulate matter and is not in solution. It also forms stable complexes with organic compounds occurring in the sea, especially sulphur-containing proteins and humic substances. In anoxic substrates, mercury may be present as Hg, HgS, and HgS_2. Microbial systems in the sea can convert all these inorganic forms of mercury into methyl mercury. This is readily released from sedimentary particles into the water and may then be accumulated by living organisms.

Mercury in algae and invertebrates

Organic forms of mercury are more toxic than inorganic salts. Table 5.6 shows

Table 5.6. Toxicity of various mercury compounds to the red alga, *Plumaria elegans*

Compounds	18 h LC_{50} (p.p.b. Hg)
Methyl mercuric chloride	44
Ethyl mercuric chloride	26
n-Propyl mercuric chloride	13
n-Butyl mercuric chloride	13
n-Amyl mercuric chloride	13
Isopropyl mercuric chloride	28
Isoamyl mercuric chloride	19
Phenyl mercuric chloride	54
Phenyl mercuric iodide	104
Mercuric iodide	156
Mercuric chloride	3120

the 18 h LC_{50} of a number of mercury compounds to the red alga *Plumaria elegans*, and there is a similar pattern of toxicity of these compounds to larvae of the barnacle *Elminius* and brine shrimp *Artemia*. As with other metals, bivalve molluscs take up mercury from the surrounding water very quickly. Figure 5.1 shows the uptake of mercury by the commercial species *Crassostrea virginica* exposed to mercuric acetate. The distribution of mercury in the tissues varies (Fig. 5.2) and in bivalves the highest concentration is in the viscera, the lowest in the muscles. Once the molluscs are returned to uncontaminated water, the mercury is lost from the body.

Mercury in fish

Most species of fish in oceanic waters contain 150 µg kg^{-1} (0.15 p.p.m.) mercury in muscles, though much higher values are found in fish from contaminated waters. Cod taken from the strait between Denmark and Sweden, which is

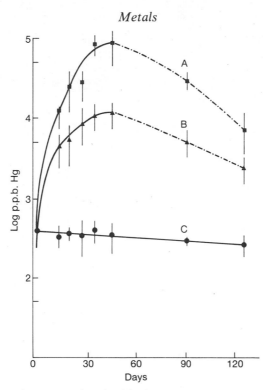

Fig. 5.1. Uptake of mercury by the bivalve *Crassostrea virginica* exposed to (A) 100 p.p.b. and (B) 10 p.p.b. mercuric acetate for 45 days (————), and subsequent loss of mercury after transfer to uncontaminated seawater (–·–·–·–). (C) Control.

heavily contaminated with mercury, contain up to 1.29 p.p.m.; those from the North Sea 0.15–0.20 p.p.m.; and those from Greenland only 0.01–0.04 p.p.m. Some species, notably tunny (*Thunnus* spp.), swordfish (*Xiphias gladius*), marlin (*Makaira indica*), and some other large, oceanic pelagic fish, naturally contain high concentrations of mercury. Concentrations of 1 p.p.m. in the muscle are common and may be as high as 4.9 p.p.m. There are several reasons for this. These fish are large carnivores at the end of food chains and their diets therefore contain high levels of mercury resulting from bioaccumulation and biomagnification. Food is not their only source of mercury. They are very active fish with a high metabolic rate. They swim continuously with their mouths open, so producing a forced flow of water across the gills. This results in a large uptake of oxygen, but also of metals (including mercury) dissolved in the water. Much of this mercury is in the form of methyl mercury and because the fish cannot excrete it, its concentration in the tissues increases with the age of the fish. It is the large, old specimens that have high body burdens of mercury, and warnings are given about the danger of eating the flesh of very large fish of these species.

Halibut (*Hippoglossus hippoglossus*) is another long-lived species that

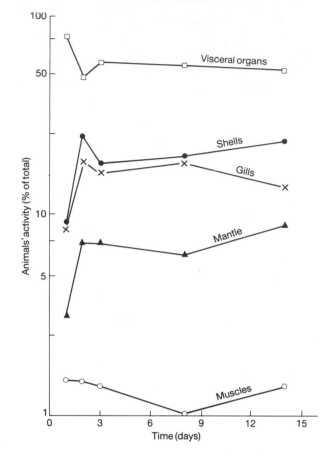

Fig. 5.2. Uptake of mercury (as ^{203}HgCl$_2$) in different tissues of the bivalve *Venerupis decussata. (Copyright FAO.)*

accumulates large concentrations of mercury. A big halibut of 300 kg may be 50 years old. All specimens over 115 kg and half those weighing more than 60 kg may be expected to contain over 1 p.p.m. muscle mercury. As with most fish, more than 90 per cent of this is in the form of methyl mercury and such fish are unsuitable for human consumption. They are either discarded or used for fishmeal. Their high concentration of mercury can then be diluted by the large mass of small fish containing little mercury that make up the bulk of fishmeal for animal feed.

Mercury in birds

Birds tend to accumulate mercury in the liver and the feathers. Most published records refer to liver or feather mercury and measurements are given on the basis of dry weight (see p. 66). Levels of contamination therefore appear far higher than those in fish for which measurements generally refer to edible parts (i.e. muscle mercury) and are given on a wet weight basis. The fact that mercury accumulates in feathers is interesting because it allows a study to be made of museum specimens, revealing levels of mercury contamination at various places and times in the past when the specimens were collected.

The larger sea birds may live for 20 years or more and those feeding at high trophic levels are likely to accumulate mercury. Species that feed on or close to shore are most at risk: black guillemot (*Cepphus grylle*) are inshore feeders and contain more mercury than common guillemot (*Uria aalge*) and Brünnich's guillemot (*U. lomvia*) which feed out at sea.

The contamination of the Baltic is reflected in the mercury levels in fish-eating birds from Scandinavia. Wing feathers of ospreys (*Pandion haliaetus*) replaced there contain more mercury than those replaced in their winter quarters in Africa. Feathers of Baltic guillemots contain three to five times as much mercury as those from Faeroese or Greenland birds. Measurements of the mercury in the feathers of museum specimens of Baltic Guillemots has shown that the level of contamination rose by two to five times in the first half of this century, though since the late 1960s it has started to decline again.

The transfer of mercury to feathers which are periodically moulted may be an important safety valve for birds exposed to heavy-metal contamination. In Sweden and Finland, the population of both ospreys and white-tailed eagles (*Haliaetus albicilla*) has declined during this century and mercury has been thought to be a factor. These are fish-eating birds and the mercury concentration in feathers of the white-tailed eagle increased from an average of 6.6 p.p.m. in Swedish museum specimens collected between 1880 and 1940, to about 50 p.p.m. in 1964–5. In the mid-1960s, white-tailed eagles are known to have died from mercury poisoning in south-west Finland, but ospreys appear not to have suffered in this way.

A study of osprey nestlings in Finland showed that there is certainly a relationship between the concentration of mercury in their diet and that in their plumage, although there is a limit to the concentration of mercury that can be acquired by feathers (Fig. 5.3). Even so, in 2.5 per cent of the nestlings examined, the mercury content of the feathers was over 30 p.p.m. Comparisons of nestlings from Lapland (uncontaminated) and from Hämeenkyrö in south-west Finland (relatively contaminated) showed that in the former the concentration of mercury in the liver (dry weight) was twice that in the feathers; in the contaminated area, the feather concentration was actually greater than that in the liver (Table 5.7). More striking, in terms of the total body burden of mercury, nestlings containing 60 µg of mercury have one-third of it in the plumage, but nestlings containing 770 µg stored two-thirds of it in the plumage. It is not known if white-tailed eagles have less ability to transfer mercury to the plumage, but in ospreys this appears to be a method of removing mercury from tissues where it

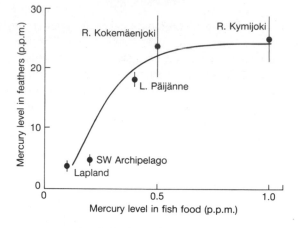

Fig. 5.3. Mercury concentration in feathers of nestling ospreys in five areas of Finland in relation to the mercury concentration in local fish.

Table 5.7. Mercury in osprey nestlings from Lapland (uncontaminated) and south-west Finland (relatively contaminated)

	Inari (Lapland)	Hämeenkyrö (SW Finland)
Liver (wet wt) (p.p.m.)	0.2	1.8
(dry wt) (p.p.m.)	0.8	7.1
Feathers (p.p.m.)	0.4	8.3
Total body burden (μg)	60.5	772.8
% in plumage	32.6	65.5

can interfere with metabolic processes. This is, in fact, a method of detoxication and excretion.

Mercury in sea mammals

Marine mammals accumulate large quantities of mercury from their food apparently without coming to harm. Selenium antagonizes the toxic effects of mercury, and in seals, sea lions, and dolphins, the selenium concentration in the tissues keeps pace with the amount of mercury. Mercury selenide found in the connective tissue of the liver of dolphins is apparently a product of a detoxifying mechanism for the methyl mercury acquired from their food.

Minamata disease

That mercury is toxic to humans has been known for centuries. Mad hatters in Victorian England got their name from convulsions and loss of neuromuscular co-ordination, symptomatic of chronic poisoning by the mercury used in the treatment of felt in the manufacture of hats. In this century, mercury has been the only contaminant introduced by man into the sea that has certainly been responsible for human deaths.

Mercury poisoning resulting from pollution of the sea occurred at the small Japanese coastal town of Minamata where part of the population is dependent on fishing for a livelihood and the only industry is a factory which began producing vinyl chloride and acetaldehyde in 1952. This illness affected only fishermen and their families and first appeared in 1953, but was not diagnosed as metal poisoning derived from fish and seafood taken from part of Minamata Bay until 1956. In all, 2000 cases were recognized; of these, 43 died during the epidemic and over 700 of the survivors were left with severe permanent disabilities. Fishing in part of the bay was banned from the start of 1957 and the epidemic halted, but it was not until 1959 that it was shown that mercury was the toxic element involved, and 1960 that the source was the effluent from the vinyl chloride factory discharged into the bay near the affected community.

A second outbreak of mercury poisoning in Japan occurred among fishermen living near the mouth of the Agamo river in 1965. Like the Minamata tragedy, this was caused by the contamination of fish by mercury from an industrial effluent, in this case, from a factory 60 km upstream.

The Minamata disaster was investigated in detail. It proved to be a classical example of methyl mercury poisoning. Methyl mercury is more dangerous to humans than inorganic mercury because it cannot be excreted. It therefore acts as a cumulative poison and, since it can cross the barrier from blood vessels in the brain into the nervous tissue ('the blood–brain barrier'), it causes progressive and irreversible brain damage. The chief danger from inorganic mercury depends on chronic exposure to it (as in some industrial processes where the victim is in daily contact with the toxin); the danger of methyl mercury poisoning resides in the total life dose.

In addition to methyl mercury produced by methylating bacteria from inorganic mercury, effluent from the Minamata factory included methyl mercury as well as the inorganic form. In the 1950s, this factory manufactured acetaldehyde by a process using mercuric sulphate as a catalyst. Typically 300–1000 g of mercury is lost for each tonne of acetaldehyde produced by this method and about 5 per cent of it is in the form of methyl mercury. Mercuric chloride is used as a catalyst in the manufacture of vinyl chloride and about 1 g of methyl mercury per tonne of product is lost in the washing process. Investigations carried out in Minamata Bay in 1959 revealed contamination of

sediment as high as 200 p.p.m. mercury near the factory outfall, declining to
12 p.p.m. at some distance. Plankton contained 5 p.p.m., bivalves from intertidal areas contained 10–39 p.p.m. (dry weight), and fish 10–55 p.p.m. (dry
weight); most of the mercury in the fish was methylated.

Public health standards

Following the Minamata disaster there was a greater appreciation of the risk of
mercury poisoning from eating contaminated seafood, and several countries
introduced legal standards for mercury in food offered for sale. The World Health
Organization (WHO) recommended a maximum tolerable consumption of
mercury in food of 0.2 mg of methyl mercury or 0.3 mg of total mercury per week.
Any standard must take into account how much fish is eaten as well as the
concentration of mercury in it. In Japan, for example, a far wider range and
quantity of seafood is eaten than in Britain where the average per capita
consumption of fish is only 20 g per day.

Standards adopted for maximum permitted mercury levels in seafood are
0.5 μg g^{-1} (p.p.m.) in the United States and Canada; 0.7 μg g^{-1} in Italy;
1.0 μg g^{-1} in Japan, Germany, Sweden, and Switzerland; and 1.5 μg g^{-1} in
Norway. No standards have been introduced in Britain because of the low
consumption of fish which generally contains no more than 0.3 μg g^{-1}
mercury.

Sweden initially intended to introduce a limit of 0.5 μg g^{-1} but discovered that
much of the fish in the Baltic and inland lakes contained more than this and to
have adopted such a stringent standard would have excluded much otherwise
wholesome fish from the market. Instead, the limit of 1.0 μg g^{-1} was set, but the
public was advised not to eat more than two fish meals per week.

In 1970, it was discovered that samples of canned tuna on supermarket shelves
in the United States contained more than 0.5 μg g^{-1} mercury. This led to a
temporary withdrawal of tuna until it was discovered that only a small
proportion of cans (presumably of older, larger fish) had such a high mercury
content.

Cadmium

Sources and inputs

Cadmium is widely distributed in the Earth's crust, but is particularly associated
with zinc and it is produced commercially only as a by-product of zinc smelting.
Cadmium has been used in quantity since about 1950 and total world production
is about 15 000–18 000 t yr^{-1}. The principal uses of cadmium are as stabilizers
and pigments in plastics and in electroplating, but substantial amounts are used
in solders and other alloys and in batteries.

Less than 10 per cent of the cadmium used in these primary products is recycled and the rest must be assumed to be released to the environment. Although they cannot be quantified, other inputs to the environment are from a variety of often diffuse sources:

- fumes, dust, and waste water from lead and zinc mining and refining, as well as from cadmium production;
- rinsing water from electroplating with 100–500 p.p.m. cadmium;
- the iron, steel, and non-ferrous metal industries produce dust, fumes, waste water, and sludge containing cadmium;
- zinc used in galvanized coatings of metals contains about 0.2 per cent cadmium as an impurity; it is estimated that all this cadmium is lost to the environment through corrosion within four to twelve years;
- wear of automobile tyres which contain 20–90 p.p.m. cadmium as an impurity in the zinc oxide used as a curing accelerator;
- phosphate rocks may contain 100 p.p.m. cadmium, and phosphate fertilizers are a source of cadmium in the environment;
- coal contains 0.25–5.0 p.p.m. and heating oils average 0.3 p.p.m. cadmium, an unknown amount of which is discharged to the atmosphere;
- sewage sludge contains up to 30 p.p.m. cadmium.

The total input of cadmium to the world oceans is estimated to be nearly 8000 t yr^{-1}, about half of it the result of man's activities, the rest natural. Rivers and atmospheric inputs are equally important. About 2900 t yr^{-1} of the cadmium is deposited in bottom sediments (most on the continental shelf) but it is difficult to account for the fate of the rest. Known fates of cadmium in the sea do not balance the marine budget and the camium content of the sea may be slowly increasing.

Cadmium in marine organisms

Cadmium is not an essential element for any organism, although for unknown reasons, it enhances phytoplankton photosynthesis and growth at concentrations up to 100 p.p.m. Because of its associations with phosphates, cadmium is assumed to be taken up by phytoplankton, but except in two instances, it does not appear to accumulate in the food chain. The euphausiid *Meganyctiphanes norvegica*, for example, feeding on phytoplankton containing 2.1 p.p.m. (dry weight) of cadmium, produces faecal pellets containing 9.6 p.p.m. (dry weight) but has a whole-body concentration of only 0.7 p.p.m. (dry weight). At higher levels in the food web, fishes and sea mammals have low concentrations of cadmium, at most a few p.p.m., stored chiefly in the kidney, and they are able to detoxify it by the production of a metallothionein.

Zooplankton in the surface layers of the ocean evidently have high cadmium levels because petrels and the hemipteran sea skater *Halobates*, both of which feed on surface zooplankton far from sources of contamination, tend to have high concentrations of cadmium. Petrels may contain 49 p.p.m. (dry weight) in the liver and 240 p.p.m. (dry weight) in the kidney; *Halobates* normally contains 33 p.p.m., but may contain as much as 330 p.p.m. (dry weight) cadmium.

Molluscs accumulate large concentrations of cadmium. This is particularly so in the bivalve Pectinidae: *Pecten novae zetlandiae* has been found with 2000 p.p.m. (dry weight) in the liver, but 1900 p.p.m. (dry weight) has been found in the oceanic squid *Symplectoteuthis oualaniensis*, and oysters, limpets (*Patella vulgata*), and dog whelk (*Nucella lapillus*) also acquire high concentrations of cadmium. *Nucella* shows clear evidence of accumulation of cadmium: in the Bristol Channel this dog whelk was found to contain 38 p.p.m. of cadmium, but the barnacles on which it feeds contained only 0.15 p.p.m.

Studies in the cadmium-contaminated Severn estuary and Bristol Channel in south-west Britain, where the input is from natural sources, and in the Sörfjord, a branch of the Hardanger fjord in Norway which receives smelter wastes, have failed to show any ecological effect beyond the contamination of some members of the local fauna.

Itai-itai disease and public health

Cadmium achieved notoriety in the aftermath of the Minamata disaster when it was suspected of being responsible for an outbreak of itai-itai disease in a Japanese village on the Jintsu river. This painful disease affected particularly the bones and joints and resulted in 100 deaths. It was attributed to contamination of rice by cadmium from the effluent from a zinc smelter. There is now doubt, however, whether itai-itai is cadmium-related or is more likely to have been associated with malnutrition and vitamin deficiency. High concentrations of cadmium (173 p.p.m.) and zinc (57 600 p.p.m.) in oysters, *Crassostrea gigas*, from the Derwent estury in Tasmania caused nausea and vomiting in people consuming them, but there is no evidence of people being permanently affected by eating fish or shellfish contaminated with cadmium. With the exception of oysters, scallops and probably other bivalves from contaminated water, seafood contains no more cadmium than other foods and does not represent a special hazard.

Cadmium and its compounds, along with mercury and some other dangerous metals, are, however, included in the 'black list' of materials which by international agreement may not be discharged or dumped into the sea.

Copper

Sources and inputs to the sea

The natural input of copper to the marine environment from erosion of mineralized rocks is esimated to be 325 000 t yr^{-1}. Inputs from human activities are localized and vary widely in their nature. About 7.5 million t yr^{-1} of copper is produced for use in electrical equipment, in alloys, as a chemical catalyst, in antifouling paint for ships' hulls, as an algicide, and a wood preservative. Several of these uses inevitably result in copper being transfered to the environment. Urban sewage contains a substantial amount of copper and this is reflected in enhanced concentrations in sediments at sludge dumping grounds (see Figs. 2.9(c) and 2.11(c)). The municipal waste from Los Angeles is estimated to contribute 510 t of copper to the sea annually. Run-off from mine tailings in tin and copper mining areas results in high copper and zinc concentrations in the river Fal in Cornwall and Rio Tinto in Spain. Antifouling paint releases all its copper to the sea. This is not a negligible amount: some antifouling paints contain 500 g l^{-1} of copper and it is estimated that 180 t yr^{-1} of copper entered the coastal waters of California between Santa Barbara and San Diego from this source alone until copper was replaced by tin compounds in antifouling paints.

Dissolved copper in the sea is in the form of $CuCO_3$, Cu^{2+}, and $CuOH^+$, but copper is one of the metals readily removed from solution by adsorption to particles and it is estimated that 83 per cent of copper in the sea is in this form.

Copper in marine organisms

Copper is an essential element for animals and the highest concentrations are found in decapod crustaceans, gastropods, and cephalopods in which the respiratory pigment haemocyanin contains copper. Excess copper is usually stored in the liver, 4800 p.p.m. copper has been detected in the liver of *Octopus vulgaris* and 2000 p.p.m. in the hepatopancreas of a lobster, *Homarus gammarus*. Oysters which lack haemocyanin may acquire very high concentrations of copper, stored mostly in the wandering leucocytes, and these blood cells may contain 20 000 p.p.m. copper and 60 000 p.p.m. zinc.

Although plankton, fish, and shellfish from areas known to be contaminated contain higher concentrations of copper than those from uncontaminated areas, copper does not generally accumulate in food chains. A predatory fish, the marlin (*Makaira indica*) at the top of a food chain accumulates mercury (see p. 87) but has low concentrations of copper: 0.3–1.2 p.p.m. (average 0.4 p.p.m., wet weight) in muscles and 0.5–22.0 p.p.m. (average 4.6 p.p.m., wet weight) in the liver.

Despite the existence of a number of detoxifying and storage systems for copper, it is the most toxic metal, after mercury and silver, to a wide spectrum of marine life, hence its value in antifouling preparations. Its damaging effect is illustrated by the case of a quantity of copper sulphate illegally dumped on the Dutch coast near Noordwijk in 1965. A body of water containing more than 0.3 p.p.m. copper moved slowly up the coast, causing the death of plankton, fish, and shellfish (Fig. 5.4). There were fears that it would reach the extensive shellfish beds in the Waddensee where the economic losses would have been very great.

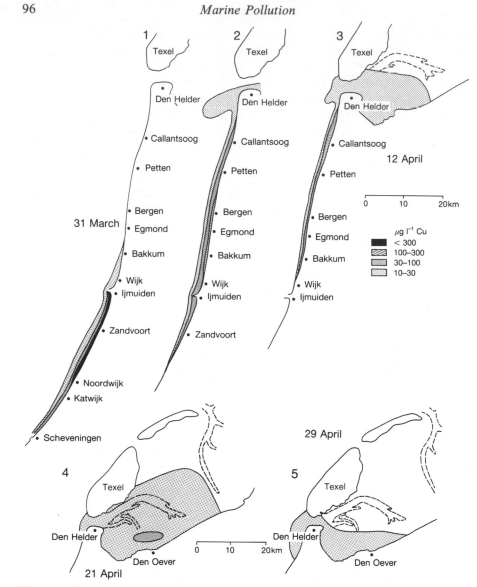

Fig. 5.4. Movement of copper sulphate on the Dutch coast after being dumped on the beach at Nordwijk, from 31 March to 29 April 1965.

Fortunately, strong winds produced the necessary mixing and dilution, and this catastrophe was averted.

The very long-standing contamination of the estuary of the river Fal in south Cornwall has been investigated in detail, with interesting results. One branch of the estuary, Restronguet Creek (Fig. 5.5), is fed by the Carnon river which drains

Fig. 5.5. River Fal and its tributaries. The Carnon river drains the chief tin mining area: 1–12 are sampling areas, △ indicates tin mines. Inset: west Cornwall, showing metalliferous areas and the study area. *(Cambridge University Press.)*

a formerly very productive tin mining area. Alluvial tin has been recovered from Restronguet Creek for several thousand years since the Bronze Age, and the river has received wastes from deep mining for several hundred years. In the nineteenth century, arsenic refining and lead and tin smelting were carried out in the Carnon valley, adding to the contamination of Restronguet Creek. Although mining activity is now reduced, drainage from ancient mine tailings continues to carry a heavy load of metals into the creek. Levels of contamination of sediments are: zinc 2700 p.p.m., copper 2148 p.p.m., arsenic 1732 p.p.m. These very high levels of contamination are about two orders of magnitude greater than for uncontaminated estuaries.

Despite this great contamination, the fauna and flora of Restronguet Creek is unexpectedly normal. Only bivalve molluscs, with the exception of *Scrobicularia plana*, and the estuarine gastropod *Hydrobia ulvae* are conspicuously absent. A variety of factors explains the presence of organisms in the water and sediment which might have been expected to be lethal.

Concentrations of copper in the polychaete *Nereis diversicolor* are closely related to those in the sediment and worms containing more than 1000 p.p.m. have been found in the creek. The copper is stored in the epidermal cells. Such levels would be lethal to *N. diversicolor* from uncontaminated estuaries (see Fig. 4.2) and it appears that a copper-resistant strain of this species exists in the Fal. The alga *Fucus vesiculosus* in upper reaches of the creek accumulates several thousand p.p.m. of copper and zinc (Fig. 5.6) and may also be a tolerant strain. Resistant strains are also know to occur in the fouling alga *Ectocarpus siliculosus* which succeeds in growing on ships treated with copper-containing paint.

The polychaetes *Nephtys hombergi* and *Glycera convoluta* and the crab *Carcinus maenas* also show increased tolerance to copper but are mobile species with distributed larvae, and they colonize the creek from less contaminated areas. There may be some selection of tolerant individuals, but copper tolerance may also be induced in these species through exposure to sub-lethal concentrations as they migrate into the creek.

Larval bivalves are very sensitive to copper and also to zinc, and it is not surprising that they are unable to survive in the high concentrations prevailing in the creek. *Scrobicularia*, which does occur there, is confined to the highest tidal levels where it is exposed to much diluted river water. Breeding of this species is in July and August, and in dry autumn conditions with a low river input, juveniles have a chance to establish themselves.

Flounders, *Platychthys flesus*, feeding in the creek, largely on *Nereis diversicolor*, appear to be able to limit the assimilation of copper in the gut and do not acquire an increased body burden of the metal, although there is some evidence of liver damage in flounders exposed to high levels of metals.

Redshanks, *Tringa totanus*, wintering in the area, feed almost exclusively on *Nereis diversicolor* and the daily intake of worms by these birds is about equal to their body weight. They receive a high concentration of metals in their diet, but it is not known if they are affected by it.

Public health

Bivalves growing in contaminated water have the capacity to accumulate copper: the concentration factor for oysters is 7500 and they may accumulate so much copper that the flesh becomes green. This commonly happens to the oyster *Ostrea edulis* in the river Fal and they have to be relaid in uncontaminated water

Fig. 5.6. Copper in brown seaweeds, *Fucus*, in three rivers in South-west England: Restronguet Creek receives mine waste, the Tamar passes through old tin mining areas, and the Dart is only slightly influenced by previous mining. ○ ─── ○ growing tips; ●──● thallus; ○·····○ stipe.

for a year before they can be marketed. There is no danger to humans of copper poisoning from seafood—the lethal dose is about 100 mg—but the human taste threshold for copper is low, 5.0–7.5 p.p.m., and the taste is repulsive. There is an ample safety margin and copper in the sea is not regarded as a health hazard.

Lead

Sources and inputs

The total world production of lead is about 43 million t yr^{-1}. Much lead in metallic form, in battery casings and plates, in sheet and pipes, etc., is recovered and recycled, but most lead used in compound form is lost to the environment.

Nearly 10 per cent of the world production of lead is used as petrol additives such as lead tetraethyl and it is lost, largely to the atmosphere. Globally, inputs to the atmosphere resulting from human activities, 450 000 t yr^{-1}, dwarf natural inputs of 25 000 t yr^{-1}.

Lead aerosols are carried to Earth in rain and snow and are widely scattered. Figure 5.7 shows the lead content of the annual ice layers in Greenland from this

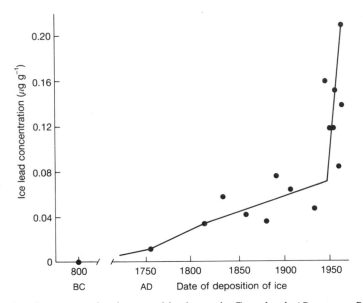

Fig. 5.7.   Lead concentration in annual ice layers in Greenland. *(Pergamon Press.)*

source. The start of the industrial revolution marks the first major increase in the deposition rate; the growth in the number of automobiles using leaded petrol since 1940 is reflected in a second marked acceleration in deposition rates. The lead content of a peat profile in Derbyshire (Fig. 5.8) shows a similar increase.

Local high concentrations of lead may be caused by special circumstances. Sea bass taken on the Californian coast near Los Angeles with its very high density of automobiles contain 22 p.p.m. (wet weight) of lead in their livers. Corresponding figures for fish caught 300 miles offshore have 10 p.p.m., and off the Peruvian coast 9 p.p.m.

Sewage sluge dumping grounds may be expected to contain high lead concentrations. Glasgow sewage sludge contains 771 p.p.m. lead, sediments in the dumping area 200–320 p.p.m., whereas the general background in the Firth of Clyde is 48–139 p.p.m. (Fig. 2.9(d)), and in an area far from sources of contamination such as Trinidad, only 22 p.p.m.

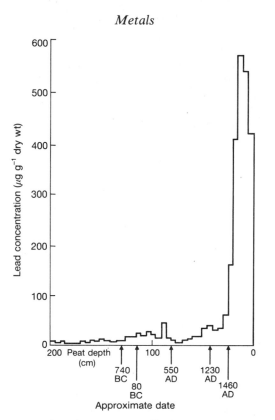

Fig. 5.8. Lead concentrations in a peat profile in Derbyshire. *(Copyright © 1973, Macmillan Journals Ltd.)*

Impact on marine organisms

Compared with other metals, lead in the sea is not particularly toxic and at concentrations up to 0.8 p.p.m., lead nitrate even enhances the growth of the diatom *Phaeodactylum* (Fig. 5.9), presumably through the nutrient effect of the nitrate. Sub-lethal effects of low concentrations include a depression of the growth of *Cristigera* (a ciliate protozoan) by 8.5 per cent at 0.15 p.p.m. and 11.8 per cent at 0.3 p.p.m. (Table 4.3, p. 72); the growth of the crustacean *Artemia* is significantly reduced at 5–10 p.p.m. and the mortality rate of the mussel *Mytilus edulis* is increased by prolonged exposure to 10 p.p.m. or less of lead salts.

Nevertheless, high concentrations of lead can be accumulated by some animals without apparent harm. The limpet *Acmaea digitalis* may contain about 100 p.p.m. on the Californian coast near San Fancisco where evidently the contamination is from aerial fall-out. In the river Gannel in north Cornwall

Fig. 5.9. Growth of a culture of the diatom *Phaeodactylum* with lead nitrate in various concentrations added after the first day.

where there is a natural input from lead deposits, estuarine sediments contain 2175 p.p.m. lead and the bivalve *Scrobicularia plana* living in them, contains 991 p.p.m. In the contaminated Sörfjord in Norway, seaweeds and animals contain high levels, the content in mussels rising to 3000 p.p.m.

Mytilus has a detoxifying mechanism for lead and stores large quantities in the form of granules in the digestive gland. Because of their tendency to accumulate metals, mussels are regularly monitored in Britain to ensure that none with a lead content exceeding the maximum allowable concentration of 10 p.p.m. are sold for human consumption. In practice, the actual value is usually considerably lower.

Fish contain little lead and the content in commercial species in Britain ranges between 0.05 and 0.15 p.p.m. The livers of fish-eating seals and porpoises contain no detectable lead. Evidently it does not present a hazard through bio-accumulation.

A rare instance of lead poisoning has occurred among sea birds wintering on the Mersey estuary: 2400 birds, mainly dunlin, died in 1979 and a smaller number the following year. The dead birds had more than 10 p.p.m. (dry weight) lead in their liver, 30–70 per cent of it in the form of tri-alkyl lead. Further investigations showed that birds with 0.5 p.p.m. tri-alkyl lead in the liver were at risk and some birds showed neuromuscular disorders symptomatic of lead poisoning. These waders acquired the lead from their food which was predominantly the bivalve *Macoma baltica* containing 1 p.p.m. lead, and the polychaete worm *Nereis diversicolor* containing 0.2 p.p.m. It is thought that a discharge of organic lead in factory effluent was responsible for contaminating the benthic fauna of the estuary.

Public health

Although lead is held responsible for serious damage to health on land, such contamination of the sea and marine products as occurs does not appear to be a matter for concern.

Iron

Iron is not usually a significant contaminant of the sea, but it has come to prominence over sea dumping of 'red mud' from the extraction of alumina from bauxite, and 'acid iron waste' from the production of titanium dioxide; both wastes contain a large amount of iron. It is unfortunate that titanium dioxide manufacture should create environmental problems because it was introduced as a white pigment in paints to allow lead pigments to be phased out, so reducing human exposure to lead. Very large quantities of these wastes are produced: western Europe produces about 7.5 million t yr^{-1} of acid iron waste, of which 5.6 million t are discharged to sea, either directly by dumping or indirectly through pipelines and rivers. Eastern Europe discharges about 2 million t yr^{-1} to the Baltic and Black Seas and inland waters.

The acid in the dumped waste has at most a very localized effect, but the iron salts are precipitated as hydrated oxides of iron which drift around as flakes and particles before settling. A heavy deposit of iron oxides, like red rust, forms on solid objects, including the shells and carapaces of animals. Particles adhere to fish eggs and larvae when they may clog delicate feeding structures. In one investigation hydrated ferric oxide caused loss of weight and increased mortality in mussels, *Mytilus edulis*, apparently through the increased production of pseudofaeces and loss of organic matter through the secretion of additional mucus. The oxides also appear to precipitate in the gills of fish, and other metals co-adsorbed with the iron are readily taken up.

It is impossible to reproduce in the laboratory the behaviour of iron oxides in the sea and studies at dump sites have yielded uncertain evidence about the impact of the iron in the wastes. A study at the dumping grounds in New York Bight in the early 1970s, after some 50 million t of titanium dioxide waste had been dumped over the previous 20 years, could detect no particular effects attributable to the iron content. On the other hand, this dump site has received a wide variety of toxic wastes for many years, it has an impoverished fauna and only hardy species remain. Studies of plankton, benthos, and fish at a German dumping ground in the North Sea also failed to show any change, although iron concentrations in the area had increased. An attempt has been made to relate the incidence of epidermal tumours and fin rot in flatfish to acid iron waste dumping in the area, but these conditions may arise in any area of waste disposal and appear to be a response to general stress and not related to a particular contaminant.

Although the total effect of this dumping cannot be assessed, the waste is in such quantity that a good deal of concern has been expressed by the fishing industry and by conservationist bodies. As a result, the US Environmental Protection Agency recommended that discharges of titanium dioxide waste should no longer be dumped in New York Bight, but 90 miles further out to sea. Holland and Germany have curtailed the dumping of these wastes in the North Sea.

Tin

Antifouling paints containing organic tin compounds tributyltin oxide (TBT) and tributyltin fluoride are much more effective and long-lasting than copper-based antifouling paints. They came into use in all classes of shipping in the 1970s and subsequently were also commonly used to treat net enclosures of mariculture installations and wooden lobster pots.

TBT is extremely toxic and is lethal to a variety of planktonic organisms, including mollusc larvae which are 10–100 times more sensitive that the adults, at concentrations of only $1.0 \, \mu g \, l^{-1}$. Such concentrations are commonly found in waters in and around yacht marinas and have been associated with recruitment failures of scallop and oysters in the affected areas.

The sub-lethal effect of low concentrations of TBT are of even greater consequence to commercial shell-fisheries. Concentrations of TBT down to $0.01 \, \mu g^{-1}$ cause reduced growth and other sub-lethal effects in very young Pacific oysters *Crassostrea gigas*. More seriously, TBT causes gross thickening of the shells of oysters, greatly reducing the size of the animal inside, and rendering them unmarketable.

A curious and equally damaging sub-lethal effect of TBT has been discovered in the American mud snail *Ilyanassa obsoleta* and the dog whelk *Nucella*. A penis and sperm duct are developed in females, a condition known as 'imposex', evidently as a result of TBT triggering changes in the hormonal system. In *Nucella*, the oviduct and female genital opening eventually become overgrown by the developing penis and blocked, so that the egg capsules cannot be laid. *Nucella* does not have a planktonic or distributive phase in its life cycle, and in areas frequented by shipping and small boats its population has been seriously reduced or eliminated altogether because of the failure of reproduction. It is not known if TBT has a damaging effect on other marine organisms, but it is likely.

In mariculture installations where TBT has been used to prevent fouling of sea pens, organotin concentrations of 0.28–0.90 µg g^{-1} (wet weight) have been detected in the flesh of chinook salmon reared in them. The organotin is not destroyed by cooking.

Because of the damage to shell-fisheries and hazard to other marine organisms, as well as its possible threat to human health, the use of TBT in mariculture installations and on small boats has been banned in several countries, including France, Ireland, the United Kingdom and the United States. For the present, its use has been permitted on ocean-going vessels on the grounds that they do not congregate in inshore waters in the way that small vessels do, and are therefore unlikely to result in a damaging concentration of TBT near shellfish beds.

TBT degrades in seawater to non-toxic compounds within a few weeks and the problems it has caused are not expected to have a lasting effect.

6

Halogenated hydrocarbons

Hydrocarbons containing fluorine, chlorine, bromine, or iodine (the halogens) differ from petroleum hydrocarbons (Chapter 3) because they are not readily degraded by chemical oxidation or bacterial action. Like metals (Chapter 5), they are essentially permanent additions to the environment, but unlike metals, most of these compounds are man-made and do not occur naturally. The great majority contain chlorine and are known collectively also as chlorinated hydrocarbons or organochlorine compounds.

Low-molecular-weight compounds

Halogenated hydrocarbons embrace a very wide range of compounds. Low-molecular-weight hydrocarbons, particularly methane, are synthesized by marine algae and possibly by a few invertebrates, and may contain chlorine, bromine or, occasionally, iodine. Elevated concentrations of these substances in seawater may therefore come from natural sources and not be the result of human activity.

Low-molecular-weight, volatile, halogenated hydrocarbons are, however, manufactured in large quantities and almost all this production is eventually lost to the environment. Those produced in greatest quantity, totalling some 30 million t yr^{-1}, are the industrial solvents dichlorethane (CH_3CHCl_2) and vinyl chloride ($H_2C{=}CHCl$). Other solvents with a world production approaching 1 million t yr^{-1} each are carbon tetrachloride (CCl_4) and perchlorethylene ($Cl_2C{=}CCl_2$) used in dry cleaning, and trichlorethane (CH_2Cl_3) and trichlorethylene ($ClHC{=}CCl_2$). Chlorofluorocarbons or freons (CCl_3F and CCl_2F_2) are used as coolants, aerosol propellants, and in foamed plastics (Table 6.1). World production of freons in 1986 amounted to over 1 million t (Table 6.2).

Some of these compounds have become very widely distributed in the atmosphere and can even be detected in the air of Antarctica, far from any possible source. They occur in detectable quantities in seawater close to centres of industrialization. Although there is concern about the effects of freons on the ozone layer in the upper atmosphere and some attempt has been made to reduce production, low-molecular-weight hydrocarbons in the sea are not regarded as

Table 6.1. European Community sale of freons (in thousand t)

Use	1976	1977	1978	1979	1980
Aerosols	176.9	162.6	150.4	136.6	126.5
Refrigeration	21.8	20.3	20.4	20.3	21.2
Foams	42.2	45.3	54.5	55.8	61.9
Other	4.2	4.9	6.1	6.9	7.4
Total	245.1	233.1	231.4	219.6	217.0

Table 6.2. World production of freons in 1986 (in thousand t)

Country	Production
European community	438
United States	295
Japan	125
USSR	100+
China	20
Others	45
Total	1038

a particularly serious threat. They appear not to accumulate in marine organisms.

Pesticides and PCBs

Attention has been focused particularly on the higher-molecular-weight chlorinated hydrocarbons which do accumulate in animal fat tissues. These include pesticides and polychlorinated biphenyls (PCBs) (Fig. 6.1).

DDT and related compounds

Although DDT (dichloro-diphenyl-trichloroethane) was known in the last century, it was not introduced as an insecticide until 1939. In many ways it is the ideal pesticide:

Fig. 6.1.   The structure of some chlorinated hydrocarbons.

(1) it is extremely toxic to insects, but very much less toxic to other animals;
(2) it is very persistent, with a half-life in the soil of about 10 years;
(3) it continues to exert its insecticidal properties for a very long time;
(4) it is relatively cheap.

Few other pesticides share the desirable properties of being reasonably specific to the target organisms, of remaining effective for a long time so that only a single application may be needed, and of being safe for the humans exposed to it.

The use of DDT prevented epidemics of typhus among refugees and in war-damaged areas in Europe during and immediately after the Second World War. It provided the basis of the very successful programmes of the World Health Organization to control malaria and other insect-borne diseases in Africa and the Far East. Its primary use, however, particularly in developed countries was pest control in forestry and in most forms of agriculture.

DDE (dichloro-diphenyl-ethane) is a derivative of DDT, involving the loss of one chlorine atom from the -CCl₃ group in the DDT molecule. It has low toxicity to insects and is not used as a pesticide. Most of the chlorinated hydrocarbon in the sea and 80 per cent of that in marine organisms is in the form of DDE and presumably nearly all of it has been derived from the breakdown of DDT.

DDD (dichloro-diphenyl-dichloroethane) is another derivative of DDT involving the loss of a chlorine atom from the -CCl₃ group in the DDT molecule. It has some toxicity to insects and is less toxic than DDT to fish. For this reason it is occasionally used as an insecticide in situations where its low toxicity to fish is important. It can be excreted by many organisms and rarely accumulates in them.

Commercial DDT is a mixture of DDT, DDE, and DDD, though with DDT predominating.

DDT has now been almost completely superseded by less persistent insecticides in the developed world, but it continues to be extensively used in developing countries because it is effective, safe to handle, and cheap.

'Drins'

This group of interrelated insecticides includes aldrin, dieldrin, endrin, heptachlor, etc. They are all extremely persistent and the degradation products are also toxic: heptachlor degrades to heptachlor epoxide which is even more toxic than the parent compound; aldrin degrades to dieldrin.

These pesticides were used as seed dressings and in situations where their high toxicity and persistence were required, as in the control of wireworms (*Tipula* larvae) in ploughed-up grassland. Their chief disadvantage is that they are toxic to mammals as well as being persistent and subject to bioaccumulation. They were largely withdrawn during the 1970s although they continued to be used to moth-proof textiles, carpets and fleeces, and for some minor agricultural purposes until the late 1980s.

Although now used only in very small quantity because of their persistence, 'drins' are widespread in the environment and continue to leach out of agricultural land into water courses and the sea.

Gamma HCH, Lindane or BCH

Gamma hexochlorocyclohexane (gamma HCH) or lindane, was formerly incorrectly known as benzine hexachloride (BHC). It came into use at about the same time as DDT and acts as a contact poison to insects. It is volatile and stable at high temperatures and so can be used as a smoke to fumigate crops in, for example, orchards. It is also used as a seed dressing. Because of its tendency to accumulate in food chains, it has been banned or its use restricted in a number of countries. However, it is still widely used in agriculture as an insecticide on crops and for seed treatment, and in veterinerary products to control sheep-scab mite. It is also used in some countries as a wood preservative against timber pests.

Hexachlorobenzene (HCB)

This product was formerly widely used as a soil fumigant and as a seed dressing for grain or as a fumigant in grain storage. It has been largely replaced by other pesticides but it occurs as a by-product in the manufacture of carbon tetrachloride and perchlorethylene and is inevitably released in the production waters from these processes.

Toxaphene

Toxaphene is the trade name for polychlorinated camphenes and was introduced as an insecticide in the mid-1940s. Its method of synthesis results in the production of a complex mixture of at least 670 camphene compounds with six to ten chlorine atoms per molecule and a total chlorine content of about 68 per cent by weight. It is used as an insecticide on cotton and vegetable crops, and in livestock dips. It is acutely toxic to fish and is occasionally used as a piscicide in freshwater lakes. Since its introduction it has been the most heavily used pesticide in the United States, with a total production not far short of that of DDT at its peak. Its use is now coming under regulation.

Polychlorinated biphenyls (PCBs)

PCBs have been in use since the early 1930s. They are not pesticides, but are used in electrical equipment, in the manufacture of paints, plastics, adhesives, coating compounds, and pressure-sensitive copying paper. Because they are chemically very stable, they resist chemical attack and act as flame retardants. They have been used in transmission fluids in fluid-drive systems, and as dielectrics in transformers and large capacitors.

The number of chlorine atoms per molecule varies from one to ten, but commercial PCBs are produced to physical, not chemical specifications and contain a mixture of isomers. The product may contain 20 per cent by weight of chlorine and average about one chlorine atom per molecule, or up to 60 per cent chlorine with different percentages of biphenyls containing three to six atoms of chlorine per molecule.

Following concern about the environmental accumulation of chlorinated hydrocarbon pesticides, a number of steps were taken to reduce the use of PCBs. In 1970, Monsanto, sole manufacturer of PCBs in the United States, voluntarily reduced production from 33 000 t in 1970 to 18 000 t in 1971. Since then, a variety of measures have been adopted to limit the use of PCBs to functions where recovery and recycling is possible: dielectrics in transformers and large capacitors and, in some countries, in hydraulic systems. In 1985, the Netherlands stopped using PCBs altogether. Up to the time the use of PCBs came under restriction, however, total world production had amounted to more than 1 million t, most of which has been dispersed in the natural environment.

Ocean incineration

Because of their persistence and toxicity, it is difficult to dispose of chlorinated organic compounds safely. The principle waste is 'EDC-tar', a liquid tar containing 60–70 per cent chlorine, which is a residue from vinyl chloride manufacture. Between 1970 and 1985, 1.75 million t of EDC-tar were produced in western Europe alone. In addition to EDC-tar, PCBs, and certain herbicides and organochlorine insecticides that have been withdrawn from use have to be disposed of.

If such wastes are dumped on land, it must be in a situation where there is no risk that they will leach out and contaminate ground or surface water. Exhausted salt mines are ideal and are used, but they have not the capacity to receive all the wastes for disposal. Up to the 1960s a proportion of such wastes were dumped at sea, but this practice has been abandoned in favour of high temperature incineration. The principal combustion products are carbon dioxide and hydrochloric acid but small quantities of heavy metals may be included in the exhaust gases, depending on the nature of the wastes.

Specialized incinerators on land, designed to burn these wastes, have scrubbers to remove the hydrochloric acid from the emissions. But incinerators, particularly those dealing with toxic wastes are never popular with the surrounding population who fear the consequences of an accidental release of dangerous material.

Partly in response to the difficulty of gaining acceptance of incinerators on land, and partly because it was cheaper, incinerator ships have been developed to burn highly chlorinated wastes at sea. Trial burns have been made in the Gulf of Mexico, the Pacific and Australia, but ocean incineration has been in regular use only in the North Sea since 1969. During most of the 1980s, 90–100 000 t of chlorinated wastes, two-thirds of them from Germany, the rest from a number of other European states, were incinerated each year at a designated site 70 nautical miles from land in the Dutch sector of the North Sea. Incineration is at more than 1200 °C and achieves 99.9999 per cent destruction of PCBs. The practice is regulated and closely monitored by the Dutch authorities.

Exhaust gases from ocean incineration are not scrubbed; hydrochloric acid, the main product, is rapidly absorbed by the sea which has an enormous buffering capacity. The metal input is tiny compared with the input of metals from the atmosphere and rivers (see Table 5.1). It has been suggested that traces of dioxins might be produced in the heated exhaust gas plume, but this has not been established. No environmental damage has been detected from this practice but there is some evidence of an accumulation of organochlorine compounds in bottom sediments in the burn zone.

Despite the advantages of incinerated chlorinated wastes at sea, the practice has not received acceptance outside Europe and agreement has been reached to phase it out altogether by 1995.

Inputs to the marine environment

Low-molecular-weight chlorinated hydrocarbons are volatile and both HCH and HCB are rapidly lost to the atmosphere in the presence of water vapour. DDT, the 'drins', and toxaphenes also adsorb strongly on to particles and are carried by wind-borne dust. Chlorinated hydrocarbons can be detected in the atmosphere even at remote oceanic sites (Table 6.3) and it is likely that deposition

Table 6.3. Average concentration (in ng m^3) of some chlorinated hydrocarbons in the atmosphere at marine sites

	PCB	Total DDT	Total HCH
South Carolina	0.25	0.036	—
North Atlantic	0.69	0.006	0.39
Enewetak	0.05	<0.006	0.26
Samoa	0.012	0.0015	0.032

from the atmosphere is an important route for the addition of chlorinated hydrocarbons to the sea.

Other important inputs to the sea are from rivers—over 3 t yr^{-1} of PCBs enter the North Sea by this route, mainly from the Rhine—and from the dumping of dredging spoil or sewage sludge which is often highly contaminated.

The uses for which pesticides and most PCBs are designed result in them being widely distributed in the natural environment, but the principal source of widespread pesticide contamination is from the agricultural use of these compounds.

- *Aerial spraying.* In the fruit- and vegetable-growing areas of California where there is heavy use of pesticides, it is estimated that 50 per cent of the pesticide released from crop-spraying aircraft never reaches the ground but forms aerosols and, as such, may travel great distances.
- *River run-off.* In addition to rain washing pesticide from the plants and soil into rivers and hence to the sea, irrigation water, particularly if it is applied by spraying, has the same effect. Floods carry very large quantities of silt to the sea, and if derived from agricultural land, the silt may carry a considerable quantity of adsorbed pesticide.
- *Blown dust.* Arid areas may be intensively cultivated with the aid of irrigation, but dry soil with its burden of pesticides is transported in dust storms.

Aerial transport has resulted in the world-wide distribution of organochlorine pesticides. DDT is an entirely man-made substance which does not occur naturally; it has been in use only since 1940. Yet within 20 years, DDT and its residues had pervaded the entire biosphere. Even king penguins in Antarctica, several thousand kilometres from any place where DDT has been used, contain detectable traces of it.

In the manufacture of chlorinated hydrocarbons, a variety of related compounds is usually produced, only one of which is the desired product. During purification, these unwanted hydrocarbons (whose identity is generally unknown) are extracted and were formerly commonly dumped at sea in considerable quantities.

Locally, chlorinated hydrocarbons appear in industrial effluent in outfalls to the sea. The Montrose Chemical Company in Los Angeles is the world's major manufacturer of DDT. The Los Angeles sewage system received the effluent from this factory and at peak production in 1971, this resulted in a discharge of 21.6 t yr^{-1} of DDT residues to the sea through the ocean outfall of this sewage system. A survey made in 1972 suggested that 200 t of DDT residues were trapped in the upper 30 cm of bottom sediment over an area of 50 km^2 around the outfall (Fig. 6.2). Discharges from the factory were substantially reduced after

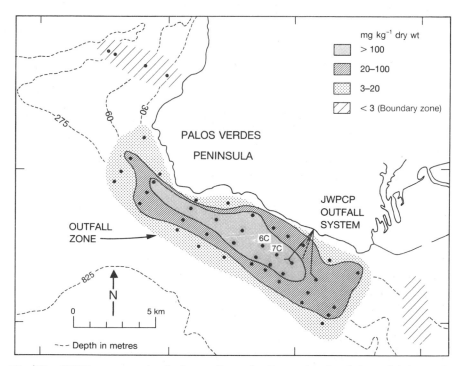

Fig. 6.2. DDT concentration in the top 5 cm of sediment (mg kg^{-1} dry weight) near the ocean outfall of the Los Angeles sewage system, October 1983. (*Pergamon Press.*)

1971 and amounted to only 0.73 t in 1977.

Sewage sludge also may contain appreciable quantities of halogenated hydrocarbons and if dumped at sea provide an additional source of contamination. Sewage sludge from Glasgow in the 1960s made a contribution of 1 t yr^{-1} of PCBs to the Clyde dumping grounds (Fig. 6.3) until brought under control.

Fats in the sea

Chlorinated hydrocarbons are extremely insoluble in water, with a saturation concentration of no more than 1 p.p.b., but they are soluble in fats and adsorb

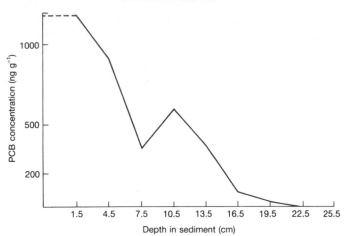

Fig. 6.3. Concentration of PCBs at various depths in the bottom sediment near the Firth of Clyde dumping ground. *(Pergamon Press.)*

strongly on to particles. Their distribution in the sea is therefore far from uniform.

Most are adsorbed on to inorganic particles or on to micro-organisms such as diatoms. This creates problems for analysis, because apart from the difficulty of distinguishing between the various halogenated hydrocarbons, there is the difficulty of deciding what is incorporated in organisms and what is adsorbed on the outside of them; the former may affect them, the latter cannot but is biologically available to animals that feed on the contaminated organisms.

Chlorinated hydrocarbons adsorbed on to inorganic particles may ultimately be carried to the seabed which then acts as a sink for these compounds. However, suspended or resuspended particles, if they are of a suitable size or density, are commonly ingested by filter-feeding animals and chlorinated hydrocarbons may enter food chains by this route.

The surface layer of the sea is a film varying from a few μm to 1 mm in thickness, and contains fatty acids. Because of their lipid solubility, chlorinated hydrocarbons may therefore accumulate in the surface film, and while the total quantity may not be great, it may be of considerable importance to surface-living organisms, or to birds such as petrels which skim off fat from the surface of the sea. For a variety of reasons, the surface layer of the sea—the site of interchange with the atmosphere—is very important, but it is extremely difficult to study and is still an area of considerable ignorance.

Halogenated hydrocarbons, most particularly DDT and its derivatives, now occur in all organisms in all environments, and a considerable quantity in total of the halogenated hydrocarbons in the sea is in the bodies of marine organisms and will continue to circulate within the food webs.

Biological effects of halogenated hydrocarbons

Problems of analysis

As with petroleum hydrocarbons, halogenated hydrocarbons embrace an enormous variety of related compounds: it may be possible to distinguish 100–150 different organochlorines in a single sample and to identify and measure most of them. Such an abundance of related compounds makes it very difficult to identify which of them is responsible for an observed biological effect. The problem is probably worst for PCBs because the commercial products are mixtures, the exact composition of which varies with the degree of chlorination, the manufacturer, and even with the production batch. Up to 70 PCB compounds may be present in a single sample and the analyst can either estimate total PCBs in the mixture or painstakingly identify and measure individual constituents. The latter approach is very expensive in time and money, so correspondingly fewer samples can be processed, besides which, unless it is known or suspected which of the many compounds is responsible for the biological effect, nothing is gained by the apparently great accuracy of the detailed analysis. The alternative use of cruder measurements of total PCB contamination may be responsible for discrepancies between reports of the biological effects of PCBs. Some other classes of organochlorines, particularly toxaphenes, present the same problem, but much less attention has been paid to them.

A second problem is more fundamental. By 1965, it was possible to distinguish DDT from its metabolites DDE and DDD, and from dieldrin, but it was not until 1966 that PCBs were first identified and a year or two later that their separation from DDT was practised in most analytical laboratories. PCBs had been in use and released to the environment for some thirty years, and they were probably present in all samples. Since PCBs can interfere with the detection and measurement of other organochlorines, many, perhaps most, early records of DDT contamination are incorrect. As late as 1980, toxaphenes, which are also widespread contaminants, were not reliably detected in analyses of chlorinated hydrocarbons. Even now, despite the refinement and sensitivity of modern analytical methods, many organochlorines are almost certainly overlooked and some may well be biologically active. Caution must therefore be exercised in interpreting observations of the biological effects of halogenated hydrocarbons.

Storage and bioaccumulation

There is evidence that chlorinated hydrocarbons are difficult to excrete and hence they tend to accumulate in the body. Because they are lipid-soluble, they tend to occur in much higher concentrations in fatty tissues than in other tissues. This introduces two risks:

(1) in times of poor feeding, animals mobilize and use fat reserves, so increasing the concentration of chlorinated hydrocarbons circulating in the body, possibly to a dangerous level;
(2) as with other bioaccumulating contaminants, there is a strong possibility of transmission through food webs and of biomagnification, as, indeed, has been established in a number of animals.

Because of the tendency of chlorinated hydrocarbons to be sequestered in fatty tissues, care is needed in comparing levels of contamination in different organisms. Different amounts and concentrations are likely to occur in fat tissue, muscles, gonads, etc. and even if the total body-burden of chlorinated hydrocarbon is known, this has quite different implications for a fat animal from an emaciated animal.

Accumulation rates for organochlorines, measured by residues in the body divided by residues in the food or the environment, vary widely between species. Figure 6.4 shows the average concentrations of PCBs and six organochlorine pesticides in five species living in the contaminated Weser estuary on the North Sea coast of Germany. The actual concentrations acquired relate to the lipid content of the animal and its position in the food chain, and the sole (*Solea solea*) with at least twice as much lipid as the invertebrates, as well as being a carnivore, is the more contaminated as a result. But while the sole, shrimp (*Crangon*), and lugworm (*Arenicola*) retain a higher proportion of PCBs than pesticides, the cockle (*Cerastoderma*) acquires relatively little PCB but proportionately much more lindane which is not preferentially accumulated by the others. *Crangon* is remarkable in accumulating proportionately less DDT and DDE than the other species. Each species, in fact, has its own profile of organochlorine accumulation.

Even within a species there may be considerable variation in the amount of organochlorine that is acquired. Mussels (*Mytilus* spp.) vary greatly in the DDT residues and PCBs they contain (Table 6.4). A number of different factors undoubtedly contribute to this variation; not all are understood but they include age, tidal level at which they live, sex, stage in the annual breeding cycle, as well as the concentration of organochlorines to which the animal is exposed. It is not only molluscs that show such unexplained interspecific variations. In the grey seal (*Halichoerus grypus*), males acquire more DDT residues and PCBs than females, but females more dieldrin than the males.

Distribution of organochlorines within the animal is not uniform. Figure 6.5 shows how DDT is distributed in different tissues of the sole (*Solea lutea*) after three days in which they had been fed 17 μg of DDT labelled with ^{14}C, and after two months in water free from DDT. The brain and, more understandably, the liver both acquire the highest concentrations and eliminate them most slowly.

Fig. 6.4. Average concentration of PCBs and organochlorine pesticides in littoral animals in the Weser estuary: (a) PCB, (b) DDD, (c) dieldrin, (d) α-HCH, (e) γ-HCH, (f) DDE, (g) endosulphan. (*Pergamon Press.*)

Table 6.4. PCB and DDT/DDE concentrations in seawater and *Mytilus*

Marine area and year	Seawater concentration ($ng\ l^{-1}$)	Concentration in mussel ($mg\ g^{-1}$)	Concentration factor
PCBs			
France:			
Valras Beach, 1974	0.94	0.25	270 000
Saintes Maries, 1974	0.95	0.45	470 000
Carro, 1974	0.68	0.20	300 000
Marseille, 1974	1.60	1.10	690 000
California:			
Los Angeles, 1972	1.20	0.23	190 000
San Francisco, 1975	0.98	0.068	69 000
DDT or DDE			
France:			
Valras Beach, 1974	0.54	0.051	90 000
Saintes Maries, 1974	0.35	0.013	40 000
Carro, 1974	0.25	0.052	210 000
Marseille, 1974	1.30	0.900	690 000
California:			
Los Angeles, 1972	5.10	1.600	310 000
San Francisco, 1975	0.11	0.005	45 000

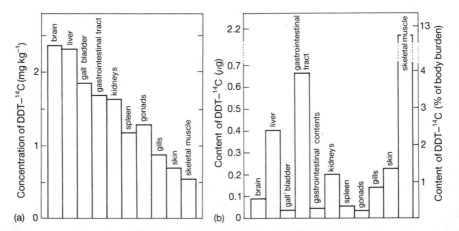

Fig. 6.5. Distribution of DDT in tissues of the sole *Solea lutea*: (a) after being given 17 µg of DDT during three days, (b) after two months in a DDT-free environment.

With so much specific and individual variation, it is difficult to generalize, but the highest concentration factors (for DDT) are found in bivalve molluscs, such as oysters and clams, where they may reach 70 000. For crustaceans and fish accumulation factors range between 100 and 10 000; for sea birds it is 10 or less.

Since organochlorines are eliminated slowly from the body they may be expected to show biomagnification in food chains. Figure 6.6 shows the average

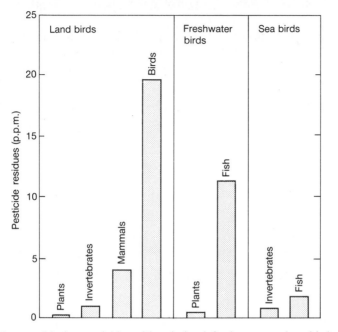

Fig. 6.6. Organochlorine pesticide residues in land, freshwater, and sea birds, in relation to their predominant diet.

concentrations of organochlorines in land birds, freshwater birds, and sea birds, in relation to the main types of food they eat. Those with most are land birds feeding on other birds (i.e. hawks); they live in an environment where pesticides are most immediately available and they are at the top of a food chain.

Biological effects

It is difficult to be precise about the effect of halogenated hydrocarbons on plants and animals. Because of the low solubility of these substances in water, there is considerable uncertainty about the dose actually received by aquatic organisms in laboratory tests unless the organochlorine is administered by mouth. Because organochlorines are stored in the fatty tissues of the body, they become biologically available and exert their influence only when the fat tissues are metabolized. Animals may therefore acquire a considerable body-burden of halogenated hydrocarbons, but show no ill effects except in conditions of starvation when fat reserves are mobilized. These facts make laboratory experimentation difficult, but if confirmation of laboratory findings is sought in natural populations, there is the additional complication that wild animals are usually contaminated with a variety of halogenated hydrocarbons and it is impossible to tell which one is responsible for whatever symptoms have been detected.

In laboratory cultures of whole phytoplankton from the Caspian and Mediterranean Seas, DDT and PCBs reduce primary production (Fig. 6.7) by as

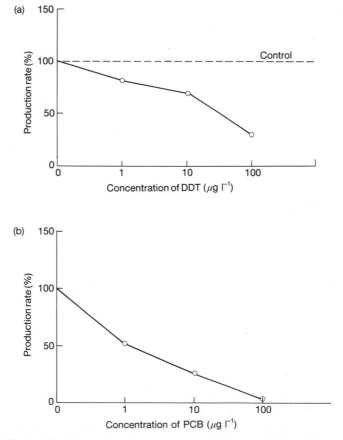

Fig. 6.7. Production (as percentage of control) of (a) whole phytoplankton from the western Caspian Sea exposed to DDT, and (b) whole phytoplankton from the Mediterranean Sea exposed to PCBs.

much as 50 per cent at a concentration of only 1 µg l^{-1} (p.p.b.) in the case of PCBs. Marine crustaceans and fish also appear to be very sensitive to organochlorines. The 96 h LC$_{50}$ of DDT ranges between 0.4 and 89 µg l^{-1}, and of dieldrin between 0.9 and 34 µg l^{-1} for a variety of teleosts: puffer (*Sphaeroides maculatus*), Killifish (*Fundulus heteroclitus* and *F. majalis*), mullet (*Mugil cephalus*), eel (*Anguilla rostrata*), silverside (*Menidia menidia*), and bluehead (*Thalassoma bifasciatum*). The values for the shrimps *Crangon* and *Palaemonetes*, and the hermit crab *Pagurus longicarpus* are 0.6–6.0 µg l^{-1} for DDT and 7–50 µg l^{-1} for dieldrin. There is, however, a wide range of toxicity among chlorinated hydrocarbons. Figure 6.8 shows the relative toxicity of this class of

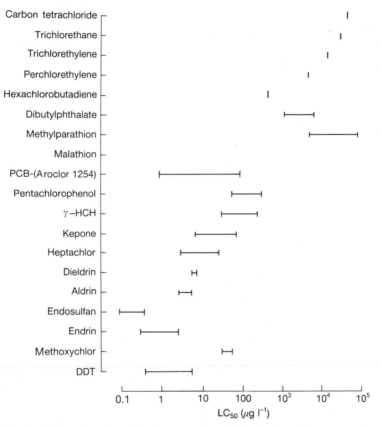

Fig. 6.8. Toxicity of organochlorine compounds to shrimp *Crangon* and crayfish *Astacus*.

substances to *Crangon* and *Astacus*. Bivalve molluscs, on the other hand, with their ability to concentrate organchlorine pesticides without coming to harm, have a 96 h LC$_{50}$ greater than 10 000 µg l^{-1}.

Since halogenated hydrocarbons are known to be subject to bioaccumulation and biomagnification, most attention has been paid to their effect on animals high in the food chain. Very large doses of PCBs and DDT amounting to several g kg^{-1} of the body-weight, are required to cause the death of mammals or birds by a single administration by mouth. Such doses are clearly not found in the natural environment where animals are exposed to much lower levels of contamination of their food, but are continuously, or chronically, exposed to them.

Two sub-lethal effects of halogenated hydrocarbons in birds and mammals appear to have some ecological significance. DDT and its residues interfere with calcium metabolism and result in the egg shells being unusually thin. In both birds and mammals PCBs have a more direct effect on reproduction, and eggs of birds contaminated with PCBs show reduced hatchability. PCBs included in the diet of laboratory rats and mice cause a reduction in the number of offspring produced and poorer survival of those young that are born. Mink are very severely affected in this respect when fed PCBs.

Environmental impact of halogenated hydrocarbons

Warning signals

During the 1960s there were increasing signs that the widespread and intensive use of pesticides, most obviously DDT, was having unforseen and unwelcome consequences for the natural environment.

In 1964 fish were found to be dying in an area around the marine outfall of a Danish factory manufacturing the pesticide parathion. Lobsters, *Homarus gammarus*, were affected over a much wider area. The factory effluent was found to be lethal to lobsters at a dilution of 1:50 000.

The Laguna Madre was a productive lagoon system on the coast of Texas, but it became heavily contaminated with pesticides from neighbouring agricultural land. The fish catch fell abruptly after 1964–5 (Table 6.5) and this was attributed to pesticide poisoning.

The Salinas valley is one of the richest agricultural areas in California, specializing in vegetable and salad crops. The Salinas river which drains the valley does not flow in summer but is blocked by a sand bar at its mouth. During the rainy season December–April, the river breaks through the bar and flows into Monterey Bay. Although it is wide open to the Pacific Ocean, the bay has a sluggish and irregular circulation and any pollutant remains there for some time. In exceptionally wet seasons the river may burst its banks and flood large areas of farmland. This happened in February 1969 and when the river burst the sand bar flood water carrying enormous quantities of silt flowed into the bay. During the previous 10 years, DDT had been used intensively (it is estimated that 50 t yr^{-1} had been used on crops in the valley) and pesticide residues were carried with the

Table 6.5. Capture of sea
trout in Laguna Madre

Year	Catch (t ha^{-1})
1964	74
1965	62
1966	30
1967	—
1968	6
1969	0.4

No sample in 1967

silt-laden flood water into the bay. This was followed by exceptionally large numbers of seabird deaths in the following months. All had remarkably high liver concentrations of DDT residues:

Brandt's cormorant	107–155 p.p.m.
Western grebe	199–222 p.p.m.
Fork-tailed petrel	313 p.p.m.
Ashley's petrel	412 p.p.m.
Ring-billed gull	805 p.p.m.

In addition, sea lions (*Talophus californianus*) were found dead or dying on beaches. They had liver concentrations of DDT up to 89 p.p.m.

The dangers of a widespread ecological impact from the use of persistent pesticides were expressed by Rachael Carson in *Silent spring* published in 1963. This book presented the case against pesticides and if some of the predictions were overstated, it drew public attention to the problems associated with the widespread and indiscriminate use of pesticides.

Population decline of predatory birds

The most reliable evidence of the damaging effect of organochlorine pesticides on wildlife was demonstrated in 1967 by Dr D. A. Ratcliffe of the Nature Conservancy in the United Kingdom. The peregrine falcon (*Falco peregrinus*) was protected in Britain after 1945 and showed a dramatic increase in numbers until, in the mid-1950s, the population went into a sharp decline. This proved to be due to reproductive failure: birds were laying eggs with abnormally thin shells and a large proportion of them were broken during incubation. Examination of museum speciens showed that egg-shell thinning had started about 1947. Thinning of egg shells can be produced in ducks and chickens if DDT is included in their diet. High concentrations of DDT residues occured in peregrines and the yolk of their eggs during the mid-1960s. There was no doubt that DDT was the cause of the population decline of these birds, and with the cessation of the use of DDT for agricultural purposes in Britain, peregrine numbers have increased to their former level.

Pesticides have persisted in the environment, however, and for some reason there has not been a marked decline in DDT residues in sparrow hawks (*Accipiter nisus*) in Britain. This species appears to have been more affected by the cyclodiene organochlorines, and the recovery of its population was delayed until the 'drin' pesticides went out of use in 1975.

The peregrine falcon is a top predator and therefore particularly vulnerable. Comparable effects of organochlorine pesticides were not found in herbivorous or insectivorous birds, but other predators were affected. The North American sparrow hawk (*Falco sparverius*) is related to the peregrine and suffered a similar fate. A number of fish-catching predators were also affected, including the American bald eagle (*Haliaetus leucocephalus*), osprey (*Pandion haliaetus*), and brown pelican (*Pelicanus occidentalis*), all of which suffered a serious population decline. Pelican colonies on the Californian coast had their first successful breeding in 1972 after nearly 10 years of reproductive failure, following curtailment of the use of DDT as an agricultural pesticide. The situation in these pelicans, however, was complicated by the scarcity of sardines, their staple food, during the breeding seasons of 1969–72 and it is not known how far this contributed to their reproductive failure.

Smaller, fish-eating sea birds appear not to have been so seriously affected by organochlorine pesticides. One example to the contrary is of Sandwich terns, *Sterna sandvicensis*, and eider duck, *Somateria mollissima*, on the island of Griend off the coast of Holland. It is thought that effluents from a chemical factory near Rotterdam producing dieldrin, endrin, and telodrin, were responsible for a decline in the size of the tern colony from 20 000 to 650 in 1965. There were many eider deaths between 1964 and 1967 when measures were taken to prevent the discharge of effluent from the factory. By 1974, the numbers of breeding terns had risen to 5000.

The difficulty in interpreting seabird deaths is illustrated by the 'wreck' of sea birds (mainly guillemots, *Uria aalge*) in the Irish Sea in autumn 1969. Over 12 000 birds came ashore in a dying condition in the space of a few weeks. Some estimates put the death toll at 50 000 or even 100 000 birds. All were emaciated and those autopsied had liver and kidney lesions similar to those caused by PCBs. While the total body-burden of PCBs was about the same in the affected birds as in other, apparently healthy birds, very much higher concentrations were recorded in the liver. This suggests a redistribution of chlorinated hydrocarbon within the body resulting from the loss of fat in these emaciated birds. These results are based on a small sample of birds which proved to be highly variable with PCB concentrations in the liver ranging from 8 to 880 μg g^{-1}. Although PCBs may have been a contributory cause of death in some birds, it cannot be concluded that poisoning by chlorinated hydrocarbons caused the 'wreck'. Furthermore, sea bird wrecks were recorded from time to time in the last century, long before the introduction of these compounds.

Impact on seal populations

Organochlorines, or more particularly PCBs, have been held responsible for the decline of some seal and sea lion populations, though the evidence is far from complete and there are a number of unexplained discrepancies.

Seal populations in the Baltic have been declining since the beginning of this century. Much of the decline was due to over-hunting, but it has continued despite protection of the seals and there is a strong suspicion that high levels of contamination by PCBs has been responsible for a failure of reproduction. Since about 1970, only 28 per cent of mature female ringed seals (*Phusa hispida*) have become pregnant each year, instead of the usual pregnancy rate of 80 per cent. Non-pregnant females contain an average of 77 p.p.m. PCBs in the blubber lipids, compared with 56 p.p.m. in pregnant females. About 40 per cent of females have one or both uterine horns blocked by occlusions, effectively rendering them sterile. Grey seals (*Halichoerus grypus*) and common, or habour seals (*Phoca vitulina*), found dead, showed the same pathological conditions and non-pregnant females contain 110 p.p.m. PCBs, and pregnant females 73 p.p.m. PCBs in the blubber lipids.

PCBs are known to interfere with ovulation and development in mammals, though this has not been confirmed experimentally in seals. PCB concentrations up to 145 p.p.m. in Californian sea lions have been suggested as a cause of abortions, but these specimens had exceptionally high concentrations of DDT residues as well (up to 5077 p.p.m. in the blubber) and cannot be compared with Baltic seals. PCB contamination may explain why the pregnancy rate of Baltic seals without occlusions is only 50 per cent, but there is no evidence to suggest that PCBs are responsible for the uterine occlusions which render 40 per cent of the seals infertile. Furthermore, seals on the Dutch coast and on the Farne Islands in north-east England with higher concentrations of PCBs than those in the Baltic do not show this pathological condition. The birth rate of the Farne Island population of grey seals, despite up to 122 p.p.m. contamination with PCBs, grew steadily until the early 1970s, when attempts were made to control the population (Fig. 6.9).

In 1988, an epidemic of viral distemper severely reduced the population of common seals in the North Sea. The epidemic started in seal colonies on the Danish and Dutch coasts and then spread to British colonies. Grey seals were less seriously affected. There has been some speculation that the establishment of the virus in the seals was facilitated in populations already weakened by pollution, but there is no firm evidence of this and lethal epidemics have been observed in seal populations in other parts of the world at various times.

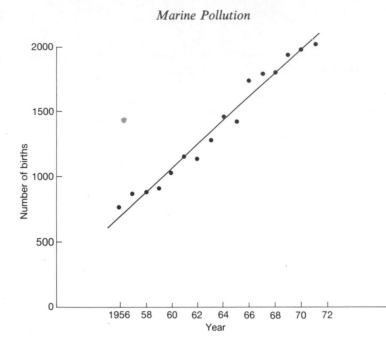

Fig. 6.9.   Number of births per year of grey seals in the Farne Islands colony, 1956–72.

Persistence of contamination

Because of the long life of chlorinated hydrocarbons in the environment, their effect may continue for some years after an input has been brought under control.

Until 1971, the ocean outfall of the Los Angeles sewerage system carried a large quantity of DDT residues from a factory manufacturing the insecticide. Offshore sediments were heavily contaminated over a wide area (see Fig. 6.2), but despite a dramatic reduction in DDT emissions after 1971, contamination of fish in the area persisted for years. Table 6.6 shows the modal concentration of DDT residues in the muscles of three species of fish sampled twice a year in the outfall areas, and also the percentage of the fish in the sample with more than the recommended limit of 5 p.p.m. for human consumption. Dover sole (*Microstomus pacificus*) which feed on invertebrates living in the bottom sediment actually contained more DDT residues (median 14 p.p.m.) in 1975 than in 1971 (4.7 p.p.m.), and throughout the period, in most samples, more than 80 per cent of the fish contained more than 5 p.p.m. Black perch (*Embiotoca jacksoni*) is also a bottom feeder, but takes organisms attached to rocks. Peak median concentrations of 24–25 p.p.m. were recorded in autumn 1972 and spring 1973; thereafter the contamination level fell to 3.2 p.p.m. in spring 1977. Even so, in the last sample, 20 per cent of the fish were above the permissible level of 5 p.p.m.

Table 6.6. Total DDT concentration (mg kg^{-1} wet wt muscle) of fish collected in the ocean discharge area, Los Angeles

	1970	1971		1972		1973		1974		1975		1976		1977
	Spring	Spring	Autumn	Spring	Autumn	Spring	Autumn	Spring	Autumn	Spring	Autumn	Spring	Autumn	Spring
Dover sole (*Microstomus pacificus*)														
Median	4.7	5.6	17	8.1	6.2	25	13	12	12	14				
% with more than 5 p.p.m.	50	80	86	80	67	100	85	82	82	83				
Black perch (*Embiotoca jacksoni*)														
Median	8.0	18	9.1	9.3	2.5	24	4.5	6.8	5.7	6.3	2.9	4.0	3.3	3.2
% with more than 5 p.p.m.	75	100	71	73	75	92	46	59	63	55	44	23	18	20
Kelp bass (*Paralabrax clathratus*)														
Median	3.3	2.6	1.8	12	4.6	8.3	2.6	3.2	2.0	3.8	7.7	0.26	0.84	3.4
% with more than 5 p.p.m.	33	33	0	100	40	73	33	7	33	45	100	0	0	40

Kelp bass (*Paralabrax clathratus*) feeds on fish and invertebrates in mid-water. Its contamination was generally less than that of the bottom-feeding species, though more variable. Even as late as spring 1977, 40 per cent of the sample were above the 5 p.p.m. limit.

None of these three species are fished commercially near the contaminated area although they are taken by sport anglers and no doubt eaten. Harmful effects of this contamination appeared in an unexpected quarter: in the Los Angeles Zoo. In early summer 1976, within four to five weeks, all but one of the collection of Brandt's cormorant (*Phalacrocorax penicillatus*) and guanay cormorants (*P. bougainvillii*) and all the Californian gulls (*Larus californicus*) died. The birds all showed loss of appetite and then, a few days later, tremors culminating in convulsions and death. On autopsy it was discovered that the gulls had 3100 p.p.m. DDT residues in the liver and the cormorants 750 p.p.m. The brain tissue of each contained 430 p.p.m. and 220 p.p.m., respectively. This is similar to the concentration in the brain of kestrels that died in convulsions after receiving an experimental diet containing DDT for 18 months. The cormorants and gulls had been in the zoo for six to seven years and it transpired that the fish on which they were fed, queen fish (*Seriphys palitus*), came from a fishery in the Los Angeles area and contained 3.1–4.2 p.p.m. DDT residues. Brown pelicans in the zoo, also fish eaters, were unaffected, but they were habitually fed surf smelts (*Hypomesus pretiosus*) which were caught elsewhere and they contained only 0.018 p.p.m. DDT residues.

Threat to human health

In 1968 rice oil contaminated with PCBs caused an outbreak of 'yusho' disease in Japan. In all, 1200 people were affected and suffered darkening of the skin, enlargement of the hair follicles, and eruptions of the skin resembling acne. A majority developed respiratory difficulties which persisted for several years. The rice oil was found to contain 2000–3000 p.p.m. of a 48 per cent chlorinated hydrocarbon and the minimum dose that produced symptoms of the disease was about 0.5 g of PCBs ingested over 120 days, or about 0.07 mg kg^{-1} body-weight day^{-1}. Similar symptoms to those of yusho disease have been observed in workers at a Japanese condenser factory. This was thought to be due to local contact with PCBs and the symptoms disappeared when the use of PCBs ceased. It is not entirely clear, though, that PCBs alone were responsible for the yusho incident because workers in Finland occupationally exposed to PCBs and having high concentrations of PCBs in their blood and body fat showed no sign of adverse effects. There have been no confirmed cases of illness resulting from ingesting PCB residues from marine organisms used as food.

Even before the outbreak of yusho disease in Japan, with the demonstration of harmful effects of DDT on top predators among birds there was naturally concern about human exposure to organochlorine pesticide residues in food. Although there was no evidence of harm to humans from this source, legal limits to contamination of foodstuffs in commerce were introduced in a number of countries as a precautionary measure. In the United States this was set at 5 p.p.m. DDT residues and 0.3 p.p.m. dieldrin. There was naturally consternation when it was discovered that human milk of some nursing mothers in Wisconsin (and no doubt elsewhere as well) exceeded that limit for DDT. Had it been cow's milk, it would have been condemned as unfit for human consumption.

Controls on the use of chlorinated hydrocarbon pesticides quickly followed. Dieldrin and related insecticides were banned or phased out in many countries in the early 1970s and DDT has been subject to a progressive withdrawal, particularly for use in agriculture, in many areas. Manufacture of DDT has, however, continued on a reduced scale for use particularly in developing countries where its effectiveness, cheapness and safety in use make it indispensable.

The World Health Organization programme of control of insect-borne diseases in the tropics and south-east Asia depended on the use of DDT, and in 1970, WHO was very concerned that anxiety in North America and Europe about the effect of organochlorine pesticides should not result in DDT no longer being available, until an equally cheap and effective substitute was developed. The continuing need for this insecticide was illustrated by the experience in Sri Lanka where in 1946 there were 2.8 million cases of malaria, causing 12 587 deaths. Following the WHO mosquito control programme using DDT, in 1960 there were 110 cases and no deaths. Against the advice of WHO, the programme was then stopped. In 1968 there were again 2.5 million cases of malaria in Sri Lanka.

In 1970, the progressive withdrawal of the use of organochlorine pesticides in the United States reached North Carolina and the use of DDT on tobacco crops was prohibited for the first time. Parathion, an organophosphorus insecticide which is not persistent but is a very potent nerve poison to humans, was widely substituted for DDT. In that season, there were 40 human deaths in North Carolina alone from the careless use of parathion, for which it is necessary to wear face masks and protective clothing. DDT, which requires no such precautions, is not known to have caused any human deaths.

7
Radioactivity

Nature of radioactivity

The nucleus of an atom contains **nucleons**, which are either positively charged **protons** or electrically neutral **neutrons**, bound together by powerful nuclear forces which overcome the electrostatic repulsion between the protons. The nucleus is surrounded by a cloud of orbiting **electrons**, each of which carries a negative charge equal to the positive charge on a proton. Normally, the negative charges on the electrons balance the positive charges on the protons, and the number of electrons, and hence the charge on the nucleus, determines the element to which the atom belongs and its chemical properties (Fig. 7.1).

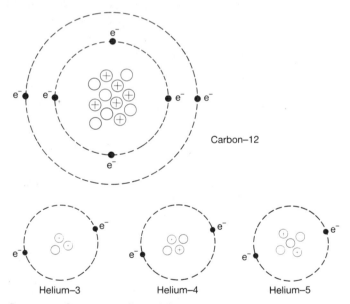

Fig. 7.1. Structure of some atomic nuclei.

An atom commonly loses or gains one or more electrons in the course of a chemical reaction, or through physical processes. It then becomes a positively or negatively charged **ion** and is chemically much more reactive than the electrostatically neutral atom. The process by which this occurs is **ionization**.

Atoms of the same chemical element have the same number of protons in the nucleus, but the number of neutrons may vary. These variants, known as **isotopes**, have the same chemical properties but differ in their nuclear mass. Thus, 99 per cent of naturally occurring carbon has a nucleus containing 6 protons and 6 neutrons and is designated carbon-12 or ^{12}C because its nucleus contains 12 nucleons; but 1 per cent contains 7 neutrons and is designated carbon-13. Both of these are stable isotopes, but some isotopes are unstable. Potassium with 19 protons in the nucleus normally occurs in a form with 20 neutrons as potassium-39; potassium-40, with 21 neutrons also occurs naturally, but is unstable. The instability of the nucleus is remedied by a change in the ratio of protons to neutrons, accompanied by the emission of particles and energy. This is known as radioactivity and the unstable forms are **radioisotopes** or **radionuclides**. Each radioisotope has its characteristic nuclear change and form of emissions.

α radioactivity The unstable nucleus emits an **α particle** consisting of two protons and two neutrons. Since the nucleus loses two positive charges, the atom becomes that of an element two places lower in the periodic table. α particles are relatively slow moving and lose their energy in a short distance; they are stopped by a few centimetres of air or only 40 μm of tissue. They are, however, intensely ionizing in the matter through which they pass and can cause more damage to living tissue than particles with a longer path. Nuclei emitting α particles are therefore of biological consequence if they are taken into the body, e.g. by ingestion or inhalation.

β radioactivity A neutron in an unstable nucleus spontaneously changes into a proton, or vice versa, and the resulting atom is that of an element one place higher or lower, respectively, in the periodic table. To conserve electrostatic charges, a **β particle** is emitted. This is a negatively charged **electron** if a neutron has changed into a proton, or its positively charged equivalent, a **positron**, if a proton has changed into a neutron. β particles vary widely in their energy but lose most of it within a relatively short distance and can be screened by a few millimetres of perspex or 40 mm of tissue. Like α particles, their biological significance is greatest if a β-emitter is taken into the body.

Spontaneous fission Nuclei of some very heavy unstable elements always have a large excess of neutrons. The nucleus breaks into two large fragments representing elements in the middle of the periodic table, accompanied by a few free neutrons. This is known as **spontaneous fission** and the fission products are themselves unstable. Neutrons are slowed down only by collisions with other nuclei and because of the infrequency of this, neutrons penetrate matter for a considerable distance. Although they carry no electric charge and do not cause ionization, the nuclei with which they collide cause intense ionization over a short

Marine Pollution

distance (like α particles) and the nucleus that finally absorbs the neutron shows strong γ radiation.

γ radiation   γ rays are similar to X-rays and, like them, are deeply penetrating and strongly ionizing. Living tissues need to be shielded from γ radiation by a considerable thickness of heavy material such as lead or concrete to absorb the radiation. In addition to being emitted by nuclei bombarded with neutrons, some of the energy released by α- and β-emitters, particularly the latter, is in the form of γ rays.

Units

The older units for measuring radioactivity have now been replaced by new SI units, although the latter have not yet come into universal use.

Curie (Ci)   Radioactivity is measured by the frequency with which radioactive disintegrations of nuclei take place in a substance. The curie is defined by the amount of radioactivity displayed by 1 g of radium (^{226}Ra), that is 3.7×10^{10} disintegrations per second. For many purposes, the level of radioactivity is more significant than the mass of radioactive material; it is then usual to express the total amount of a substance in terms of the number of curies it contains.

Becquerel (Bq)   The curie is a very large unit for some purposes; levels of radioactivity in the sea are often measured in picocuries (1 pCi $= 10^{-12}$ Ci). The SI unit that replaces the curie is the becquerel, or 1 nuclear disintegration per second. 1 Bq $= 27.03$ pCi; 1 TBq (terabecquerel) $= 10^{12}$ Bq $= 27.03$ Ci.

Half-life   The radioactivity of a substance declines with the passage of time. After one half-life, the radioactivity is halved. Each radionuclide has its characteristic half-life which may be a fraction of a second, hours, days, months or millions of years. The half-life of radium-226 is 1602 years. Radioactivity is inversely related to the half-life and a substance with a short half-life is intensely radioactive, while one with a long half-life displays low radioactivity.

Rad   The curie takes no account of the nature of the nuclear disintegration, merely its frequency. For biological purposes it is more important to know the amount of radioactivity absorbed by a tissue or organism. This is measured by the rad, defined as the amount of radiation causing 1 kg of tissue to absorb 0.01 joules of energy.

Gray (Gy)   This SI unit replaces the rad and is defined as an energy absorption of 1 J kg^{-1}; thus 1 Gy $= 100$ rad.

Rem Different kinds of radiation do different amounts of damage to living tissue for the same energy, and neutrons or α particles have about ten times the effect of β or γ particles for the same number of rads. The rem is an arbitrary unit designed to take account of this difference. Thus a dose of 5 rem could be made up to 5 rad of γ particles or 0.5 rad of neutrons.

Sievert (Sv) This SI unit replaces the rem as the unit of dose equivalence; 1 Sv = 100 rem.

Inputs of radioactivity to the sea

Background radioactivity

Radioactivity is a natural phenomenon. Seawater is naturally radioactive, largely through the presence of potassium-40, but it also contains decay products of uranium and thorium, and receives a continuous input of tritium (^{3}H, the radioactive isotope of hydrogen) through the activity of cosmic rays (Table 7.1).

Table 7.1. Natural levels of radioactivity in surface seawater

Radionuclide	Concentration ($Bq\ l^{-1}$)
Potassium-40	11.84
Tritium (^{3}H)	0.022–0.11
Rubidium-87	1.07
Uranium-234	0.05
Uranium-238	0.04
Carbon-14	0.007
Radium-228	$(0.0037–0.37) \times 10^{-2}$
Lead-210	$(0.037–0.25) \times 10^{-2}$
Uranium-235	0.18×10^{-2}
Radium-226	$(0.15–0.17) \times 10^{-2}$
Polonium-210	$(0.022–0.15) \times 10^{-2}$
Radon-222	0.07×10^{-2}
Thorium-228	$(0.007–0.11) \times 10^{-3}$
Thorium-230	$(0.022–0.05) \times 10^{-4}$
Thorium-232	$(0.004–0.29) \times 10^{-4}$

Heavy radionuclides have a low solubility in water and tend to be adsorbed on to particulate matter. They therefore accumulate in sediments, and fine sediments, with their large surface area, tend to adsorb more than coarse sediments. Thus while oceanic seawater has a radioactivity of about 12.6 Bq l^{-1}, marine sands have a radioactivity of 200–400 Bq kg^{-1} and muds 700–1000 Bq kg^{-1}. In parts of the world with very high natural levels of radioactivity, marine sands have correspondingly high radioactive levels. The best known examples are in Kerala in south-west India and in the provinces of Espirito Santo and Rio de Janiero in Brazil. At one popular bathing beach at Guarapari near Rio de Janiero, the visitor is exposed to a dose rate of 20 μGy h^{-1}.

Weapons testing

Inputs of radioactivity to the sea from human activities began in the later stages of the Second World War with the explosion of the first nuclear weapons, and continued with nuclear weapons testing until the signing of the test ban treaty between the USA, USSR, and UK in 1963. Subsequent weapons tests by France in 1965 and China in 1968 made minor contributions. These nuclear weapons contained enriched uranium and plutonium, and when exploded under water or near the ground produced over 200 different fission products and isotopes. These were carried in fine dust into the stratosphere where they circled the globe many times before settling back to Earth again as fall-out. Many of the radioisotopes produced do not occur naturally; some have a very short half-life, but the longer-lived radioisotopes allow the extent and distribution of contamination from this source to be detected. The most important of these are strontium-90 and caesium-137 with a half-life of about 30 years, and plutonium-239 with a long half-life of 24 400 years.

Because of the global pattern of atmospheric circulation, most of the fall-out has occurred between latitude 45 °N and 45 °S, with higher levels in the northern hemisphere where most of the explosions took place. There has been a negligible input from this source since the mid-1960s (Fig. 7.2) and radioactivity from this source has been subject to natural decay ever since then. The average radioactivity of ocean water in the north Atlantic in the early 1970s, attributable to fall-out is shown in Table 7.2, but its distribution is far from uniform. The highest levels occur in surface waters, and, depending on water movements, are slowly carried to deeper water (Fig. 7.3).

Liquid wastes

Radioactive substances are included in cooling water and other liquid wastes from nuclear reactors and may be discharged into the sea.

Nuclear-powered ships and submarines release some radioactivity, but the amounts are trivial compared with the discharges from nuclear power stations

Fig. 7.2. Monthly deposition of strontium-90 in the northern hemisphere, derived from weapon testing.

Table 7.2. Average (and range of) radioactivity in north Atlantic waters in the early 1970s due to fall-out from nuclear weapon tests

Radionuclide	Radioactivity $(Bq\ l^{-1})$	
Tritium (^{3}H)	1.78	(1.15–2.74)
Caesium-137	0.008	(0.001–0.03)
Strontium-90	0.005	(0.0007–0.02)
Carbon-14	0.0007	(0.0004–0.015)
Plutonium-239		(0.0001–0.0004)

Fig. 7.3. Vertical distribution of caesium-137 in the north Atlantic.

and fuel-reprocessing plants. Furthermore, such discharges as these are widely distributed in the oceans, not confined to one area as in the case with discharges from land-based installations.

By 1987, 433 nuclear reactors for generating electric power were in operation or under construction in 30 countries. Several types of reactor are in use, but all depend on the energy derived from the fission of uranium, usually in the form of uranium dioxide. The core of the reactor containing the fuel rods generates great heat, and a coolant passes through the core to maintain a uniform internal temperature. The coolant may be light or heavy water, carbon dioxide, or molten sodium. The heat is transferred indirectly to water and used to generate steam to drive turbines which generate electricity in the conventional way. This water is then condensed and recycled, but large volumes of cooling water are required for this process and are then discharged into the sea in the case of coastal or estuarine nuclear power stations.

The discharged cooling water inevitably acquires some radioactivity and the discharge also contains liquid wastes with low radioactivity from processes involved with the handling of spent fuel rods from the reactor. In Britain, the total radioactive discharge and the discharge of particular radionuclides are limited by regulations for each nuclear power station, depending on local circumstances. Thus the nuclear power station at Bradwell on the Blackwater estuary in Essex is permitted to discharge 7.4 TBq yr^{-1} of radioactivity, plus 55.5 TBq yr^{-1} of tritium, but because of the presence of commercial oyster beds in the area, the discharge of zinc-65 which the oysters accumulate, is limited to 0.185 TBq yr^{-1}. At Hinkley Point on the southern shore of the Bristol Channel, where there is no such commercial interest, levels are limited to a total discharge of 7.4 TBq yr^{-1} and 74 TBq yr^{-1} of tritium, with no stipulation about zinc-65. In practice, actual emissions are a good deal less than the permitted levels. In 1986, for example, Bradwell nuclear power station discharged 10 per cent of the permitted total radio-activity and only 1 per cent of the permitted zinc-65. Other power stations have a similar performance.

The fuel elements remain in the reactor for two to three years, by which time they have lost efficiency but still contain large amounts of uranium-235 which has not yet undergone fission, together with a variety of other radionuclides, including plutonium-239 and americium-241. Spent fuel rods may be removed for permanent safe storage on land, as is the current practice in Canada and the United States, or more commonly are taken to a reprocessing plant where the uranium is recovered for reuse and the plutonium and fission products are extracted. Major reprocessing plants in Europe exist at Sellafield on the north-west coast of England, La Hague near Cherbourg on the French Channel coast, and at Karlsruhe in Germany. There are others in India, Japan, and the United States of America. They discharge large quantities of waste water with a low radioactive content, but because of the quantities involved, these dwarf the output from power stations.

Discharges from Sellafield rose to a peak in the early 1970s when the maximum permitted release of α emitters was 222 TBq yr^{-1} (6000 Ci yr^{-1}) and of β emitters 11 100 TBq yr^{-1} (300 000 Ci yr^{-1}). Since that time discharges have been greatly reduced and by 1986 the maximum permitted discharge for α emitters was 14 TBq yr^{-1} and for β emitters 950 TBq yr^{-1}. In practice, actual discharges have been substantially below these limits. The most significant discharges because of their long half-life are caesium-137 and -134, ruthenium-106, strontium-90, and americium-241, and separate maximum permitted discharges are set for these and a number of other radionuclides. In recent years there has been some concern about the possibility of human exposure to α emitters, primarily plutonium and americium, and discharge of these has now been reduced to a very low level (Fig. 7.4).

The behaviour of these radionuclides in the sea depends on their chemical form and physico-chemical characteristics. Caesium-137 remains in solution and has a half-life of 30 years. Since the isotope does not occur naturally, it can serve as a marker for Sellafield liquid emissions, showing their course and dilution in the Irish Sea (Fig. 7.5(a)) and round the north of Scotland into the North Sea (Fig. 7.5(b)).

Other radionuclides, particularly those of ruthenium and plutonium, tend to adsorb strongly on to particulate matter and so are carried to the seabed where they accumulate in fine substrata. Some seabed sediments in the area influenced by the Sellafield discharge are contaminated with up to 3.9 Bq g^{-1} of plutonium-239. Resuspension of particles and the local hydrography results in some accumulation of radioactive particles in estuarine muds and salt marshes on the Cumbrian and Solway coasts and this has to be taken into account in calculating the radiation exposure of fishermen in the area who regularly work on the mud-flats.

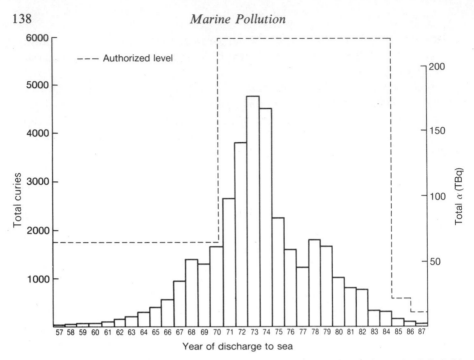

Fig. 7.4.   Permitted and actual discharge of α-radioactivity to the sea from the Sellafield fuel-reprocessing plant. *(Published with the permission of the Controller of Her Majesty's Stationery Office.)*

Solid wastes

Sea dumping of radioactive solid wastes has been practised since 1946, but has increasingly come under international control. The 1972 London Dumping Convention, now ratified by 91 states, regulates all dumping at sea and this agreement prohibits the dumping of high-level radioactive wastes. High-level waste is now defined as that containing, per tonne of material: more than 1 million Ci (37 000 TBq) tritium; 1000 Ci (37 TBq) β and γ emitters; 100 Ci (3.7 TBq) of strontium-90 and caesium-137; or 1 Ci (0.037 TBq) of α emitters with half-lives over 50 years.

Intermediate and low level radioactive waste continued to be dumped at sea until 1982. Between 1946 and 1967, the United States used a site 2800 m deep in the western Atlantic; a small amount was also dumped in deep water off the Pacific coast. Eight European countries (Belgium, France, Germany, Italy, Netherlands, Sweden, Switzerland, and the United Kingdom) used 10 sites in the north-east Atlantic until 1971 when all dumping was centred at a site 900 km from the nearest land and 550 km beyond the edge of the continental shelf in 4400 m of water. The amounts of radioactivity dumped until use of this site was suspended in 1983 are shown in Table 7.3. Japan prepared a plan to dump low

Fig. 7.5. Concentration of caesium-137, in Bq kg^{-1} in filtered seawater (a) in the Irish Sea in April 1987, and (b) in the North Sea in August–September 1987. (*Crown copyright reserved.*)

level radioactive waste in deep water in the western Pacific, but this plan has not been proceeded with.

The waste consists of contaminated piping, concrete and building material, glassware, protective clothing, etc. and is derived from nuclear power stations and reactors operated by industry and nuclear research centres, from universities, research institutes, and radiological services in hospitals. For disposal it is packed in concrete-lined steel drums, either embedded in resin or bitumen, or with a pressure equalization device. This ensures that the container reaches the seabed intact without imploding under the great pressures. Ultimately, the containers will corrode and leach their contents out into the surrounding water, but the delay results in a loss of radioactivity as the shorter-lived radionuclides decay, and the slow release of the contents ensures great dilution.

As on land, ocean disposal sites are selected to ensure that the radioactive waste does not present a risk to the human population. At such great depths, there is no risk of drums of waste being accidentally trawled by fishermen. There are no known food chains linking the abyssal fauna, which might eventually become contaminated with radiation, with pelagic fisheries and even if such a link does exist, the abyssal fauna is so sparse that the contamination of human food supplies would be insignificant compared with other exposures to radiation. Bottom currents on the abyssal plane flow slowly towards the Antarctic where

Marine Pollution

Table 7.3. Amount of intermediate and low level radioactive waste dumped in the north-east Atlantic

Year	α emitters (TBq)	β/γ emitters (TBq)	Tritium (TBq)
1974	15.5	40 700	
1975	28.9	1 130	1 100
1976	32.6	1 200	775
1980	70.3	3 075	3 630
1981	77.7	2 930	2 750
1982	51.8	1 830	2 860
Total 1948–82	660	38 000	15 000

they surface; Antarctic plankton is potentially a more important route to the human population, though still insignificant. Peak exposure from this source will be 200 years from now.

Exposure of marine organisms in and around the dump site are all at or below the natural background level of radiation and well below the dose rates at which harmful effects to individuals or populations of marine organisms have been observed.

These predictions are based on theoretical models. It is impossible to check them because no measurable radioactivity has yet been released at the dump sites. Even after the first drums of waste begin to disintegrate, it will be difficult to measure an increase in radioactivity against background levels because of the slow rate of discharge and dilution of soluble radionuclides and adsorption of others on to bottom sediments.

Ecological impact of radioactivity

Lethal doses

The measurement of acute lethal doses of radioactivity is complicated by the fact that damage inflicted on test organisms may not be revealed for some time after exposure to radiation, and sub-lethal genetic damage cannot be detected until the next or later generations. This is less of a problem for micro-organisms with a very short lifespan, but for these, measurement of the LD_{50} is hardly appropriate and, instead, the LD_{90} is used. In practice this is a measure of the dose at which almost the entire culture dies. For macroscopic animals, the LD_{50} is based on the mortality occurring within a given time after exposure to radiation. This time is arbitrarily selected, but 30 days is a convenient period and most animals surviving so long stand a good chance of living an appreciable time longer.

The LD values given in Table 7.4 are therefore intended only to give an impression of the susceptibility of different organisms to radiation damage. There is wide variation, but as a rule, the more advanced and complicated the animal, the lower the radiation dose necessary to cause it fatal damage. Gametes and larval stages are more susceptible to radiation damage than adults.

Bioaccumulation and food webs

Radionuclides behave chemically in the same way as their non-radioactive, naturally occurring isotopes, but the possibility of bioaccumulation and biomagnification in food chains has greater significance if the substance accumulated is radioactive.

Algae are able to acquire large concentrations of substances from the surrounding water. *Porphyra umbilicalis*, since it is the only seaweed eaten in quantity by sections of the human population in Britain, has attracted particular attention. In the neighbourhood of Sellafield, where it is exposed to a considerable variety of radionuclides from the marine outfall from the reprocessing plant, it accumulates 10 times the concentration of caesium-137 found in the water, 400 times the concentration of zirconium-95 and niobium-95, 100 times the concentration of cerium-144 and 1500 times the concentration of ruthenium-106. Concentrations of radionuclides in *Porphyra* collected near Sellafield at the period of maximum discharges in 1974 are shown in Table 7.5. Other seaweeds in the area also accumulate radionuclides, but different elements predominate: *Enteromorpha* and *Ulva* accumulate much higher concentrations than *Porphyra* of zirconium, niobium, and cerium, and also accumulate plutonium-239. Fucoids, although they are rather poor accumulators of ruthenium-106, accumulate very much higher concentrations than *Porphyra* of plutonium-239 and for this reason have proved to be useful monitors of this radionuclide. Despite the high concentrations of radioactive materials in these algae, they are unaffected by them.

Planktonic crustaceans appear to be poor assimilators of radionuclides received in their food and they lose a high proportion of their intake in faeces. The fact that they moult at frequent intervals means that radionuclides adsorbed on to them are regularly shed. Planktonic crustaceans are therefore not an important pathway for radionuclides in pelagic food webs. Most inshore fish are, however, benthic feeders and in an area with a localized input of radioactive material, as at Sellafield, sedimentation processes ensure that there is an accumulation of radionuclides on the seabed with corresponding contamination of the infauna. Crabs, *Carcinus maenas*, accumulate much greater quantities of plutonium-237 than plaice, *Pleuronectes platessa*, when fed on *Nereis diversicolor* labelled with this radioisotope (Fig. 7.6); most of the radionuclide was accumulated in the digestive gland of the crab, but in the plaice was found adhering to the gut wall but not accumulated in other organs.

Table 7.4. Acute lethal radiation doses for adults of marine organisms

Organism	Dose (Gy)	Type of experiment
Blue-green algae	4000–12 000+	LD_{90}
Other algae	30–1200	LD_{90}
Protozoa	up to 6000	LD_{90}
Mollusca	200–1090	LD_{50}
Crustacea	15–566	LD_{50}
Fish	11–56	LD_{50}

LD_{50} values are based on total mortality observed during 30 days following exposure to radiation

Table 7.5. Radioactivity of *Porphyra* collected near Sellafield in 1974

Radionuclide	Concentration (Bq g^{-1})
Ruthenium-106	8.29
Cerium-144	0.90
Zirconium-95/Niobium-95	1.37
Caesium-137	0.093
Plutonium-239, -240	0.051
Americium-241	0.023
Strontium-90	0.016

Bivalves are notorious for their ability to accumulate very high concentrations of metals, though specific abilities vary widely. Scallop, *Pecten maximus*, accumulate large quantities of manganese, oysters, *Ostrea*, large amounts of zinc, and mussels, *Mytilus*, iron. The very small amounts of the radioisotopes of these elements included in the discharges are readily taken up by these species.

Exposure levels

Bottom-living fish are likely to be exposed to higher levels of radioactivity than pelagic species because of the adsorption of radionuclides to particles that accumulate in the seabed. Experiments have been conducted to measure the exposure of plaice in the north-east Irish Sea by attaching dosimeters to their ventral surface. Individuals caught up to two and a half years after release proved to have acquired a mean dose of 3.5 μSv h^{-1}, with occasional individuals that had received a dose of 25 μSv h^{-1} (Fig. 7.7). This maximum figure is about the

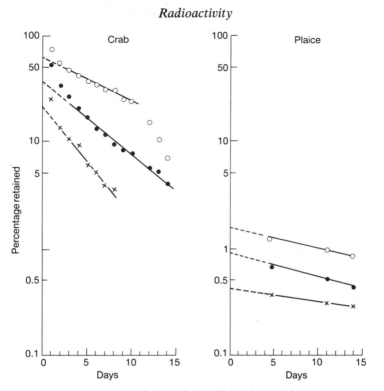

Fig. 7.6. Percentage retention of plutonium-237 by three crabs, *Carcinus maenus*, and three plaice, *Pleuronectes platessa*, after being fed with *Nereis diversicolor* containing the radionuclide. *(Copyright © 1977, Macmillan Journals Ltd)*

same as the calculated dose based on the seabed radioactivity near the Sellafield outfall. Evidently, the migrations of the fish result in the great majority of them receiving a much smaller dose. The minimum dose at which minor radiation-induced disturbances to physiology and metabolism can be demonstrated in the laboratory is 100 µSv h^{-1}, and it is evident that bottom-living fish, even in the most heavily contaminated areas, receive far less than such minimally damaging exposures.

Population effects

Even though marine organisms have generally a relatively high tolerance of radioactivity, it must be expected that damage to some susceptible individuals and genetic disturbances are an inevitable consequence of any level of radiation exposure, whether the source of it is natural or man-made. This would be manifested in increased mortality of adults or eggs and larvae, but in view of the enormous natural mortality this would be very hard to detect.

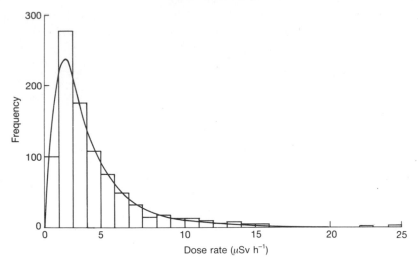

Fig. 7.7. Dose of radiation received by plaice, *Pleuronectes platessa*, in the north-east Irish Sea.

In one Canadian experiment, eggs and larvae of the chinook salmon, *Onchorhynchus tschawytscha*, raised in a salmon hatchery were subjected to 5–200 mGy per day, and returns to the river were measured in subsequent years. Large batches of eggs and young were used in the experiments and there was an increased number of abnormalities in young fish at all dose rates, but no decline in the number of adults returning to the river for spawning was ever detected.

Existing levels of radiation in the sea have so far produced no measurable environmental impact on marine organisms or ecosystems. This is not to say that there are no particularly sensitive organisms or ecosystems that might be adversely affected, but it will evidently require detailed investigations to expose them.

Hazard to human health

The natural environment appears to be unaffected by present levels of radioactivity, but there is naturally more concern about risks to the human population.

Humans are currently exposed to radiation from a variety of sources, natural and man-made. The average annual dose to members of the general public in Britain is estimated to be 2390 μSv and is derived from radioactive fall-out, food stuffs, from medical irradiation, cosmic rays, building materials (brick, stone, etc.), and from radon gas seeping from the ground; radon provides about one-third of the annual dose. Exposure to radioactivity from the sea is either through the consumption of seafood that has accumulated radioactive substances or by external exposure to radioactive substrata on beaches. In either case, since levels of radioactivity are low, exposure must be prolonged to be significant.

Chronic exposure to ionizing radiation may produce **somatic** effects, most importantly leukaemia and cancer of the bone, thyroid, lungs or breast; or **genetic** damage manifested in some abnormalities or defects in the next generation, resulting from irradiation of the gonads. While these effects undoubtedly occur, it is always difficult to establish a connection between low-level chronic exposure and the incidence of an effect in any individual. Such diseases do not usually reveal themselves until long after the period of exposure, there is not a strict relationship between the intensity and duration of exposure and the incidence of disease or effects in the individual at risk, and all these diseases occur in any normal population, whether or not it is exposed to a particular source of radiation. Equally, genetic effects show a dose relationship only at the level of the population and the consequences of exposure for the individual are unpredictable. The nature of the genetic damage resulting from radiation does not differ from genetic defects that occur spontaneously.

Different radionuclides present different kinds of health hazard, depending on their chemistry. In the same way as the stable isotopes, depending on the form in which radioisotopes are presented to the organism, they differ in the ease with which they are assimilated, in the organs in which they accumulate, and the length of time they remain in them. The existence of **critical organs** in which particular substances accumulate is particularly important for α- and β-emitters which have an intensely ionizing effect but are damaging only over a short distance. The critical organ for the radioisotope iodine-131 is the thyroid because the thyroid accumulates 600 times the iodine concentration of other tissues in the body. The critical organ for strontium-90, which behaves chemically like calcium, is bone. For manganese-54 the critical organ is the liver.

A great many factors must therefore be taken into account in assessing the possible impact of radioactive effluents on a section of the population:

(1) the nature of the radionuclide;
(2) the nature of the emitted radiation;
(3) its half-life;
(4) the decay scheme;
(5) the chemical form in which the radionuclide is encountered;
(6) the fraction that is assimilated;
(7) the organ in which it may accumulate and the concentration that may be reached.

The principal source of guidance about radiation exposure is the International Commission on Radiological Protection (ICRP). This body grew out of an international commission set up in 1928 to advise on tolerable levels of X-ray and radiation exposure. There is no evidence that there is a threshold level of radiation exposure below which there are no harmful effects, and when setting tolerable levels of exposure it must be assumed that any increase in radiation levels above the inescapable natural background, carries some risk of damage. No human activity is without some degree of risk, however, and a degree of risk is acceptable if the benefits of an activity are great enough. The use of X-rays in medical diagnosis, for example, entails some risk of radiation damage, but given the safeguards that are in use, the risk is an acceptable one.

Limits to radiation exposure recommended by ICRP are designed to safeguard those who are regularly exposed in the course of their work. An overall limit of 50 mSv (5 rem) yr^{-1} is prescribed, but particular tissues should not receive more than a particular fraction of this and there are detailed recommendations about the annual exposure to 240 different radionuclides that may be ingested or inhaled. Occupational exposure at the ICRP-recommended limits would, on a statistical basis, entail 340 additional deaths per million workers. In practice, occupational exposure is well below the recommended limits. For comparison, in the United Kingdom in 1986–7 there were 300 accidental deaths per million workers in metal mining, 106 per million in coal mining, 95 per million in metal manufacture, and 92 per million in the construction industry.

Members of the general public are much less regularly exposed to radioactivity from man-made sources than those employed in nuclear installations. The whole-body dose limit recommended for them by the ICRP is 5 mSv (0.5 rem) yr^{-1}, or one-tenth that for occupational exposure, and this entails a risk of 1–10 radiation-induced deaths from cancer per million of the exposed population. Allowing for the fact that there is wide variation in the levels of exposure among the population, such an upper limit means that the average dose received by members of the public is 0.5 mSv yr^{-1}. This is about the same dose as might be expected from medical diagnosis or from living in a brick house rather than a wooden one.

A more stringent safeguard is provided in setting limits to radioactive discharges to the sea by directing attention to the most likely route by which radionuclides may reach the human population, and the dose likely to be received by that section of the population most at risk. This **critical path** approach is exemplified by the way in which it has been applied to discharges from the fuel reprocessing plant at Sellafield.

A large range of radionuclides is included in the liquid effluent, which is discharged from the reprocessing plant by a 2.5 km long pipeline into the Irish Sea. The Irish Sea supports a variety of commercial fisheries and the most critical pathway to man through the consumption of contaminated seafood from the area proved, surprisingly, to be by the seaweed *Porphyra*. *Porphyra* was collected along the coast near Sellafield and shipped to South Wales where, along with *Porphyra* harvested in other parts of Britain, it was processed into laverbread, a delicacy whose consumption is almost entirely limited to South Wales. *Porphyra* accumulates a variety of radionuclides from seawater (Table 7.5), the most important being ruthenium-106. Surveys carried out in South Wales showed that 26 000 people consumed up to 75 g day^{-1} of laverbread regularly, but a small group of 170 adults was identified with individual consumption rates of about 160 g day^{-1}, with a maximum of 388 g day^{-1}.

The critical tissue for ruthenium-106 is the lower large intestine, and for strontium-90, plutonium-239, and americium-241, it is bone. Because of the variety of radionuclides in the *Porphyra*, calculations were made for individual radionuclides, on the most pessimistic assumptions, ensuring that the total exposure did not exceed recommended limits.

The recommended annual dose limit recommended by the ICRP for the lower large intestine was 15 mSv yr^{-1}; estimated doses received by the critical sub-group of laverbread eaters in 1962–7 was 4–7 mSv yr^{-1}. The recommended genetically acceptable dose was calculated to be 1.3 mSv yr^{-1}; the dose resulting from laverbread consumption was 1 μSv yr^{-1}. These calculations were based on the very conservative assumption that all *Porphyra* used in the manufacture of laverbread came from the neighbourhood of Sellafield, and ignored the water added during its preparation, which dilutes the radioactive component.

Use of the critical pathway approach requires constant vigilance to take account of changing circumstances and increasing knowledge of the behaviour of radionuclides. *Porphyra* ceased to be a significant pathway in the mid-1970s when the last two commercial collectors of the seaweed retired and Sellafield *Porphyra* was no longer used in the preparation of laverbread. Locally caught fish then assumed the critical position: the maximum exposure of an individual in the critical population from fish consumption was 34 per cent of the dose limit recommended by ICRP. Caesium-137 contributes substantially to radiation exposure from eating fish caught around Sellafield, and caesium discharges rose substantially in 1974–5 as a result of changed practices at the reprocessing plant. In 1976, the critical group among members of the public received 25 per cent of the ICRP-recommended dose limit of caesium-137 from this source. In subsequent years, this figure was reduced to about 10 per cent of the ICRP limit. Further reassessment of exposures was necessary in 1982 when a new survey by the Ministry of Agriculture, Fisheries, and Food revealed that the estimated consumption of molluscs by the critical group of seafood consumers had increased threefold. Their intake of plutonium and americium had increased by a similar factor. It has also been discovered that the uptake of plutonium from food by the human gut is five times higher than was formerly thought. Thus the dose of plutonium received by members of the critical group must be increased by a factor of 15, bringing their total exposure from 24 per cent to 39 per cent of the ICRP annual dose limit, of which actinides (plutonium and americium) contribute 26 per cent rather than the 4 per cent previously estimated. Steps were then taken to reduce the discharges of α radioactivity accordingly.

Critical pathway analysis is used to determine discharge standards in a number of countries and this accounts for the great variation in the limits set for each installation, which must take account of local circumstances and the critical pathways of exposure of the human population to radioactivity. The nuclear power station at Lake Trawsfynydd in Wales discharged 5.18 TBq in 1975 and individuals in the critical group consuming fish from the lake are estimated to have received 8 per cent of the ICRP limit. The reprocessing plant at Sellafield, on the other hand, discharged 10 000 TBq in that year when maximum exposure of a member of the critical group of seafood consumers was estimated to be 34 per cent of the ICRP limit, only four times as much despite the enormously greater discharge.

8

Solid wastes and heat

Dredging spoil and industrial solid wastes

Dredging spoil

Ports, harbours, rivers, and approach channels often need regular dredging to keep them open to shipping. The dredged material may be used in land reclamation, but is more often dumped at sea. In England and Wales alone, 28 million tonnes of dredging spoil is dumped annually at 60 licensed offshore sites. The composition of the spoil is varied: for routine dredging it is usually fine silt, but if new channels are constructed or old ones deepened, it may consist of boulder clay or chalk, etc. Unlike other solid wastes dumped at sea, the spoil cannot usually be distinguished from the surrounding substratum at the dumping ground and, depending on the bottom currents, it may not stay where it was dumped, but gradually be transported to other areas, including the place it originally came from.

Dredging spoil is often anoxic and contaminated with metals and persistent oils. Pollutants accumulating in estuarine sediments are transferred elsewhere in the course of dredging. Table 8.1 shows the quantity of heavy metals included in

Table 8.1. Quantities of metals (kg day^{-1}) in dredging spoil dumped in the North Sea in 1981

Country	Cadmium	Mercury	Chromium	Copper	Lead	Nickel	Zinc
Belgium	0	31	6 978	1761	4422	1448	27 216
Holland	151	32	2 693	1457	3789	873	11 486
UK	14	19	1 149	804	1213	390	3 425
Total*	165	82	10 821	4026	9425	2711	42 141

* Including small quantities contributed by Denmark

dredging spoil dumped in the North Sea each year by Belgium, the UK, and Holland. These totals conceal a wide variation. Spoil from harbours and estuaries with intense shipping activity and heavy industry is much more contaminated than that from other areas. Dredging spoil from docks on the Manchester Ship Canal, for example, contains 20.7 p.p.m. mercury and 5080 p.p.m. lead. The Tees estuary spoil contains 7 p.p.m. mercury and 3000 p.p.m. zinc, but only 320–460 p.p.m. lead. Swansea docks spoil contains a high concentration of cadmium (18 p.p.m.). At the other extreme, the chromium concentration in the spoil from Newhaven is 1 p.p.m., compared with 1500 p.p.m. in one sample from the Tees estuary.

The immediate impact of dumping dredging spoil is a smothering of the benthic fauna in the dumping grounds, though some animals are able to burrow to the surface of the dumped material without much difficulty. One study was carried out in the fjord at Uddevalla on the west coast of Sweden (Fig. 8.1) where dredging was going on in an area where surveys of the benthic fauna had been made in 1971–2. Immediately after the dredging of a new channel, there was a loss of diversity at stations near the site of operations due to a failure of recruitment of several bivalves, probably because of the increased sediment in the water, but the position was restored a year later. Benthic animals in the area accumulated high concentrations of metals when dredging was in progress, but returned to former levels within 18 months.

In all, it is concluded that while dumping of dredging spoil at sea transfers contaminants from one site to another, it has little effect on the fauna of the dumping grounds.

China clay waste

China clay deposits in south Cornwall near St Austell have been used since the middle of the eighteenth century as a source of fine clay for the manufacture of porcelain. The waste which the extraction of the clay produces consists of fine sand, kaolin and flakes of mica, and has been discharged into the rivers Fal, Luxulyan, and St Austell (Fig. 8.2), though the Fal ceased to be used for this purpose many years ago. About 1.5 million t yr^{-1} of mica waste is produced, about half of it being discharged into the St Austell river (which is known locally as the White river for this reason), 25 per cent into the Luxulyan river, and the rest disposed of on land.

Most of the river-borne waste is deposited in St Austell Bay and Mevagissy Bay (Fig. 8.3(a)). The substratum in the area is naturally one of coarse sand, shell, pebble, and rock but about three-fifths of the seabed is now covered, sometimes to a considerable depth, with micaceous clay waste and this has caused faunistic changes. Some bivalves, such as *Venus fasciata* (Fig. 8.3(b)) and *Dosinia exoleta*, are intolerant of the clay waste but there is a characteristic fauna of the china clay waste, including the polychaete *Melinna palmata*, the bivalves *Tellina fabula* and *Cultellus pellucidus*, the heart urchin *Echinocardium cordatum*, the holothurian *Labidoplax digitata*, and the ophiuroid *Amphiura filiformis* (Fig. 8.3(c)). Plaice,

Fig. 8.1. (a) Dredged and disposal areas in the Byfjord, western Sweden, (b) diversity (Shannon–Wiener index) and (c) number of species at stations 10–12 before and after dredging; station 12 represents the control site. *(Pergamon Press.)*

Pleuronectes platessa, dab, *Limanda limanda*, and sole, *Solea solea*, feed on this specialized fauna.

Fly ash

Ash from coal-fired power stations consists of large, fused lumps of clinker and a considerable amount of very fine powder. This includes 'pulverized fuel ash' from

Fig. 8.2. Area from which china clay is produced near St Austell, Cornwall, and the discharge routes for the china clay waste. *(Pergamon Press.)*

the boilers but is mainly 'fly ash' extracted from the exhaust fumes in the smoke stacks by air pollution control equipment. This fine material is composed mainly of silicon dioxide with oxides of aluminium and iron, and a variety of metals present in trace concentrations. There is some use for fly ash in the construction industry but the supply greatly exceeds demand; the surplus is dumped generally

Fig. 8.3. St Austell and Mevagissey Bays, Cornwall: distribution of (a) clay waste fractions in bottom sediments, (b) the bivalve *Venus fasciata*, intolerant of clay, and (c) the brittle star *Amphiura filiformis*, clay-tolerant. *(Cambridge University Press.)*

on land, but power stations in Newcastle and Blyth in north-east England dump 600 000–700 000 t yr^{-1} at sea. The particle size of fly ash is 2–200 µm and similar to that of fine silt, but because of its homogeneity, it offers low niche diversity and at the Blyth dumping ground some species such as the gastropod *Turritella communis*, and the foraminiferan *Astrorhiza*, common at the time dumping started in 1959, are now rare or eliminated. Unlike the situation at St Austell Bay with an input of clay waste, the main dumping ground receiving fly ash shows extreme impoverishment of the fauna, presumably because of the daily disturbance of dumping by barge. As in Cornwall, the fine sediment has sifted into rock crevices to the detriment of the lobster fishery, but there appears not to have been a compensating development of a rich benthic soft-bottom fauna.

Colliery waste

Waste from collieries near the north-east coast of England has been dumped on beaches or barged out to sea for dumping since the start of this century. The waste is predominantly shale with some sandstone, but includes small fragments of coal and because of this has a high metal content. The waste is mainly in gravel-sized fragments of larger, 2–30 mm. Material dumped on beaches is not subsequently dispersed, but that dumped offshore is subject to considerable movement. There is great depletion of the fauna in the areas of dumping.

Plastics

Plastic particles

Small pellets of polyethylene, polypropylene, and sometimes polystyrene, 3–4 mm in diameter, are widespread in the oceans. Their presence has been reported on beaches and in surface waters near centres of industry or major shipping routes since the early 1960s, but they have also been found in the south Atlantic and south Pacific, several thousand kilometres from any industrial source, and it must be assumed that their distribution is now worldwide. They are probably derived from plastic 'feedstock' for the plastics industry and reach the sea through accidental spillages at ports, or at factories whence they reach rivers. They are virtually indestructible and buoyant, and are presumably steadily accumulating in the sea and on coasts.

They are too small to cause an aesthetic nuisance on beaches, unlike other plastic debris. It is not certain if they are harmful to marine organisms but they are certainly ingested by surface-feeding marine birds. Prions, *Pachyptila*, are small petrels from the southern oceans, which have a sieving arrangement on the lower bill and feed on plankton. They commonly have numerous plastic pellets packed in the gizzard. Larger petrels and shearwaters rarely contain plastic pellets, but carnivorous birds such as great skuas, *Catharacta skua*, acquire them from their food and regurgitate them along with other indigestible material in their pellets. Plastic particles have also been found in the pellets of gulls and terns.

It is possible to speculate that an accumulation of pellets in the gut may be harmful, but the only evidence of this is a negative correlation between body fat and the number of pellets in migrating red phalaropes, *Phalaropus fulicarius*, on the Californian coast. If ingested pellets are responsible for impairing feeding, this would obviously be detrimental to birds facing a long migration.

Plastic litter

Larger plastic debris, mostly primary and secondary packaging, occurs in great abundance in the sea. Much of it is derived from shipping and it is estimated that 1.1–2.6 kg person^{-1} day^{-1} of plastic waste is generated and nearly all thrown overboard. Plastic wrappings of cargo add another 290 t ship^{-1} yr^{-1} and the total amount of plastics discarded by ships may be 6.5 million t yr^{-1}, most of it within 400 km of land.

Plastics are not biodegradable and although some may be subject to photodegradation when exposed to ultraviolet light, most are extremely durable and have a long life in the sea. Judging from plastic litter on beaches, the average age of containers is 2.9 years; older material is generally in fragments and stranded high on the shore. Over half the stranded plastic is as containers for lavatory and household cleansers, which are made of polyethylene, and a substantial minority are polyvinyl chloride mineral water containers, but there is a great variety of plastic containers for other substances made of a variety of plastics.

Plastic are inert to marine organisms, and floating articles that have been at sea for some time may acquire a fauna of barnacles and other encrusting organisms. Large fish have been discovered with plastic cups lodged in their stomachs, and the blanketing of the seabed, to the exclusion of the burrowing fauna, by discarded polythene sheeting is an increasing problem on fishing grounds. Generally, however, plastic litter is an aesthetic nuisance on amenity beaches but is not a hazard in the marine environment.

Drift nets

Diving sea birds, seals, and dolphins become entangled in drift nets when pursuing fish, and they are drowned. Drift nets that break free continue to catch fish automatically and continuously until they are washed ashore or rot, and they are a danger to birds and sea mammals as well as to fish. This is not a new problem, but it has been greatly increased by the introduction of nylon monofilament gill nets.

Such nets are virtually indestructible and they are very efficient at catching fish, perhaps because the fish cannot detect them. It is claimed that for the same fishing effort, the catch of bass, *Dicentrachus labrax*, on the south coast of Cornwall has increased from 100 kg to 3000 kg per fishing vessel per day through the use of monofilament gill nets. Unregulated use of these nets may have seriously reduced the stocks of white sea bass on the Californian coast, and the Canadian, New Zealand, and South African fishery authorities have all found it necessary to ban or closely regulate their use.

Unfortunately, the nets are equally efficient at catching sea birds. The Danish salmon drift net fishery in the north Atlantic is estimated to have killed 500 000 ± 250 000 sea birds, mostly Brunnich's guillemot, *Uria lomvia*, each year during the period 1965–75 when the fishery was exploited. The Japanese salmon fishery in the north Pacific and Bering Sea is estimated to have taken an annual toll of between 214 500 and 715 000 birds during 1952–75, and 350 000–450 000 in 1975–8. Such losses are of an order of magnitude greater than the estimated losses of sea birds in the north Atlantic from oil pollution.

Monofilament gill nets trap a considerable variety of fish, birds, and sea mammals. Northern fur seals, *Callorhinus ursinus*, dall porpoises, *Phocoenoides dalli*, and sea otters, *Enhydra lutris*, and on the south-east African coast, Cape fur seals, *Arctocephalus pusillus*, have been recorded as being killed by becoming entangled in discarded or lost nets. There are reported to be 130 000 small cetaceans caught in nets each year, but the actual number may be much higher. Birds trapped by them include the laysan albatross, *Diomedea immortabilis*, fulmars, *Fulmarus glacialis*, shearwaters, *Puffinus griseus* and *P. tenuirustris*, and tufted puffins, *Lunda cirrhata*. Since the monofilament gill nets used in the Japanese northern Pacific salmon fishery are 6 m deep and average 15 km long, their scope to inflict damage after they have broken free is very great indeed.

Munitions

In the past, many countries have disposed of defective, obsolete or surplus munitions by dumping them at sea. Accidental losses from wartime, and smaller losses of explosives and target ammunitions seaward of firing practice ranges, also remain on the seabed. The wreck of the ammunition ship *Richard Montgomery*, containing 3500 t of aerial fragmentation bombs and 1100 t of high explosives, which lies in the Thames estuary only 4.8 km from the Isle of Grain oil terminals, it but one example of a continuing major hazard.

Dumping grounds and known dangers are indicated on charts, but except for large bombs and shells these munitions, often in a dangerous condition, are shifted from their original dumping site or lose position by water movements. A considerable number are recovered in the course of fishing or dredging operations or subsequently appear on the shore, and there are periodic reports of human injuries resulting particularly from chemical warfare agents. Munitions in the sea have no material impact on living resources.

Figure 8.4 shows the main sites of munitions inputs to British coastal waters; coastal waters of other countries harbour similar hazards but the information about them has not been analysed. A wide range of such material is recovered (Table 8.2), and a substantial proportion is in a sufficiently dangerous condition that it has to be destroyed *in situ* instead of being removed for safe disposal elsewhere.

Marine disposal of unwanted munitions is now regulated and deliberate dumping in coastal waters is not authorized except in emergency. The accidental or deliberate inputs over many earlier years, however, remain a hazard to users of the sea.

Heat

Cooling water and often other industrial effluents are discharged at a higher temperature than that of the receiving waters. By far the greatest amount of heat discharged to the sea is in cooling water from coastal power stations. About 20 million m^3 of cooling water, 12 °C above the ambient sea temperature, are discharged for 1000 MWe of electricity generated by oil or coal-fired power stations. Nuclear power stations are a little less efficient and the cooling water from them is about 15 °C above ambient.

In the tropics there is little fluctuation in the power demand or the sea temperature, but in temperate regions, the peak load, and so the greatest discharge of cooling water, is in winter when the sea temperature is low and falling. In subtropical areas, particularly those of North America, the peak load is in summer because of the extensive use of air conditioning. The maximum discharge of hot water is thus at a time when sea temperatures are near their maximum which may be as high as 30–35 °C. Not only is the added heat dissipated more slowly than in cold seas, but the sea temperature is already near the thermal death point for many organisms and, with these additions of heat, may easily exceed it.

Cooling of the heated discharge is almost entirely by mixing with the receiving water. The area affected is limited to the plume of hot water and its immediate surroundings, although the direction taken by the plume may change with changing tidal currents and so the total area under its influence is greater than appears at first sight. Even so, the outfall from the Diablo Canyon nuclear power station on the Californian coast affects only 0.7 ha and the 250 MWe Bradwell nuclear power station in Essex discharging 2 million m^3 day^{-1} into the enclosed Blackwater estuary raises the temperature of the surface water by only 0.2–1.7 °C. A succession of power stations using and reusing the same water along the tidal Thames have a total capacity of 8000 MWe, but do not cause a build-up of water temperature. In contrast, in subtropical waters, much larger areas may be affected: at Turkey Point, on the Atlantic coast of Florida, nearly

Fig. 8.4. Main sites of munitions inputs to British coastal waters. *(Pergamon Press.)*

Table 8.2. Types of munitions recovered and the proportion that had to be destroyed *in situ* in the Portsmouth and Medway Command Area (PMCA), 1969–77

Class of munitions	Number	% destroyed
Bombs	422	81.5
Land service mortars and grenades	141	37.5
Mines and torpedoes	51	26.0
Anti-submarine weapons	11	23.4
Shells	1303	21.1
Rockets and propulsion units	23	13.6
Pyrotechnics	46	6.9
Total	1997	24.4*

* Percentage of all finds destroyed

40 ha are affected by the cooling water discharge from a power station complex (Fig. 8.5).

It is difficult to separate the effects of hot water from other features of the discharge. Cooling water is usually treated at least intermittently with chlorine to discourage the settlement of organisms in the heat-exchange system. The scour of the seabed caused by the water flow in the plume is likely to change the nature of a soft substratum and so influence the fauna. Metals are leached from the cooling system and the disapperance of abalones (*Haliotis*) from the neighbourhood of the Pablo Canyon power station is attributed to copper in the cooling water, not to the elevated temperature.

The Turkey Point power station complex discharges cooling water in a situation where quiet, shallow soft-bottom areas are dominated by turtle grass, *Thalassia*. This marine grass forms the basis of a specialized community supporting a characteristic fauna. The temperature of the sea around the discharge is 30–35 °C in summer and a further increase of 5 °C or more is damaging to *Thalassia*. About 9.3 ha of *Thalassia* has been destroyed by this outfall and a further 30 ha shows reduced growth.

Here and elsewhere it has been found that tropical marine animals are generally unable to withstand a temperature increase of more than 2–3 °C, and most sponges, molluscs, and crustaceans are eliminated at temperatures above 37 °C, though intertidal species appear to be more tolerant of high temperatures than benthic species. It is not surprising that there is a reduction in benthic diversity in the area of cooling water discharges from power stations on the Florida coast and in Guanilla Bay, Puerto Rico; the temperature of the discharge reaches 40–45 °C in summer.

In temperate regions, hot water discharges, far from being damaging, enhance

Fig. 8.5. Increase in surface sea temperature resulting from the discharge of cooling water from power stations at Turkey Point, Florida. (*Pergamon Press.*)

the growth of bivalves and fish and advantage of this is taken for mariculture of a number of organisms. In enclosed areas receiving heated effluent, several species breed continuously and this has been observed in the ascidians *Ciona* and *Ascidiella* and the amphipod *Corophium*; others have an unusually long breeding season as in *Balanus amphitrite* and *Elminius modestus*, both exotic species to Britain. Zooplankton blooms earlier in heated water: near the Hunterston nuclear power station in the Firth of Clyde, the copepod *Asellopsis intermedia* blooms two months earlier than elsewhere in the region. Unfortunately, the phytoplankton on which the copepod depends, blooms in response to increasing day length, not sea temperature, so that the copepod does not benefit from its earlier appearance.

Strong-swimming fish are able to avoid the intake of seawater cooling systems,

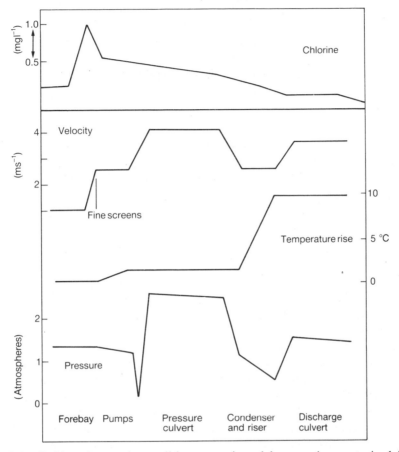

Fig. 8.6. Sudden changes in conditions experienced by organisms entrained in the cooling water flow at a power station.

but smaller fish and plankton are entrained in the flow of water and organisms small enough to pass through the screens are swept through the cooling system. They may be exposed to sudden injections of chlorine, sudden and large temperature changes, and to mechanical buffeting (Fig. 8.6). There is conflicting evidence about the impact of entrainment in the cooling water circuit. The most serious insult to entrained organisms appears to be the mechanical stresses imposed on them; small organisms, such as a polychaete larvae appear to be little affected, but very large numbers of fish eggs and larvae may be killed.

9

The state of some seas

In this chapter, a brief view is taken of five seas, the North, Mediterranean, Baltic, Caribbean, and Caspian Seas. All receive a considerable volume of effluents but because of difference in climate, physiography, and hydrographic regimes, the problems in each differ.

The North Sea

The total area of the North Sea is 575 000 km^2. The southern end is constricted at the Straits of Dover, but there is no geographical northern boundary, although for practical purposes this can be regarded as a line from Shetland to the Norwegian coast near Bergen. The south and south-eastern parts are shallow, with depths mostly less than 50 m. The northern part is 120–145 m deep, with deeper water off the Norwegian coast. It is not a homogeneous body of water and a number of areas can be distinguished between which water exchange is relatively slow (Fig. 9.1). Flushing time in these areas varies between 46 and 333 days, though surface water to a depth of 10 m is exchanged more rapidly. Overall, there is an excess of precipitation over evaporation, but in winter the lee-effect of the British Isles produces a net loss of water by evaporation in the western and south-western parts of the North Sea. During summer, all parts of the North Sea receive an excess of water by precipitation and with surface water becoming less saline, stratification of warm, less dense water over the deeper water is encouraged. A thermocline sometimes develops in the eastern North Sea and German Bight, particularly in calm weather, and this results in reduced oxygen concentrations in the bottom water (see Fig. 2.13, p. 30).

The North Sea is used as intensively for as great a variety of purposes as any sea area in the world. The Straits of Dover and southern North Sea are among the most heavily trafficked sea lanes in the world; gravel and sand for the construction industry is dredged in a number of areas; gas and oil are extracted in the central and northern North Sea. A largely urban and industrialized population of 31 million lives around the North Sea and its estuaries, and to these are added an influx of summer visitors, particularly to the sandy beaches of the eastern side of the sea. The North Sea receives the wastes from this population, together with those carried in a number of major rivers, the Rhine, Elbe, Weser,

Fig. 9.1. Areas of the North Sea between which there is little water exchange.

Scheldt, Ems, Thames, Trent, Tees, and Tyne. It also provides the site of highly productive fisheries which are intensively exploited.

Inputs

Much of the sewage from the population surrounding the North Sea is discharged untreated or given only primary treatment, although an increasing number of towns are introducing secondary treatment. Sewage sludge is discharged from the Netherlands coast and dumped at sea by the United Kingdom. These sources, together with the very large input from rivers, contribute over 1 million t yr^{-1} of BOD to the North Sea (Fig. 9.2(a)). Rivers are also a major source of the 1.5 million t yr^{-1} of nitrogen and 1 million t yr^{-1} of phosphorus input, much of it derived from run-off from agricultural land (Fig. 9.2(b,c)).

Estimates of inputs of heavy metals to the North Sea vary widely (see Table 5.1, p. 81). It is clear, though, that the atmosphere, rivers, and dredging spoils are the major contributors and that metal inputs from sewage sludge and industrial

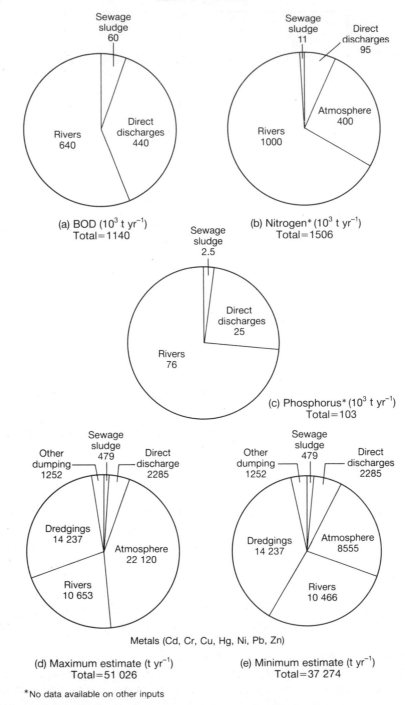

Fig. 9.2. Estimated inputs to the North Sea by various pathways.

waste are small in comparison. It is uncertain how much of the contaminated dredging spoil (see Table 8.1, p. 149) is a permanent addition to the sea and how much is recycled back into the estuaries and shipping channels from which it was dredged. If the maximum estimates of metal inputs are accepted, atmospheric inputs are particularly important (Fig. 9.2(d)), but if minimum values are used, inputs from the atmosphere, rivers, and dredging spoils are all of the same order (Fig. 9.2(e)).

The input of organochlorine pesticides and PCBs is small, following the phasing out of the pesticides and control of the use of PCBs. However, DDT and 'drins' continue to be leached from agricultural land where they were formerly used and perhaps 200 kg yr^{-1} enter the North Sea via rivers. Rivers are also responsible for an input of 3 t yr^{-1} of HCH and 3 t yr^{-1} of PCBs.

Atmospheric inputs, although large (see Table 5.3, p. 82) are dispersed throughout the whole of the North Sea. The effect of river inputs is most evident in the eastern North Sea and German Bight. Unlike inflows from British rivers which disperse rapidly, water from the continental rivers remains in a coastal strip as it flows northward up the Dutch, German, and Danish coasts. This is reflected in the higher metal concentrations in continental coastal waters than in British waters (Table 9.1). Mercury and lead tend to become associated with

Table 9.1. Typical dissolved concentrations (μg l^{-1}) of trace metals in North Sea areas

Metal	Netherlands coast	German Bight	UK coast	Central North Sea	Average ocean
Cadmium	0.10	0.05	0.03	0.02	0.01
Copper	0.60	0.60	0.30	0.20	0.10
Zinc	5.0	2.0	4.0	0.6	0.1
Nickel	1.0	0.8	0.7	0.3	0.2
Mercury	0.01	0.01	0.01	0.001	0.001
Lead	0.05	0.05	0.05	0.03	0.003

particulate matter rather than remain in solution and they are in low concentration but contaminate coastal bottom sediments. The central North Sea is relatively isolated from these inputs, though it has a higher metal concentration than open ocean water. The continental coastal waters also receive a large river input of plant nutrients and, since this is an area where a summer thermocline often develops, are subject to phytoplankton blooms and oxygen depletion of the bottom water (see Fig. 2.13, p. 30).

Oil inputs to the North Sea are estimated to be between 71 000 and 150 000 t yr^{-1}, the chief uncertainties being the size of atmospheric and river inputs. The North Sea has had its share of oil tanker accidents, resulting of releases of

1000–5000 t in the worse cases, though since the Straits of Dover are too shallow to allow the passage of a fully laden VLCC, it has escaped catastrophic spillages on the scale of the *Amoco Cadiz* (see p. 37). The worst spillage was in the 1977 Ekofisk blow-out (see p. 38) when 20 000–30 000 t of crude oil were discharged, although that had no detectable effect. Discharges of oil production water from offshore platforms and the disposal of drill cuttings contaminated with oil-based drill muds account for 29 000 t yr^{-1}, but their effect is very localized. It is impossible to estimate the amount of oil discharged by shipping in the course of discharging oily ballast water and bilge water, but these practices are responsible for the large number of small oil slicks that are reported in the North Sea.

Impact on fisheries

Since the resumption of fishing in the North Sea after the end of the Second World War, there was a steady increase in the annual catch of most species. In 1971 the total catch was almost 3 million t; but in 1984 it was 2.4 million t. The fishing is monitored and regulated, and catch quotas are agreed each year, depending on the strength of recruitment to the fish stocks, but these quotas are often exceeded. Over-fishing has depressed the catch of some species, but a more important development has been the introduction of 'industrial' fishing of small fish for conversion to fish meal. Since the 1960s, Norway pout and sand eels, which were not previously fished, have formed the basis of industrial fishing, and these catches partly accounted for the continuing increase in the total North Sea catch. Young herrings were also taken for fishmeal after the early 1950s and this over-exploitation led to a serious decline in the herring fishery in the 1960s and contributed to its collapse at the end of the 1970s.

Although the strength of recruitment varies from year to year, the practices of the fishing industry have a dominating influence on the size of exploitable fish stocks in the North Sea. Against this background, it is impossible to detect any effects pollution may have on the fishery.

There is some concern about the effects of sand and gravel extraction in the North Sea, since gravel beds are the spawning grounds of herring, and sand eels live in them permanently. Some 30–35 million t yr^{-1} of sand and gravel are dredged from European waters, much of it from the North Sea. Exhaustion of gravel beds on land and the projected needs of the construction industry suggest that the rate of exploitation of marine deposits will continue to increase. Besides destroying a vital habitat, this dredging may have indirect effects on fisheries. Ground containing as little as 30 per cent gravel can be mined and the fine material which is washed out increases the turbidity of the water and causes siltation which may blanket the bottom fauna as well as release toxic materials from the sediments. Recovery of the fauna in the dredged areas is slow; one study off the south coast of England showed only slight recovery with a few polychaete species a year after dredging.

Because of the possible threat to human health and the known input of metals to the North Sea, contamination of food fish has been closely monitored. In most places, mercury concentrations in the muscle of cod and plaice is below 0.1 µg g^{-1} (p.p.m.), zinc contamination averages 5.2 µg g^{-1}, copper 0.65 µg g^{-1}, and cadmium 0.02–0.7 µg g^{-1}. These are all very low values and there is no evidence of serious contamination. The highest values occur in fish caught off the coasts of northern France, Belgium, and Holland, and in the Thames estuary, reflecting industrial inputs. Herring contain less mercury (0.06 µg g^{-1}) than the demersal species, but slightly higher concentrations of copper and zinc. Because of their high fat content, herring contain greater amounts of organochlorine pesticides and PCBs than occur in cod or plaice, with the PCB content 2–5 times greater than pesticides; but the content varies widely in different samples and is nowhere very high. As might be expected, mussels acquire greater concentrations of these conservative materials than fish do, generally about three times greater. These, too, reflect local inputs, but commercial harvesting or culture of mussels and other bivalves takes place in uncontaminated areas.

Impact on sea birds

In addition to a large resident bird population, the North Sea and its coasts provide wintering grounds for very large numbers of shore and sea birds. The dense flocks of birds are vulnerable to oil pollution and there are numerous casualties each winter. The worst case was in 1955 when a tanker, *Gerd Maersk*, grounded near the mouth of the river Elbe and spilled 9000 t of crude oil. Estimates of the numbers of birds killed ranged from 50 000 to 500 000. In February 1969, a few hundred tonnes of fuel oil drifted among the Dutch islands and through the Waddensee, killing 35 000–41 000 birds, including a large part of the breeding population of eider. Small quantities of oil may also cause heavy casualties—12 000 on the east coast of Scotland in 1971 and 30 000 in the Skagerrak in 1981—but regular counts of dead oiled birds on North Sea coasts indicate that casual, small-scale oil pollution is a continuing hazard to birds in the North Sea. The greatest number of casualties is in winter and the prevailing westerly winds drift both floating oil and birds towards the continental coast where 70–80 per cent of dead birds on the beaches have been oiled (Fig. 3.10). Despite these great and continuing losses, earlier fears that they were causing a reduction in the breeding populations of a number of sea-ducks (scoter, long-tailed ducks, etc.) and auks, now appear to be unfounded. Sea bird colonies around the northern North Sea, in fact, appear to be stable or have increased in size.

More insidious threats to the wintering bird flocks are the reclamation of coastal wetlands and shallows, destroying irreplaceable feeding grounds, and the depletion of fish stocks upon which the birds depend for food. It is not possible to say if these activities have had any impact on bird populations so far, but the destruction of their food resources cannot be expected to continue without some adverse consequences.

International action

Atmospheric and river-borne inputs account for a considerable fraction of the wastes entering the North Sea, and these are derived from much of central and western Europe, not simply the population of the coastal zone. The river Elbe carries wastes from Czechoslovakia and East Germany, as well as West Germany into the North Sea; the Rhine receives inputs from Switzerland, France, Germany, Luxemburg, and Holland; the Scheldt arises in Belgium, but flows into the North Sea through Holland. While it is within the power of individual states to improve the quality of some of their waters, in many cases, particularly in areas influenced by the outflow from continental rivers, only international action can achieve any improvement.

In 1974, under an international convention, the Oslo Commission was established to control discharges and dumping from ships into the North Sea. The comparable Paris Commission was set up a little later to regulate direct discharges from land. In addition, since most of the North Sea states are members of the EEC, the European Commission has some power to regulate waste inputs and has acted, e.g. by stipulating maximum permissible contamination of shellfish for human consumption and bacterial contamination of bathing beaches.

The International Council for the Exploration of the Sea (ICES) includes representatives of all the countries fishing in the North Sea and since the early years of this century has been responsible for evaluating fish stocks and recommending annual fishing limits. For the last 20 years, it has also had an important role in arranging monitoring programmes and collecting together scientific information about pollution levels and impacts.

In recent years there has been increasing disagreement about the impact of wastes discharged into the North Sea; to agree future action, the Environmental Ministers of the North Sea states met in 1984 and 1987, and intend to meet regularly in the future. As a result of these meetings, there is now agreement about the extent and source of the more important wastes reaching the sea, and for phased reductions of inputs, particularly those affecting the most vulnerable areas in the eastern North Sea.

The Mediterranean Sea

The Mediterranean is a deep, virtually tideless sea with a surface area of 2 965 000 km^3. Much of it is more than 200 m deep, with a number of deep basins below 3000 m. The eastern and western Mediterranean, separated by the relatively shallow straits between Sicily and Tunisia, show differences in resident fauna and flora, indicating a degree of isolation between the two regions. The Aegean, and particularly the Adriatic, are semi-enclosed extensions from the main body of the Mediterranean.

Evaporation is about three times greater than the input from precipitation and the deficit is made good largely by an inflow of Atlantic water at Gibraltar. There is negligible input to the eastern Mediterranean and, as a result, the salinity in the west is near oceanic levels, approaching 37 per mille, but near the cost of Asia Minor it is 39 per mille. This dense saline water sinks to a depth of 100–200 m, flows westward and leaves the Mediterranean as a deep current at Gibraltar. Through most of the year there is good vertical mixing of the top 200 m and sometimes 600 m of water.

The main centres of coastal population are on the northern side of the western Mediterranean and around the head of the Adriatic (Fig. 9.3). These are also the most industrialized areas and receive the majority of the 100 million tourists that inflate the summer population of Mediterranean countries. The North African coast, by contrast, is for the most part arid with little urbanization or industrialization. Pressures on the marine environment therefore vary widely depending on the local and human environment.

Fisheries

The Mediterranean is only moderately productive and the demand for fish in the Mediterranean countries substantially exceeds the local supply. The deficit is only partly filled by imports from the Atlantic and other fisheries, and the cash value of the Mediterranean fisheries is therefore high, with prices five to seven times above average world prices. Bottom-living (demersal) species such as mullets, hakes, etc. are most in demand. The main stocks of these are along the northern coast and these are fully exploited. A number of pelagic fish (anchovy, sardines, mackerel, etc.) in the north-western Mediterranean are also intensively fished. Mariculture is practised in some places, but is not widespread.

Oil pollution

All parts of the Mediterranean are chronically polluted with tar balls; a high value of 500 l km^{-2} has been recorded south of Italy, and many tourist beaches are irritatingly contaminated with specks of tarry oil. The main sources of oil pollution are deballasting and tank-washing operations of oil tankers and the discharge of oily bilge water by other shipping. Refinery wastes are a secondary, but important, source of chronic oil pollution. Offshore oil extraction and tanker accidents have been of minor significance. Some 250 million t yr^{-1} of oil are transported through the Mediterranean, about 150 million t yr^{-1} from North

Fig. 9.3. Sewage and industrial waste discharges to the Mediterranean Sea.

Africa to European ports (Fig. 9.4). The cross-Mediterranean journey time is too short to allow efficient operation of the load-on-top system (see p. 33), and there have been inadequate slop-reception facilities in ports. A ban on the discharge of oily wastes in 1976 and stricter enforcement has proved effective and the quantity of floating tar in the eastern Mediterranean has declined from 37 000 μg m^{-2} in 1969 to 1175 μg m^{-2} in 1987.

As a result of oil pollution, tainting of a variety of fish and bivalves, rendering them unmarketable, has been reported from the neighbourhood of oil ports in Spain, France, Italy, and Yugoslavia. Spiny lobsters have been killed by oil pollution around Bizerte in Tunisia. The Bay of Izmir and the Sea of Marmora on the Turkish coast have suffered adverse effects from oil and the spawning grounds of bonito and mackerel have been damaged. The most serious effects of oil pollution have been noted in the Gulf of Naples, Cagliari, and the Venetian lagoons where fish populations have been reduced. The Bay of Muggia at Trieste, once rich in fish and molluscs, now described as being biologically almost a desert because of the impact of petrochemical wastes.

Domestic wastes

A survey made in 1972 found the most coastal communities discharged untreated sewage to the sea and the rest usually gave only minimal treatment. The worst affected areas were the riviera coast from the river Elbo in Spain, across the French riviera to the river Arno in Italy (Fig. 9.3). It was estimated that the discharge amounted to 336 t km^{-1} yr^{-1}. The Israeli coast was found to be similarly affected. A vigorous attack on this problem was mounted, especially in France and Israel and on parts of the Spanish and Italian coast, but it is doubtful if the situation has much improved elsewhere. One difficulty is the need to provide sufficient sewage treatment facilities to cope with the enormous influx of population for a few summer months.

Apart from damage to the tourist industry for aesthetic reasons, discharges of untreated sewage are a threat to public health. In 1973, there was an epidemic of cholera, centred around Naples and spread by the consumption of infected shellfish, and lesser gastric disorders have been a common hazard to visitors to Mediterranean coasts for many years.

Other pollutants

It is estimated that 85 per cent of anthropogenic inputs to the Mediterranean is from the land, and inputs from rivers dominate. The organic load (BOD) from rivers equals that from coastal towns and most of the phosphorus and nitrogen inputs are from rivers. The input of 90 t yr^{-1} of organochlorine pesticides is almost entirely derived from the drainage areas of rivers. The most considerable input of heavy metals and PCBs is from the rivers Rhone and Po, added to those

Fig. 9.4. Activities of the oil industry in the Mediterranean.

Legend:

● Loading port for crude oil
■ Unloading port for crude oil
▲ Refinery
A Areas where oil discharge is permitted
░ Existing or offshore production
S Natural seepage

Scale:
0 200 400 600 km
0 200 400 miles

Map labels:
Algeciras, Malaga, Cartagena, Sagunto, Tarragona, Marseilles, Milan, Genoa, Porto Torres, Ancona, Zagreb, Rome, Naples, Taranto, Augusta, Palermo, Bizerta, Bedjaia, Algiers, Arzew, Oran, La Skhirra, El Sider, Alzwaitina, Marsa El Brega, Tobruk, Thessaloniki, Athens, Izmir, Izmit, Mersin, Larnaca, Homs, Tripoli, Hafa, Tel Aviv, Suez, Alexandria

from the heavily industrialized zones near their mouths, at Marseille and Toulon and at the head of the Adriatic, respectively.

The Gulf of Fos influenced by the Rhone and its industrial belt, and the upper Adriatic, together with the Saronikos Gulf receiving the effluents of Athens and Piraeus, have been studied in some detail and all show some impact of the effluent load they receive. There is most concern about the conditions of the Venetian lagoons and upper Adriatic which, because of the low rate of water exchange and their relative isolation from the rest of the Mediterranean, are least able to accept a heavy load of effluents without damaging consequences.

Phosphorus is the limiting nutrient for phytoplankton in the upper Adriatic and inputs of phosphorus to the area have increased markedly. The upper Adriatic now receives abut $30\,000\,t\,yr^{-1}$ of phosphorus, of which 60% is contributed by the river Po. Half the phosphorus is derived from detergents and agricultural fertilizers which came into intensive use after 1945. The progressive eutrophication resulting from this is shown by the increased oxygen concentration in surface waters and oxygen depletion of bottom waters, which first became apparent in 1955 around the mouth of the river Po but now includes much of the western and northern parts of the upper Adriatic (Fig. 2.14, p. 31).

Despite the existence of small areas where conservative materials accumulate in undesirably high concentrations, neither the water nor the organisms in the Mediterranean appear to be seriously contaminated and concentrations are generally comparable to those in the open Atlantic. In the early 1970s, a few fishing communities on the Italian Adriatic and French coasts were found to be exposed to high levels of mercury due to local inputs contaminating seafood organisms in the area. These inputs were subsequently brought under control. Mercury levels in two species of tuna have also been found to be high, at 2–3 p.p.m., or three times greater than those in Atlantic tuna. This appears to be due to natural causes, perhaps from the greater level of seismic activity in the Mediterranean. Mussels from the coast near Marseille contain high concentrations of copper (95 p.p.m.), and high concentrations of zinc (200 p.p.m.) occur in coastal waters in a number of areas, but neither constitute a health risk.

There is evidence that PCBs in the Mediterranean are subject to 'demagnification'. Microplankton strongly accumulate PCBs in areas with a large local input, but contamination of animals at higher trophic levels is progressively reduced. The faecal pellets contain ten times the concentration of PCBs found in the animals that produce them and they sink to the seabed in the deeper parts of the Mediterranean where they are removed from pelagic food chains. The same phenomenon has been reported for radionuclides.

International action

Many of the problems in the Mediterranean are local in character and are susceptible to local solutions. While the financially important fisheries have not been generally affected by pollution and fish catches continue to grow, the Mediterranean receives a very heavy effluent load which, because of the restricted water exchange, poses a continuing threat. The United Nations Environment Programme (UNEP) has provided a focal point for international co-operation in cleaning up the Mediterranean and this culminated in the 1976 Barcelona Convention to do this.

Subsequent progress has been slow for a variety of reasons. There are no less than 18 Mediterranean states (21 if Black Sea states are included) and it is difficult to achieve concerted action by so many countries. The problem is compounded by severe political obstacles in some cases, and by the great diversity in the degree of development of different coastal states with corresponding differences in the priority accorded to environmental protection.

The Baltic Sea

The Baltic is the largest body of brackish water in the world, with an area of 370 000 km². It consists of several basins of various depths, the greatest being 459 m, separated from each other by relatively shallow sills (Fig. 9.5). Communication with the North Sea is through the narrow Oresund between Denmark and Sweden, which is only 7–8 m deep, and the Belt Sea between the Danish Islands of Fyn and Zealand, where the depth is 17–18 m.

The annual input of freshwater from the land varies between 440 and 470 km³, depending on climatic factors, and the inflow of salt water from the North Sea is about the same. These inputs are balanced by an equivalent outflow into the Kattegat. Surface salinity is below 5 per mille in the inner parts of the Gulfs of Bothnia, Finland, and Riga, 5–7 per mille in the main part of the Baltic, and 7–9 per mille around the south of Sweden. This brackish water floats on denser more saline deeper water and, while wind and thermal convection currents produce some vertical mixing in autumn and winter, there is a permanent halocline at a depth of about 40 m in the south-western basins, and at 60 m in the central basins, separating the surface layer from the deeper water (Fig. 9.6).

Brackish Baltic water flows out to the North Sea, generally over an inflowing deeper current of North Sea water, but depending on wind direction and speed, the flow over the sills in the Oresund and Belt Sea may be entirely of Baltic water flowing seaward, or of North Sea water flowing inward. The latter is important because it is only during strong inflows of North Sea water that water in the deepest parts of the basins is replaced. At such times a second halocline develops at a depth of 110–130 m. Once the deep basins have been recharged with salt water, the density of the new bottom water must be substantially reduced by mixing before a new influx can replace it. This may take five years and during this period the bottom water is essentially stagnant.

During these periods of stagnation, the deep basins become depleted of oxygen

Fig. 9.5. Deep basins of the Baltic Sea, contours at 50 m, 100 m, and 200 m. A, Gulf of Bothnia; B, Gulf of Finland; C, Baltic proper; D, Gulf of Riga; E, Belt Sea; F, Oresund; G, Kattegat.

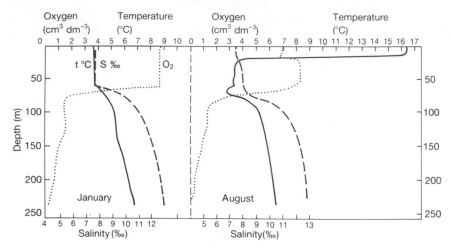

Fig. 9.6. Distribution of temperature (*t*) (*solid line*), salinity (*S*) (*dashed line*), and oxygen (*dotted line*) with depth in the Gotland Deep in January and August 1978. (*Pergamon Press.*)

through the bacterial degradation of organic material present in the sediment and drifting down from the surface layer. Extensive areas with anoxic conditions and the production of hydrogen sulphide therefore occur at irregular intervals (Fig. 9.7), and at such times the benthic fauna disappears until a new influx of water allows recolonization.

Organic wastes

In the 1960s when severe and increasing deoxygenation of bottom waters was detected, there were fears that the Baltic had become catastrophically polluted and was dying.

The Baltic is naturally oligotrophic (i.e. with a small natural organic input and low production) but receives a large quantity of organic wastes and shows some signs of eutrophication. A population of 17.5 million people living around the Baltic is responsible for the direct input of 2.3×10^6 m^3 day^{-1} of domestic sewage, of which 40 per cent is untreated. A further 1.2×10^6 m^3 day^{-1}, 20 per cent of it untreated, reaches the Baltic via rivers. Domestic sewage is the most significant organic input in the Gulf of Finland and the south-west Baltic where there is the greatest density of population. In the Gulf of Bothnia the chief input of organic matter is from the paper and wood pulp industries. The principal inputs of nitrogen and phosphorus, in both inorganic and organic forms, are largely from agriculture in run-off to rivers, but on the south coast of the Gulf of Finland also from several fertilizer factories. The installation of industrial and urban treatment plants in the 1970s reduced the input of phosphorus by 50 per cent, but despite the reduction of inputs from these sources, nitrogen from agricultural

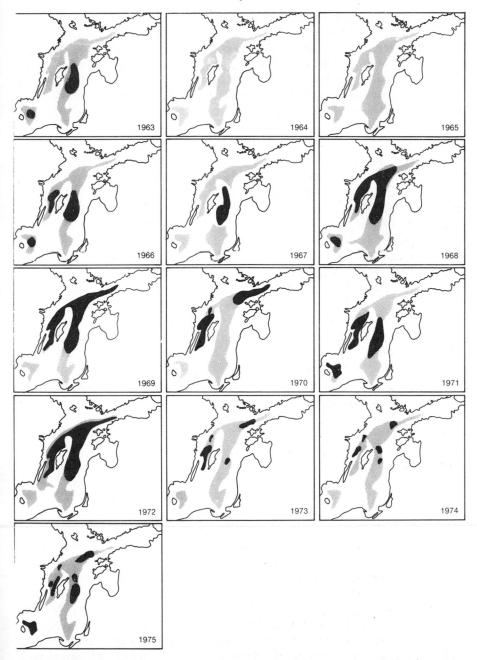

Fig. 9.7. Areas with bottom water containing less than 2 mg l^{-1} dissolved oxygen and (in black) anoxic areas with hydrogen sulphide, in the Baltic, 1963–75.

run-off increased and between 1969 and 1977 the net input of nitrogen to the Baltic increased by 10 per cent.

The effects of the increased input of organic matter and plant nutrients have been studied in coastal waters. In inshore waters, the primary production of phytoplankton has greatly increased, reducing the transparency of the water. On the shore, green algae and emergent plants in shallow water show enhanced growth. There is some evidence of an increase in zooplankton biomass throughout the Baltic, as a result of the phytoplankton increase, but in coastal waters this has been accompanied by a change in species composition of the zooplankton. The relative importance of predatory fish has decreased and although the total fish biomass has increased, catches in coastal waters, though high, are of less desirable species and so of reduced value. Less is known of the effect of the enrichment of offshore waters, though heavy phytoplankton blooms, particularly of blue-green algae, have increased and there are fears that the increased input of detritus to deep water that results from the blooms may accelerate the development of anoxic conditions.

To a degree, enrichment of the waters is beneficial to fisheries and the incursion of North Sea water allows the greater penetration of herring, sprat, and cod into the Baltic, although they do not live in the gulfs where salinity is below 5–6 per mille. These marine species make the most significant contribution to fish biomass in the Baltic and account for 90 per cent of the landings. The fishery for migratory eel and salmon is financially important, although the total weights landed are small. Freshwater commercial species, perch, pike, roach, and white fish (*Coregonus*) are caught in the waters of lowest salinity, but are of secondary importance. The overall yield of fish from the Baltic is fairly low, 2.2 g m^{-2}, compared with 5.2 g m^{-2} in the North Sea, and Baltic fish grow more slowly; but there is no evidence that the offshore fisheries have suffered from eutrophication of the waters. There is some sign, however, that sprat and herring stocks are over-exploited and may decline for that reason.

Conservative pollutants

In the 1960s, along with fears about the effects of eutrophication, there was great concern at high concentrations of mercury in fish from the inland and coastal waters of Denmark, Finland, and Sweden, and in Sweden, commercial fishing was banned in areas where the fish contained more than 1 µg g^{-1} of mercury. Fish in the open sea were not affected. The mercury was derived mainly from pesticides, and particularly from fungicides and slimicides used in the paper and wood pulp industry in Finland and Sweden.

Following these incidents, the use of mercurial pesticides was much reduced and the occurrence of heavy-metal contamination in sediments and a number of marine organisms has been closely monitored in most parts of the Baltic.

Much of the metal input (Table 9.2) is carried to the seabed by sedimentation

Table 9.2. Total metal inputs to the Baltic Sea (t yr^{-1})

Mercury	Cadmium	Lead	Nickel	Copper	Zinc
30*	250*	4300–6200*	2100–5100†	4500–8500*	15500–18900†

* 50–80 per cent atmospheric
† 50–80 per cent from rivers

and recent benthic sediments contain 200 per cent more mercury and 100 per cent more cadmium than the natural background. Lead, zinc, and copper levels are also significantly higher. The most contaminated sediments are in the Kattegat, Oresund and Arkona basin, in the Gdansk Bight, and the Gulf of Bothnia. Metal contamination of fish (Table 9.3) has now fallen to a more

Table 9.3. Heavy metals in marine organisms from the Baltic

	Mercury (p.p.b.)	Cadmium (p.p.b.)	Copper (p.p.m.)	Zinc (p.p.m.)
Cod	20–880	2–50	0.08–2.4	1.2–9.2
Herring	4–90	2–200	0.30–1.9	3.4–32
Flounder	10–450	2–100	0.10–0.89	3.5–11.3
Mussel	4–300	130–560	1.0–16	16–110

acceptable level and is not significantly higher than in fish from the north Atlantic. The highest concentrations, as might be expected, are found in the neighbourhood of the Oresund, Gdansk Bight, Gulf of Finland, and Gulf of Bothnia. For cadmium, in particular, contamination is higher in inshore animals than offshore.

Halogenated hydrocarbons on the other hand, continue to cause damage. The use of DDT has generally ceased and residue levels in fish and guillemot eggs continued to fall during the period 1974–82. Despite restrictions on their use, there are still land-based inputs of PCBs, particularly near Turku, in Finland, and Stockholm, and contamination of fish and guillemot eggs by these compounds has not shown a reduction since 1974. Apart from a few hot-spots, there appears to be no geographical gradient in the contamination of fish by DDT or PCBs and the level of contamination is not unduly high. The principal dangers of halogenated hydrocarbons are to fish-eating birds and mammals, and in the 1970s concentrations in seals and birds of prey were ten times higher in the Baltic than in areas west of Sweden. The sea eagle, *Haliaetus albicilla*, was threatened and the reduction of the breeding populations of ringed seal, *Pusa hispida*, and grey seal, *Halichoerus grypus*, in the Baltic, both of which are heavily contaminated with PCBs, still gives cause for concern (see p. 125).

International action

The Helsinki Convention, which came into force in 1980, is concerned with the protection of the Baltic Sea. All eight states with Baltic coastlines are active members of the Commission which puts the Convention into effect. Like the Oslo and Paris Commissions for the North Sea, the Helsinki Commission regulates discharges and dumping from ships and direct discharges from land. It also has wider responsibilities and has been concerned with such matters as atmospheric inputs, emergency action against oil spills, the use of antifouling paints containing tributyl tin, co-ordinating monitoring programmes, and seal conservation. It frequently arranges meetings of experts to evaluate the scientific evidence on which its recommendations are based. The Helsinki Commission has proved to be very effective, and through its efforts the Baltic is, with the North Sea, one of the most thoroughly studied seas in the world.

The Caribbean

The Greater Caribbean area includes the Caribbean Sea and the Gulf of Mexico. The total surface area is 4.24×10^6 km^2 and it consists of a number of deep basins separated by major sills. It lacks a shallow continental shelf, except in the Yucatan Gulf, off the US Gulf coast and part of the South American shelf; 80 per cent of the water is deeper than 1800 m and half is deeper than 3600 m, with the greatest depth of 7100 m in the Cayman Trench.

The Caribbean Sea and southern half of the Gulf of Mexico are tropical and experience little seasonal change. The surface water temperature is 27 °C with a seasonal fluctuation of less than 3 °C. The northern part of the Gulf of Mexico, however, has a winter surface sea temperature of 16 °C, rising in summer to 28 °C. Over much of the whole area there is a permanent thermocline at a depth of about 100 m and upwelling is not a dominant feature, although there are some local areas where bottom-water comes to the surface.

Because of the existence of the thermocline and lack of upwelling, much of the area is deficient in nutrients, and significant fisheries, particularly for penaeid prawns, are confined to the shallows off the Mexican and US coasts. These are associated with the highly productive coastal ecosystems of mangroves, seagrass, and coral reefs. The US commercial fishery in the Gulf of Mexico is worth $400 million per year and the income from recreational fishing is at least as great.

Seagrass beds (Fig. 9.8), principally of turtle grass, *Thalassia testudinum*, can contribute 3000 g dry weight m^{-2} yr^{-1} of primary production, of which two-thirds is due to seagrass growth and one-third to the associated algae. This is

Fig. 9.8. Distribution of seagrass beds in the Caribbean.

Seagrass beds

0   200   400   600 km

0   200   400 Miles

the same as, or even greater than, the production of mangrove swamps. On coasts fringed by mangroves, with seagrass beds beyond them and coral reefs to the seaward side, very high levels of productivity are reached, with fish leaving the shelter of the reef to feed in the seagrass beds, and both seagrass and mangroves, besides harbouring a large and varied fauna, providing important nursery grounds for prawns and fish.

Another feature of mangroves and seagrass beds is that their root systems stabilize the seabed and prevent coastal erosion. They also clarify the water by trapping sediments.

In the Caribbean region as a whole, there is relatively little coastal urbanization or industrialization, and there is no widespread pollution except from oil. In a number of areas, however, there has been severe local impact from a variety of pollutants (Table 9.4).

Table 9.4. Incidence of severe local pollution damage in the Greater Caribbean

Location	Pollutant
Cartagena, Colombia	Mercury
Colon, Panama	Oil
Veracruz, Mexico	Thermal effluent
Galveston, Texas	Oil
New Orleans, Louisiana	Industrial waste
Tampa Bay, Florida	Sewage
Kingston, Jamaica	Bauxite waste
Port-au-Prince, Haiti	Sewage
Santo Domingo, Dominican Republic	Urban run-off
San Juan, Puerto Rico	Sewage
Port of Spain, Trinidad and Tobago	Oil
Cumana, Venezuela	Sewage
Havana Bay, Cuba	All the above

Oil pollution

The principal oil-producing areas are Trinidad and Tobago, Venezuela, and the Gulf of Mexico. Nearly one-third of the production is from offshore oilfields and there are more than 2000 fixed offshore platforms in the US sector of the Gulf alone. Blow-outs, overflows, pipelines fractures, and other accidents at the platforms are the major source of oil pollution in the area.

Studies of the benthic fauna in oilfields off the Louisiana coast have failed to reveal any significant differences from other areas, and the platforms themselves, providing the only hard structures in a generally sedimentary region, attract an exotic attached fauna and flora, as well as sheltering a variety of sport fish. Despite the spillages and some contamination of sediments, offshore activities appear not to have a serious environmental impact.

The largest oil spill in history was that following the blow-out in the Ixtoc I field in the Bay of Campeche off the Mexican coast, between June 1979 and March 1980 when the well was finally capped. Altogether 350 000 t of crude oil were released into the sea. Prevailing offshore winds prevented fresh oil coming ashore on the Mexican coast, but 80 km of the Texas coastline, some 800 km away, was seriously affected and clean-up costs there exceeded $4 million. Entrances to the biologically sensitive Laguna Madre were boomed off to protect the breeding grounds of the endangered brown pelican, *Pelicanus occidentalis*, and 10 000 baby Kemp's Ridley turtle, *Lepidochelys kempii*, another endangered species, were air-lifted from the only breeding ground of this species on beaches on the north coast of Mexico to another area of the Gulf of Mexico free from oil. The total cost of capping the well and containing the environmental damage, including lost oil revenues, amounted to $219 million, but despite the enormous quantity of oil spilled, the environmental consequences were remarkably small. The $230 million per year Mexican and US shrimp fishery in the Gulf escaped long-term damage.

Heated effluents

The sea temperature is close to the upper thermal limit of many organisms and they are therefore vulnerable to thermal pollution. This is not a widespread hazard because of the low level of industrialization of coasts in the Caribbean, but cooling water discharges from two power stations in Puerto Rico have caused extensive damage to seagrass beds in Guayanilla Bay. Plants are killed and production is reduced in areas where the sea temperature is 5 °C above the ambient temperature of 30 °C. The benthic fauna in shallow waters is completely eliminated at this or higher temperatures.

Sedimentation

Turbid waters reduce the productivity of the seagrass beds and heavy sedimentation is lethal to corals. The Mississippi and a number of lesser rivers flow into the Gulf and Caribbean and most of the water from the Orinoco travels north and enters the southern Caribbean. These rivers carry a heavy sediment load, particularly from areas where bad farming practices result in soil erosion. The damaging effects of these inputs is limited to the areas, sometimes large, around the mouths of the rivers.

More widespread damage is caused by coastal developments involving dredge and fill, or the dredging of shipping channels. Dredging operations cause increased turbidity of the water and marine dumping of the spoil extends the damage over a wider area.

The common practice of extracting beach sand for construction purposes, as well as coastal developments, largely for the tourist trade, leads to destruction of mangrove forests and seagrass beds and had caused severe coastal erosion in a number of places. This, in turn, leads to increased turbidity of the water and increased sedimentation elsewhere.

Tourism

The Greater Caribbean receives about 100 million tourists annually and tourism represents a major industry, particularly in the eastern islands (Fig. 9.9). The attractions are sun, white sandy beaches, and warm clear waters. Hotel development is almost entirely on the coasts and often in isolated places. There is a general lack of awareness about the environmental impact of such developments, and while some hotels install their own sewage treatment plants, many do not or have inadequate treatment facilities. If, as is commonly the case, the coastal developments have resulted in the loss of seagrass beds and mangroves, leading to increased turbidity of the water, this combined with sewage pollution is detrimental to the interest of the tourist industry, even though the effects are quite local.

International action

Under the Regional Seas Programme of the United Nations Environment Programme (UNEP), an Action Plan for the greater Caribbean was adopted by 22 states of the region in 1981. UNEP provides the co-ordinating secretariat for the plan. Since then, a survey has been made of the special needs and problems of the Caribbean, and in 1983 a Convention was adopted by the major coastal states, which requires the signatories to prevent, reduce, and control pollution, safeguard sensitive environments, and collaborate in scientific research and monitoring. Particular emphasis is placed on oil pollution.

The Caspian Sea

The Caspian is by far the world's largest land-locked body of water, with a total area of 436 000 km^2. The northern part is very shallow, only 10–12 m deep, but the central Caspian has depths to 700 m and the southern part, separated from it by shoals in the region of the Apserhon peninsula, has depths to 1000 m.

The surface sea temperature is 24–27 °C in summer, but in winter falls to 9 °C in the south and to 0 °C in the north where extensive sea ice is formed. Rivers flowing into the Caspian add 350 km^3 yr^{-1} of freshwater, three-quarters of it

Fig. 9.9. Estimated population and tourist arrivals in Caribbean countries, 1977.

from the Volga, but an amount equivalent to this, plus the 100 km^3 of precipitation directly on to the sea, is lost in summer by evaporation. There is little variation of salinity with depth, but it differs widely in different parts of the Caspian. In the northern shallows it is 5–10 per mille, falling to 2 per mille near the Volga delta; and in the central and southern parts it is 12–13 per mille. The eastern side of the sea receives little precipitation and has negligible river input, and the rate of evaporation is high. Bays and semi-enclosed areas of the sea here have very high salinities, reaching 200 per mille in the Kara-Bugaz Gulf which is almost completely separated from the Caspian proper. The composition of the salt differs from that of open ocean water, with much more sulphate and more magnesium and calcium, but less sodium and chloride.

There is little vertical circulation of water and this leads to serious depletion of oxygen below 200–300 m, and zero concentrations near the bottom, resulting in the production of hydrogen sulphide in the deeper sediments. The benthic fauna of the central and southern parts of the Caspian is therefore impoverished and, in parts, totally missing (Fig. 9.10). That of the northern Caspian is dominated by molluscs and previously was conspicuously lacking in polychaetes. The former have a lower nutritive value than the worms to fish and growth rates of commercial fish species such as bream and sturgeon were lower than in the productive Sea of Azov which has a typical benthic fauna with abundant worms and crustaceans. In 1939–41, 65 000 *Nereis diversicolor* were introduced in an attempt to restructure the benthic ecosystem. By 1948 this worm had become established over 30 000 km^2, especially in the north-western area of the sea where densities of 1800 m^{-2}, representing a biomass of 86 g m^{-2}, occurred. Molluscs still dominate the benthos, but with the availability of polychaetes, sturgeon now feed almost exclusively upon them instead of, as formerly and still in other parts of the Caspian, on chironomid larvae, crustaceans, fish, and molluscs. *Nereis* now forms 50 per cent of the diet of the bream.

The Caspian is subject to wide fluctuations in sea-level and salinity depending upon river inputs of freshwater. Prolonged drought in the Volga basin during the 1930s caused a fall in level of 2 m and a corresponding increase in salinity, leading to a crash in the average biomass of the benthic fauna in the northern Caspian from 36.84 g m^{-2} in 1935 to 4.74 g m^{-2} in 1938. There was a subsequent recovery in the early 1940s, but dams constructed on the Volga, Terek, and Kura rivers for hydroelectric and irrigation schemes have again reduced the flow of the rivers into the Caspian Sea.

Pollution

Throughout the 1960s there was great concern about the effects of lowered sea-level and increasing salinity, coupled with severe pollution on the important Caspian fisheries.

A principal source of pollution in the northern Caspian has been the Volga

Fig. 9.10. Distribution of benthic biomass in the Caspian Sea.

itself with 15 towns on the river and its tributary, the Kama, discharging untreated sewage and a large number of industrial plants also discharging their wastes.

The Azerbaijan coast is the site of a major oil industry, with numerous offshore oil wells, refineries, and petrochemical plants on the coast, and a large urban population around Baku. Together they have been responsible for very damaging pollution of the productive western parts of the central and southern Caspian Sea. In the mid-1960s it was estimated that 1 million tonnes of oil and petroleum products were released into the sea from accidental spillages, seepages, pipeline fractures, industrial effluents, and in refinery waste water. Added to this the Caspian Steamship Line, the Caspian tanker fleet, and fishing vessels discharged tank washings, oily bilge water, and fuel oil to the sea. Sewage from Baku received only mechanical treatment before discharge, but 36 sewer outfalls discharged untreated sewage, and 23 000 m^{-3} day^{-1} of untreated industrial effluent were discharged into the nearby Bakinskaya inlet.

These discharges caused severe contamination of the water and seabed with petroleum hydrocarbons: 27 mg l^{-1} around Sumgait, 46 mg l^{-1} in the Neftyanye Kamni region, and 148 mg l^{-1} in the Bakinskaya inlet. Phytoplankton diversity in the western Caspian fell from 74 to 40 species and biomass from 8.7 to 2.1 g m^{-2}. The biomass of benthic organisms in coastal areas fell from 1724 g m^{-2} in 1961 to 21 g m^{-2} in 1969, and the principal decline was observed in breeding and nursery grounds for sturgeon, bream, pike, crucian carp, and other commercial fish species.

For a variety of reasons—fall in sealevel, increased salinity, and pollution (and over-fishing cannot be excluded)—fish catches dropped dramatically. In the mid-1930s the total catch from the Caspian was 300 million kg (herring were not then taken); by 1970 the total catch was 110 million kg, of which 100 million kg were herrings. Catches of sturgeon in the Azerbaijan region fell from 2100 kg yr^{-1} in 1931–35 to 350 kg yr^{-1} in 1961–64.

In 1972, a series of measures was announced to provide sewage treatment for towns on the Volga, to treat industrial wastes, and to reduce oil pollution in the Azerbaijan region of the Caspian. These measures have not proved effective, however, and waste discharges and contamination levels in the southern Caspian remain high. Fish catches have continued to decline and by the mid-1980s salmon and shad were reported to have almost completely disappeared, catches of bream and carp to have fallen by a further 80 per cent; low value herring now comprise four-fifths of the total catch. Experience since the 1950s has shown the difficulty of carrying on a valuable fishery together with rapid industrialization, massive irrigation schemes, and exploitation of offshore oilfields in a sea subject to the natural pressures of high evaporation and a variable river input of freshwater.

10

Assessing pollution damage

The need for quantitative assessment

At first sight, since pollution is by definition damaging, the obvious remedy is to stop discharging the polluting substances. Pollution problems are rarely so easily solved. Usually for reasons of practicality or cost, or because the remedy would be worse than the disease, we cannot abolish pollution but have to manage waste disposal in such a way as to reduce pollution to a tolerable level and mitigate its worst effects. This demands careful assessment of the impact of a particular discharge. Both quantifying and assessing an impact introduce technical problems and call for clear thinking about what is meant by pollution.

Practicality

The distressing loss of sea birds by oil pollution is almost entirely due to human or equipment failure leading to accidental spillages or to deliberate, but usually illegal, discharges of waste oil or oily water at sea. It is not difficult to devise safeguards to reduce oil pollution, but the only way to prevent all losses of sea birds from this source is to stop transporting or using oil at sea. This would eliminate the use of oil and oil products in many countries and effectively ground all aircraft. Most people would regard that as too high a price to pay. Some sea bird mortality must be accepted as a consequence of using oil.

This may appear an extreme example of the impracticability of abolishing a form of pollution, but a similar argument can be used for many other pollutants.

Cost

The principle on which pollution abatement costs are allocated in Britain and many other countries is that the polluter pays. It seems only just that those responsible for polluting the environment should bear the cost for not doing so. However, the polluter often turns out to be the community at large. Urban sewage represents by far the greatest volume of organic waste entering the sea and is responsible for the anoxic state of industrialized estuaries; one-third of the mercury entering the sea as a result of human activities comes from burning coal; and half the lead from the use of leaded petrol. The cost of reducing pollution falls on the community at large, directly through taxes or indirectly through other costs.

We have already seen that the cost of pollution abatement can rise steeply if high environmental standards are demanded (see Fig. 1.1). For most industrial processes, it is very costly to fit pollution-control equipment or to modify manufacturing processes in existing factories to meet new and more stringent environmental standards. The manufacturer has no alternative but to pass the costs on to the consumer in the form of higher prices for his product. The cost of pollution abatement can often be absorbed in the design of a new factory or a new process, but to wait for new technology to be introduced or a new factory to be built may delay the improvement of environmental conditions for a decade. In extreme cases, the cost of pollution abatement may make an industrial process or even a whole factory uneconomic. The result can then achieve the objective of reducing pollution but at a social cost, for example the closure of the factory.

Best practicable environmental option

Different users of the sea may well have different and conflicting needs:

- fisheries require relatively uncontaminated water, but also freedom from interference by yachtsmen and water-skiers;
- yachtsmen have no particular need for unpolluted water so long as conditions are not offensive or a hazard to sailing, but they require marinas and harbours which occupy coastal land as well as being a source of local chronic pollution;
- nature conservation in the sea demands uncontaminated water, but also freedom from the depredations of fisherman and skin-divers, and from the pressure of tourists;
- industry needs cooling water and, if possible, water in which to discharge and dilute waste products.

Satisfying the needs of one interest may therefore only create problems for another and it is almost certain that it will be impossible to satisfy all needs in the same place. As on land, it may be necessary to dedicate different areas of sea to different functions, or some compromise may be necessary to satisfy several requirements in the same place with least environmental damage.

Industrial societies inevitably produce a great variety of wastes in large quantities. By fostering industrial processes that produce little or no waste (**low waste and no waste technology**) and by withdrawing damaging substances (e.g. some pesticides) from use, it is possible to reduce pollution. Even so, large quantities of waste will always be produced (e.g. sewage) and have to be disposed of somewhere; if not in the sea, then in another environment. Waste disposal always has some impact on the environment, and in dealing with pollution problems in one environment—the sea—it is only too easy to suggest remedies that simply transfer the problem to a different environment.

In countries like Britain or Holland, where land is relatively scarce, it is important not to solve a problem in the sea by creating a greater one inland. What we seek is the means of disposing of the wastes that will cause least environmental damage. That is known as the **Best Practicable Environmental Option**. It may mean that in some instances disposal of a waste to the sea, even though it causes some damage to marine resources, is preferable to any other method of disposal.

Environmental Impact Assessment

In most developed countries, waste discharges require some kind of official consent or licence. Whether or not a formal Best Practicable Environmental Option approach is used, the environmental consequences of a discharge are increasingly taken into account before consent is given. When a new discharge into the sea is proposed in North America, the discharger must provide a detailed **Environmental Impact Assessment** which predicts the effect the proposed discharge will have on the surrounding area. On the basis of this, a permit may be issued or denied, or modifications of the discharge required. In countries where formal Environmental Impact Assessments are not required, very much the same enquiry is made before a permit to discharge a waste to sea is granted.

The Precautionary Principle

The use of the Best Practicable Environmental Option or Environmental Impact Assessment does not guarantee that marine pollution will be avoided. This is unacceptable to some, particularly with regard to the North Sea. It is argued that we cannot safely predict the effect of new discharges to an area that already receives a very large volume of wastes. As a precaution, no wastes should be discharged into the sea unless it can be shown that they are harmless. This is the **Precautionary Principle**. This is a very stringent requirement since it is almost impossible to prove that a waste is harmless and, indeed, there are few wastes that will not cause some environmental adjustment where they are discharged.

Assessment of pollution

Practical solutions to the problems created by waste disposal in the sea require a knowledge of what damage is caused by a discharge and the way in which the damage is caused. In addition to measuring the impact of a pollutant in the sea, we also have to assess its effects, i.e. to decide upon its seriousness. A number of factors enter into this assessment, several of which cannot be measured in any direct way. The final assessment therefore involves judgements about which there may be legitimate disagreements, and this is where the controversy about marine pollution arises.

The seriousness of pollution damage

Danger to public health

First and overriding priority is given to controlling a pollutant which poses a threat to human health. In the sea, conservative pollutants (most immediately mercury), pathogenic bacteria and viruses, and radioactivity are in this category. A distinction must be made between the **perceived risk** posed by these and the **actual risk**: the perceived risk reflects the gravity with which the hazard is viewed by the general public, and this does not necessarily accord with the statistical reality which is the actual risk. The perceived risk from radioactivity is very high, that from traffic accidents very low, although the actual risks are overwhelmingly in the other direction. For the most part, human exposure to harm from marine pollutants is through eating contaminated seafood, and humans generally appear to be particularly sensitive to tainting or stale flavours in seafood, or even to the suggestion that seafood is tainted, and reject it. The perceived risk to health from marine pollution is therefore very high and, for the most part, only very low actual health risks are acceptable.

This draws attention to the fact that since the principal risk is from eating contaminated seafood, coastal communities whose diet includes a significant proportion of marine organisms are most at risk. This is particularly true of cumulative poisons such as mercury and it is not surprising that the best-known cases of mercury poisoning that originated from contamination of the sea should have involved fishing communities in Japan who subsisted almost entirely on food from the sea.

Mortality and morbidity

A good deal of pollution research is concerned with measuring the toxicity of substances which are, or may be added to the sea. The nature and the limitations of toxicity tests are described in Chapter 4. They are valuable in giving warning of potentially damaging substances, they may help rank substances in order of toxicity, or, when damage is known to be caused by a complex effluent, they may indicate which of the constituents is most likely to be responsible for it. Generally, however, they have little value in assessing the impact of a pollutant in any particular situation.

Sub-lethal damage or delayed mortality, particularly if it is not revealed until the next or a following generation, escapes detection in conventional toxicity tests. While it may be concluded that greater mortality will be caused by pollutant than that suggested by the LD_{50} measured in a short-term test, and the results of an investigation of sub-lethal effects provide a more urgent danger signal, they suffer the same shortcomings as other toxicity tests.

Whatever fears may be aroused by toxicity or sub-lethal studies in the laboratory, often the first sign and sometimes the only visible evidence of pollution is the sudden death of plants and animals in the affected environment. This may be only the tip of an iceberg; many more organisms may have been killed than were seen, particularly if there is an additional delayed mortality as a consequence of initial sub-lethal damage.

It is a relatively straighforward matter to assess the extent of damage when impounded fish and other species in mariculture are killed, because the fish or shellfish have a commercial value and compensation can be based, with reasonable justice, on the estimated cash value of the lost crop or the days of fishing lost. Very much greater difficulty is experienced when the casualties have no commercial value and attempts to quantify them in cash terms have, not unexpectedly, met with little success. A prime example was the assessment of damages when the tanker *Zoe Colocotroni* ran aground on the coast of Puerto Rico in March 1973, spilling part of its cargo of crude oil and contaminating some 20 acres of mangrove and shoreline. The shipowners were found guilty of negligence and in assessing damages the judge concluded that 92 109 720 animals had been killed and proceeded to assess their value by reference to the cost of replacements (or equivalent animals) if purchased from a biological supply house. This gave rise to the so-called 'ten-cents-a-barnacle' approach to assessing pollution damage. In the *Zoe Colocotroni* case, the court's judgment was later reversed by the appeal court on the grounds that the destroyed plants and animals would have replaced themselves in the natural course of events within a relatively short time. Indeed, most had done so by the time this decision was reached.

A far greater problem is created when the casualties can be regarded in some sense, as lost 'amenities'. Oiled sea birds and the death of seals and cetaceans fall in this category. While the strength of feeling—at least in some countries—caused by sea bird deaths from oil cannot be doubted, and is an indication of the strength with which this consequence of pollution is viewed, it has no scientific basis and cannot be quantified.

Population change

From a strictly biological point of view, when pollution causes the death of organisms, what matters is not the initial mortality, but the numbers and fate of the survivors.

Many marine organisms reproduce on a lavish scale: the American oyster produces 115 million eggs, and the cod 3–7 million eggs a year and it may breed several times during its life. Their reproductive strategy is geared to enormous pre-adult mortality and for such animals pollution-induced mortality may be totally insignificant beside such natural mortality. Indeed, it has been calculated that a major oil spill at the time and place of the main fish spawning in the North Sea, using 'worst case' assumptions at each stage, would result in a small reduction in the overall yield for only one year, and that reduction would be difficult to detect against the background of the normal year-to-year variation in fish catches. Practical verification of this can be seen in the lack of any detectable impact of oil from the *Torrey Canyon* on the Cornish pilchard fishery despite the heavy loss of eggs and larvae (p. 62).

Species with a different reproductive strategy, that of producing few young which lead a protected early life, may not have the capacity to withstand heavy juvenile mortality. This is particularly true of species with a boreal reproductive pattern which is characterized by erratic breeding, low fecundity, slow growth and late maturation, but a long adult life. The breeding biology of sea birds such as guillemots exemplifies this arctic pattern (p. 54).

The consequences of heavy mortality on a population depend on the population dynamics of the affected species. Additional losses through pollution may cause a large and persistent population reduction or be totally obscured by natural mortality. While the immediate mortality may be damaging for commercial or other reasons in some circumstances, from a biological point of view, unless the mortality has an impact at the level of the population it is of no consequence.

Assessment of damage

Even when it is established that pollution-induced mortality has resulted in a population decrease in a species, assessment of the seriousness of this damage depends on what species is affected. A reduction of the population of a species of commercial importance or 'amenity' value would be regarded much more seriously than a reduction in the population of an obscure worm. Apart from species that are of particular interest to humans, others which play a critical role in their ecological community and whose loss has repercussions in the community are of particular importance. The nature of the repercussions and the length of time they continue must also be assessed in making a final judgement of the seriousness of a pollution-induced change.

Key species in ecosystems

The reduction in the number of breeding auks in the colonies of south-west England and Wales during this century appears to have had no wider impact; and if the 1967 year-class of Cornish pilchards had been catastrophically reduced by *Torrey Canyon* oil and dispersants (see p. 62), although the commercial fishery might have suffered, there is no reason to suppose that it would have had widespread ecological repercussions. The loss of limpets (*Patella*) on some Cornish beaches, on the other hand, led to major ecological change with algal domination of the rocks for several years following the loss of the dominant herbivores (see

p. 48). A similar ecological succession was observed in the sub-tidal rocks of a small bay in Baja California following the wreck of the *Tampico Maru* (see p. 48).

A potentially far more serious ecological change following the severe reduction in numbers of a key species has been recorded on the coast of Nova Scotia. Here there was a stable kelp bed ecosystem with *Laminaria* spp. as the main producers responsible for about 90 per cent of the coastal production most of which was exported offshore as detritus. The coastal area supported a population of herbivores, mainly the sea urchin, *Strongylocentrotus droebachiensis*, which was preyed upon and controlled, chiefly by lobsters, *Homarus americanus*, and crabs, *Cancer*. The lobster population declined greatly after 1968 due, it was thought, to over-fishing rather than pollution. With the reduction in predation, *Strongylocentrotus* increased greatly in numbers, and considerable areas of *Laminaria* forest were destroyed. It might have been expected that having eaten out their food source, the sea urchins would then decline in numbers. They did not; instead growth and gonad production were both reduced (Fig. 10.1) and the population

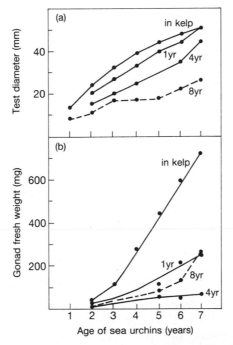

Fig. 10.1. Body growth and gonad development of sea urchins living in healthy kelp beds, and at sites where kelp has been destroyed by over-grazing one, four, and eight years previously.

remained large. Since areas denuded of *Laminaria* do not provide a suitable habitat for young lobsters and crabs, the population of these predators was not restored and the continued settlement of *Strongylocentrotus* remained unchecked. This urchin-dominated barren ground appears to be a new, stable configuration which could persist for a considerable time. The loss of primary and secondary production on substantial parts of the Nova Scotia coast which this represents is a serious threat to inshore, and possibly also to offshore fisheries.

Recovery and duration of impact

Recovery of a damaged community begins as soon as the pollution is abated. Restoration is from the vegetative growth of survivors *in situ*, immigration of mobile species from outside the area, and recolonization of the area by the distributive stages of the relatively sedentary species. Unless the damage has been slight, and for nearly all organisms except plankton and fish, the last of these restoration sources is overwhelmingly the most important. As the physical and chemical environment returns to normal, it will first become available to hardy species and later to those which can tolerate only a degree of contamination. Species that breed, or otherwise have distributive stages throughout much of the year are likely to recolonize before species with a restricted breeding season and re-establishment of the latter may be delayed for a year or more. The earliest colonizers which reproduce at most times of the year and are tolerant of adverse conditions are **'opportunistic' species** and they flourish in the absence of competition or predation. As the environmental conditions improve, a succession of other species may follow until a stable, balanced community is built up. The polychaete *Capitella capitata* is such an opportunistic species in muddy substrata and because of its tolerance of organic enrichment is regarded as a pollution **indicator species.**

Recovery of rocky substrata is more complex and less predictable, but follows a similar pattern of early colonization by opportunistic species and then the establishment of greater species diversity in the community. However, since rocky substrata are subject to greater wave action and water movement than soft substrata, the pollutant is more quickly removed from them and faunistic and floristic successions that can be observed during the recovery period are more concerned with the availability of colonizing stages and interactions between plants and animals, than with the steady improvement in environmental conditions.

With few exceptions, the most important consideration in assessing the environmental impact of pollution is neither the immediate mortality, nor the perturbation that this may cause to the population of the affected species or the community of which it is part, but the length of time the damage lasts. Damage that is restored within a few months is viewed quite differently than if it persists for years.

Experience following the wreck of the *Torrey Canyon* off the Cornish coast suggests that a considerable degree of recovery is possible on impacted rocky shores and is achieved within two or three years, but where dominant herbivores were killed and *Fucus* became established, it inhibited re-establishment of limpets for several years. Restoration of the former community took seven or eight years, and for some years after that subtle impoverishment of the fauna could still be detected. Recovery of damaged benthic communities is slow, possibly because in those physically quiet conditions, the pollutant is slow to be removed. An ecological succession continued for six years before the sub-tidal benthic community began to resemble that of unaffected sites following the reduction in oily discharges from a Finnish refinery. A similar period elapsed following an oil spill in Buzzard's Bay, Massachusetts, and even then the benthic fauna showed fluctuations and instability. Recovery of a benthic community in a sea loch in west Scotland, after discharges of organic waste from a pulp mill stopped, followed a similar course and time-scale.

In temperate waters, severe pollution damage may be restored within two to three years, but in most situations it is more likely that six to ten years will be required before something that may be regarded as a 'normal' community is re-established. Some investigators claim that subtle damage persists for even longer periods. We know much less about arctic and tropical waters, but there is reason to expect that recovery processes will be different in them from those observed in temperate regions.

Arctic fauna and flora are characterized by erratic reproduction and very low fecundity. The great majority of marine invertebrates lack distributive phases and either brood eggs and young or lay eggs in a protective attached capsule. In these circumstances, if a substantial area is damaged by pollution, recolonization will be very slow indeed because of the relative immobility of most marine organisms and their young. Terrestrial arctic habits are known to be extremely fragile and slow to recover, and the marine environment is likely to be the same. The time required for substantial restoration of pollution damage is unknown; 100 years has been suggested and could well be correct.

In the tropics, it is common for marine organisms to have pelagic larvae or other distributive phases, and breeding seasons are longer. Many species which breed only annually in temperate waters breed several times a year in the tropics, or tropical species have a much shorter generation time than their temperate water counterparts. It is also common for tropical species to have briefer lives than their temperate water or polar relatives. There is a much faster turnover in tropical ecosystems and colonizing forms are available at most, if not all times of the year. Pollution damage is therefore rapidly made good and instead of the decade that might be required for complete recovery in temperate waters, one to two years is probably a more realistic period in the tropics. There is some concern that mangrove forests and coral reefs may be more vulnerable tropical marine habitats than most, and not recover so readily from damage. Both mangroves and reef-building corals provide the physical conditions on which the large and varied associated fauna depend. Destruction of these structural elements would therefore have far-reaching consequences which might be prolonged. Whether these fears are justified remains to be discovered as more experience is gained of pollution impact in tropical waters—as unfortunately seems likely to happen.

Evaluation of change

Materials accidentally or deliberately discharged into, or otherwise reaching the sea, may cause greater or lesser biological change, of long or short duration. In evaluating this pollution impact, it is necessary to decide whether the change is desirable, undesirable, or neutral. There is a temptation to regard any change as necessarily undesirable, as most of the examples cited in this book would probably be judged. But if the ways in which the change is undesirable have to be enumerated and evaluated, it becomes less obvious that all change is necessarily for the worse.

The reduction or disappearance of auk colonies in Brittany and south-west England is biologically neutral. They are fringe populations which appear to be contracting as part of a northward recession of these birds in response to climatic change. This is small consolation to bird watchers in the affected areas for whom the decline in local sea bird populations is a loss of amenity. It has been possible to re-stock a colony of puffins on the coast of Maine with Canadian birds, and a similar re-stocking programme with Faeroese birds has been attempted in the Sept Iles Nature Reserve on the coast of Brittany. Positive conservation measures of this kind may, with difficulty, maintain a population of a formerly abundant species in protected areas like nature reserves, but cannot reverse a climatically induced trend.

The change from barnacle domination on some rocky beaches on the coast of Cornwall to an algal covering for a number of years as a consequence of killing grazing limpets with toxic oil dispersants constituted the greater part of the ecological 'disaster' following the wreck of the *Torrey Canyon*. The effected shores were in an area heavily dependent upon tourism and it is true that most tourists prefer barnacle-covered rocks to a beach covered with a dense growth of wet, slippery seaweed. From that point of view, the change was undesirable. It is less clear in what biological sense an alga-dominated beach, with its associated fauna, is more or less desirable than a *Patella–Balanus* assemblage.

The prolonged discharge of china clay waste into St Austell Bay in South Cornwall (p. 150) converted a considerable area of seabed from rock and gravel to a soft substratum. A hard-bottom fauna was replaced by a soft-bottom fauna of polychaetes and bivalves, with flatfish preying on them. This was damaging commercially because of the greater market value of lobsters than flatfish. From a biological point of view the change in the nature of the ecosystem was probably neutral.

Sea urchin domination of the Nova Scotia coast and destruction of the *Laminaria* forest as a consequence of over-fishing lobsters has resulted in a tremendous loss of production and this appears to be a long-term, if not permanent, change. Failure of the lobster fishery to recover after fishing for them stopped is commercially harmful. The loss of primary production is biologically damaging and, if it leads to an impoverishment of offshore waters, may inflict further commercial damage on offshore fisheries.

Chronic discharge of refinery effluent at Fawley, in Southampton Water, caused severe environmental deterioration measured by a reduction in species diversity in the salt marsh over which the oily effluent flowed (p. 54). Biologically, this change was very damaging, but in this case no human interest appears to have suffered as a result of it.

It would be possible to multiply these examples, but it is evident that environmental change resulting from the addition of wastes to the sea requires dispassionate consideration before the extent and nature of the damage it represents can be assessed. As shown below, ecosystem changes on at least the same scale and often of a similar nature to these induced by pollution sometimes occur from natural causes. These help to put pollution damage in perspective and have to be taken into account when making a final assessment of the significance of an observed ecosystem adjustment.

Problems of measuring pollution impact

Environmental science and many matters relating to pollution in the sea are contentious, and reputable scientists may arrive at quite different evaluations of marine pollution. When scientists disagree in this way it is usually because the question that is posed is not clearly defined, or else the data on which the answer is based are inadequate.

Much of the effort in pollution research has been directed towards collecting the following data:

- measuring the concentration of contaminants in the water column, sediments, and marine organisms;
- studying the behaviour, degradation, or modifications of these contaminants once they reach the sea;
- discovering their transmission through food webs;
- measuring their effects through toxicity tests of varying degrees of refinement and sophistication, and by studying the physiological, developmental, or behavioural responses of organisms exposed to them.

No-one would deny the importance of knowing the quantity and source of inputs to the marine environment and their behaviour after they get there, but the fact remains that much of the enormous volume of quantitative data that is being accumulated cannot be applied to any real-life situation.

When is recovery complete?

One area of disagreement among pollution scientists is the length of time required for the recovery of a damaged ecosystem; this is because of uncertainty about when recovery is complete.

Like the auks in southern England, a variety of British marine organisms are near the fringe of their geographical range. If a population of such a species is destroyed by pollution, its replacement is a matter of chance and as in the case of the sea bird colonies, it may not be replaced at all. The British Isles, lying near the southern limit of arctic and sub-arctic species and the northern limit of warm-water species, has many such precarious fringe populations. Ecologically, such populations are of little significance, though they may have considerable scientific interest. But it would be unrealistic to wait for the reappearance of such a species in a community before regarding recovery complete.

It is also unnecessary to wait for a balanced age structure to be re-established in a damaged community. Lobsters may live for 10 or 20 years; it would obviously be unrealistic to wait 20 years to get a few old specimens in the population. In any case, many marine species do not show regular recruitment and an actuarial age structure. Populations are often dominated by a particular year class and may show little new recruitment for several years (Fig. 10.2).

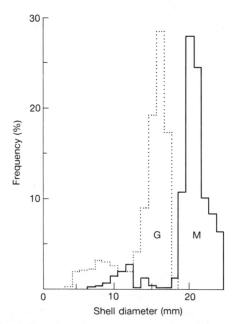

Fig. 10.2.   Size distribution of the intertidal gastropods *Gibbula* (G) and *Monodonta* (M) in a population on the Pembrokeshire coast, October 1981.

In other words, recovery is marked by the re-establishment of a healthy community, but not necessarily one that is identical in composition and age structure to the community that was present before the pollution damage. Unfortunately, we cannot define a healthy community in any rigorous way and hence there is room for considerable disagreement about the recovery of an ecosystem.

Natural population fluctuations

It is now becoming clear that there are very wide population fluctuations in marine ecosystems from purely natural causes, although the latter are rarely understood in detail. Not only is it extremely difficult to distinguish pollution-induced change against this fluctuating background, but sometimes the natural fluctuations are sufficient to produce a major ecological change comparable to that resulting from what would be regarded as a catastrophic pollution incident. The same problems are encountered in 'baseline' studies, many of which are conducted for too short a period to reveal the full range of fluctuations in the ecosystem, and therefore have little value.

The extent of this problem was dramatically shown by Dr J. R. Lewis following several years' continuous study of a rocky coastal area in north-east England. This beach with moderate wave exposure is equally suited for colonization by *Mytilus*, *Fucus*, and *Patella* with barnacles, each excluding the others. Its population changes are outlined below:

1965–6: A cold winter stopped the growth of the 1965 class of the carnivorous gastropod *Nucella lapillus* (the dog whelk), which was eaten in large numbers by the purple sandpiper, *Calidris maritima*.

1966–7: The winter was milder and the 1966 class of *Thais* fed and grew continuously, becoming too large to be eaten by the sandpipers. A large population of *Nucella* survived the winter, feeding on *Mytilus* and seriously reduced its numbers, so making space available for colonization by *Balanus*.

1967: Before *Balanus* had a chance to settle, there was an exceptionally heavy spatfall of *Mytilus* which smothered all other species on the rocks, filled the gaps and excluded *Balanus*. The *Mytilus* were so dense that there was severe competition for space, resulting in the mussels growing in unstable hummocks.

1969: In March, storms swept many *Mytilus* away, so leaving space once more for a *Balanus* settlement in June. But because the dense growth of *Mytilus* had excluded the limpet *Patella*, diatoms and ephemeral algae developed quickly and abundantly and prevented the settlement of *Balanus*. The rocks then became dominated by algae.

The important role of *Patella* in determining the rocky shore community is revealed by prolonged studies of the abundance of *Balanus* or *Mytilus* at individual sites in the same area (Fig. 10.3). The wide and erratic fluctuations are

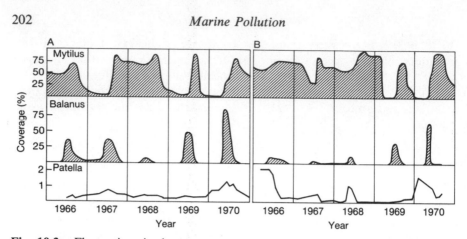

Fig. 10.3. Fluctuations in the percentage cover or rocks by mussels, barnacles, and limpets at two sites (A and B) on the north Yorkshire coast, 1966–70 *(Copyright FAO.)*

due to the operation of a variety of influences, but an important factor is the success of *Patella* recruitment. The success of recruitment in any year is not much affected by the number of gametes produced but is probably influenced by the climatic factors during the first few weeks after the young have settled on the shore (Fig. 10.4).

Fig. 10.4. Relation between the recruitment of limpets, *Patella vulgata*, and the duration of the frost-free period after spawning for the years 1967–73. *(Cambridge University Press.)*

Faunistic changes, also apparently due to the influence of climatic factors, have been detected in the benthic soft-bottom fauna off the Northumberland coast (Fig. 10.5). The assemblage of polychaetes in the community is a balanced one,

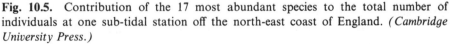

Gaining species 1972–6 (G)		Losing species 1972–6 (L)		Neutral species 1972–6 (Nt)
Species	Gain m^{-2}	Species	Loss m^{-2}	Species
Paraonis gracilis	238	*Spiophanes bombyx*	219	*Ampharete finmarchica*
Prionospio malmgreni	144	*Chaetozone setosa*	129	*Glycera rouxi*
Myriochele oculata	129	*Ampelisca tenuicornis*	112	
Thyasira flexuosa	115	*Amphiura filiformis*	50	*Goniada maculata*
Owenia fusiformis	104	*Nephtys hombergi*	31	
Magelona minuta	100	*Scoloplos armiger*	26	
Tharyx multibranchiis	27	*Rhodine gracilior*	24	
		Ammotrypane aulogaster	17	

Fig. 10.5. Contribution of the 17 most abundant species to the total number of individuals at one sub-tidal station off the north-east coast of England. (*Cambridge University Press.*)

but the relative abundance of different species changed as the average winter sea temperature increased from 6.25 °C in 1965–70 to 6.75 °C in 1971–6. Some species increased in abundance, others decreased, and a few were unaffected. No species was eliminated and there seems to have been little change in community production; the available energy was simply transferred from one suite of species to another which thrived better in response to the environmental change. Presumably if the former environmental conditions were restored there would be no obstacle to a return to the original balance of species in the community.

Long-term trends in the abundance of various species of north Atlantic zooplankton were detected in a 22-year Continuous Plankton Recorder Survey from 1948 to 1969 (Fig. 10.6). Some species, such as *Pleuromamma borealis* (a) and *Euchaeta norvegica* (b) showed an upward trend; *Spiratella retroversa* (j) and two calanoid (k) species showed a significant downward trend; *Temora*

Fig. 10.6.   Changes in the abundance of zooplankton species in the North Atlantic. The organisms are: (a) *Pleuromamma borealis*; (b) *Euchaeta norvegica*; (c) *Acartia clausi*; (d) *Temora longicornis*; (e) *Clione limacina*; (f) *Calanus helgolandicus* and *C. finmarchicus* stages V and VI; (g) *Metridia lucens*; (h) *Candacia armata*; (i) *Centropages typicus*; (j) *Spiratella retroversa*,; (k) *Pseudocalanus* and *Paracalanus*. *(Copyright FAO.)*

longicornis (d) and *Clione limacina* (e) showed no trend at all. All the species were subject to erratic and sometimes very large fluctuations in abundance—some fluctuations extending over several years—and the long-term trends would not have been detected without this very long time-series of observations. It has not been possible to relate these long fluctuations and trends to any known climatic or human factors.

   Historical records show that fish stocks have undergone the most dramatic changes. Good and bad periods for a number of herring stocks can be traced back for 600 years (Fig. 10.7) and seems to be related to climatic changes which were reflected also in the extent of the Arctic ice-cap, severity of winters, and similar phenomena. Shorter-term, wide fluctuations in the abundance of cod in the north-east Atlantic are known to have occurred during the last century and have been reflected in landings in the Lofoten Islands between 1860 and 1955, and in total landings for the north-east Atlantic cod fishery between 1945 and 1978 (Fig.

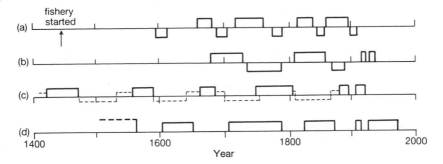

Fig. 10.7. Periods of good and bad years (above and below the line, respectively) for (a) Hokkaido herring, (b) Japanese sardine, (c) Bohuslan herring, (d) Atlanto-scandian herring.

10.8). The weight of fish landed depends on the amount of effort put into catching them, as well as upon their abundance, and there is no guarantee that fishing effort remained constant throughout these periods. The observed changes in landings have been so abrupt and so great, however, that enormous changes in fishery practices would have had to take place to account for them. Whatever changes of fishing effort may have taken place, they were certainly not on such a scale as to do this and there can be no doubt that the size of the annual catches gives a fair guide to the abundance of fish.

Several lessons can be learned from these studies of natural ecosystem fluctuations. Had a fisheries biologist begun to monitor fish stocks at the beginning of a downturn, he could well have seen over a period of five years or more, an apparently catastrophic and irretrievable collapse of the fishery. In the present climate of opinion, the collapse would no doubt be attributed to pollution, over-fishing, or some other human activity. A longer-term perspective indicates differently.

A survey made at a place which receives an effluent and is suspected of being polluted by it may well show signs of some change in the ecosystem. It would be natural to conclude that the local contamination caused the change, but unless the survey has been carried out over a long enough time and on a sufficient geographical scale, it is impossible to be sure. The change that has been detected may have been caused by pollution, but equally it may be part of a wider, natural change.

Even the worst pollution damage is no greater than, and often not much different from, ecosystem changes caused by natural events. A pollution-induced change is avoidable whereas a natural one is not, but fears that pollution is causing irreversible damage or that life in the seas is being destroyed appear to be exaggerated.

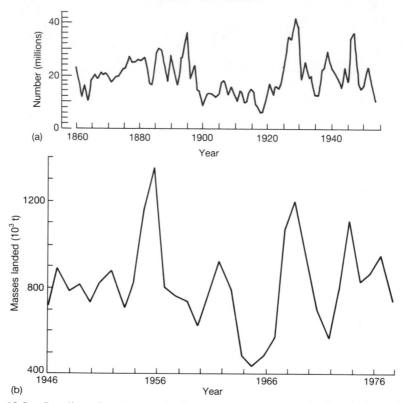

Fig. 10.8. Landing of cod (a) in the Lofoten fishery and (b) in the whole north-east Atlantic fishery.

Genetic variability

Marine invertebrates, in general, show a high degree of genetic variability and fish are genetically the most varied of all vertebrates. Views about the adaptive significance of this condition are still largely speculative, but there is some evidence that for some organisms genetic variability is an adaptation to surviving in unpredictably variable environments.

Estuaries undergo regular, predictable, short-term fluctuations with the tidal regime, and the organisms living there have been able to evolve physiological tolerance or regulatory mechanisms to survive the changes in their physical and chemical surroundings. This is not possible in environments where the changes are unpredictable or occur at intervals comparable to the life-span of the individual. If the species is genetically varied, however, there may be on-the-spot selection of whichever genotype is adapted to the conditions prevailing at the time. Some individuals do not survive a change in environmental conditions but are replaced by a different genotype that can do so.

Many marine habitats, instead of showing temporal variability where conditions change from time to time, show spatial variability and are a mosaic of microhabitats. In each microhabitat, there may be selection of larvae after they have settled, and the survivors be those genotypes that are adapted to a somewhat different set of conditions at each site.

There is great variation in size and structure of the stipe of *Laminaria* and while to some extent this is the result of a phenotypic response to water movements, there is also a strong genetic selection of different kinds of plants with different growth characteristics at different sites representing different microhabitats.

There are genetic differences affecting the withdrawal reflex of the small tubicolous polychaete, *Spirorbis borealis*, in open coast and sheltered rock pools only a few hundred metres apart, and in sunlit and shadowed pools.

Littorina populations show genetic differences with respect to shell shape, to withstand wave action and desiccation.

Oysters, *Crassostrea virginica*, from different sites show genetic differences in growth rate and salinity tolerance.

Selection of successful genotypes may also be one method of adjusting to contamination of the environment. There is, for instance, very rapid selection of alleles resistant to water-soluble components of crude oil in the copepod *Tisbe* (Fig. 10.9). Organisms living in Cornish estuaries contaminated with copper accumulate very large quantities of the metal (Fig. 5.6), such as would be lethal to members of the same species living in uncontaminated habitats. It is likely that copper-tolerant genotypes have been selected.

The same strategy for survival may underlie the success of opportunistic species, which show rapid population changes and are able to respond to environmental disturbances. The polychaete, *Capitella 'capitata'*, for example, is now known to be a complex of sibling species, several of which are themselves genetically very variable. With a reproductive pattern which ensures that colonizing young are available at most times of the year, one or other of the siblings or genotypes will be among the first animals to re-occupy a polluted area, and they will then flourish in the absence of competition.

One strategy for survival in the marine environment thus appears to be not so much an efficient machinery for tolerance or regulation so that the individual withstands environmental change, but a genetic flexibility that ensures that there is a range of genotypes available so that one can be selected to flourish in whatever environmental conditions are encountered. The existence of clusters of sibling species in *Capitella*, *Ophryotrocha*, and other polychaetes (and no doubt more are yet to be discovered) is an extension of the same phenomenon.

This phenomenon may explain the surprising robustness of many marine ecosystems to substantial levels of contamination from human activities. There may well be subtle adjustments, but if they involve the replacement of one genotype or sibling species by another, they are unlikely to be detected by ecologists. But this genetic flexibility poses practical problems for environ-

Fig. 10.9. Changes of gene frequency for two alleles in the copepod *Tisbe holothuriae* in oil-contaminated water.

mental studies and even greater difficulties for laboratory studies of pollution effects.

The selection of genotypes that will thrive in local conditions which vary within the space of a few metres or even on the opposite sides of the same boulder results in a mosaic. Figure 10.10 shows the growth rates of the algae *Laminaria* and *Agarum* at three places on the Nova Scotia coast of Canada. Although several hundred individual plants were measured in each sample, there are still standard deviations of ± 100 per cent of the mean values. With such inherent variability in the system, very large numbers of samples and measurements are needed to get valid results from an investigation. This is very time-consuming and has rarely been attempted. The variability is usually ignored or concealed, and because of this it is possible that many published results are meaningless.

The extreme complexity and variability of the natural environment makes pollution studies and monitoring in the field very difficult. This has led to a greater concentration on laboratory studies, but there the implications of the natural variability of marine organisms are even more serious. The whole philosophy of experimental biology is to obtain reproducible results under

Fig. 10.10. Seasonal growth of seaweeds (means and standard deviations) on the Nova Scotia coast.

known, controlled conditions. Experimentalists expect to get low standard deviations and, indeed, experimental results with a standard error of ± 100 per cent of the mean (as with the *Laminaria* growth rates) would be quite unacceptable. Genetic variation between the experimental organisms is to be avoided if at all possible, and the use of the laboratory white rat in genetically pure strains is an answer to that problem. In experimental pollution research, the equivalent has been the use of:

- a small number of 'standard' animals, as in toxicity tests, etc.; laboratory-cultured animals in preference to natural populations;
- genetically pure strains of *Ophryotrocha* developed in Sweden;
- cloned hydroids *Campanularia* which are, of course, genetically identical and have been used for the bioassay of pollutants in low concentrations.

This approach is in the best traditions of experimental biology, but if, as it now appears, genetic variability is an essential feature of natural populations and on-the-spot selection of successful genotypes the key to their survival in varying environments, experiments on genetically homogeneous animals may completely falsify the natural situation. It makes it virtually impossible to translate the results of such laboratory studies into real-life terms. Because of the inadequacy of our knowledge of the response of populations and communities of marine organisms to toxins and other stresses in the natural environment, experimental results at best cannot be interpreted and, at worst, may be totally misleading.

The place of science in pollution assessment

In all science, the right answers emerge only if the right questions are asked, and the answer to one question should lead to further questions. Pollution science is a little more complicated than that. Effluents discharged to the sea, or reaching it by a circuitous route, constitute pollution only when they have some undesirable effect, but that raises many questions about what is undesirable or acceptable, and to whom. Those questions are political, not scientific. The primary scientific questions relate to environmental change. Before a sensible political decision can be taken, it would be desirable to discover the nature, extent, and duration of an environmental change, and to identify the causative agents and possible remedies. That takes time, and political decisions often have to be taken without waiting for the scientific evidence to be gathered. Scientists must therefore be prepared to give a balanced appraisal on the basis of what is already known. Even when the necessary information is available, there is no guarantee that wise political decisions will be taken, but if scientists cannot even begin to provide it, the chance of adequate and economical remedial action being taken are remote indeed.

Pollution control measures are certainly not always undertaken on a rational basis. Because of the uncertainties of the situation, there is a temptation to play safe and remedial action is sometimes instituted before it is known if a waste product is damaging in any material way, or if the action taken will have a beneficial effect. Aroused, but ill-formed, public opinion may insist that 'something' be done to remedy a situation and an industry or government body be obliged to undertake completely useless activities so that they can be seen to be active. Such activities may be harmless, but they are expensive and wasteful of resources that might be better spent for some other purpose. In other respects, irrational attempts at pollution control may be positively harmful. Awareness of possible dangers stemming from pollution of the sea has encouraged the view that nothing should be discharged or dumped into it. But human society creates wastes and these have to go somewhere. Care has to be taken to ensure that in solving one problem we are not simply creating a worse one in a different environment. There is obviously a great need for scientific judgement in assessing pollution dangers and prescribing remedies, even if the scientist is only one contributor to the debate.

The pollution scientist is still faced with a number of fundamental problems. Some, possibly all, marine ecosystems show wide erratic, natural fluctuations caused by climatic or biological events which we are only just beginning to understand. They can be on a scale comparable to the effects of the most severe pollution damage, sometimes, as in the case of the loss of dominant herbivores, producing exactly the same kind of change or, as in the case of the exceptionally severe and prolonged winter of 1962–3 in Britain, causing even greater and more widespread change. These are only the most conspicuous natural fluctuations and no doubt there are constant adjustments in ecosystems on a much smaller scale. Against such a background it is difficult to detect pollution-induced changes unless they are very obvious and large or are clearly related to a single-point input. To get early warning of pollution damage, particularly from diffuse inputs, requires a much more detailed and profound knowledge of ecosystem structure and performance than we usually have. In addition to this need, it must be remembered that the collection of data is complicated by the genetic variability of organisms which is now coming to light. To collect reliable data in the field much larger numbers of samples and measurements are needed than would normally be contemplated. A concentration on the simpler and more controlled situation in the laboratory is no solution to this problem if, as sometimes seems likely, the laboratory studies lack realism and give misleading results or, at best, yield results which can be applied to a real-life situation only with the greatest difficulty.

Because of these difficulties it is understandable that scientists should have turned attention much more to short-term surveys, and to experimental studies and chemical monitoring of the pathways, concentrations, and fates of additions to the marine environment for which sensitive analytical equipment can be used. Unfortunately it is now becoming clear that although we need the results of these kinds of investigations, they do not provide the answer to the crucial question of the safe limit of effluent discharge to particular areas of sea. The situation is not likely to change until we achieve a better balance between ecological and experimental studies of the consequences of marine pollution. When we have a more secure knowledge of the response of ecosystems to stress, it will be possible to give a focus to studies in the laboratory and allow that work to produce results that can be applied to real situations in the sea.

Further reading

There is an enormous scientific literature, of variable quality, on matters relating to pollution in the sea, and a wide range of popular books on environmental matters, although the latter are mostly concerned with putting forward a particular point of view. The following titles give more technical detail on subjects discussed in this book and guide the reader to important works in the scientific literature.

Clark, R. B. (ed.) (1987). *The waters around the British Isles: their conflicting uses.* (Oxford University Press). This book examines in detail commercial activities in and around western European waters, conflicts of interest that arise, and the national and international legal regimes that regulate these activities.

Cormack, D. (1983). *Response to oil and chemical pollution.* (Applied Science, London). At the time this book was written, Dr Cormack was Chief Scientific Adviser to the UK Marine Pollution Control Unit, responsible for co-ordinating the response to major pollution accidents. The book deals comprehensively with the merits of the various methods employed to deal with oil and chemical spills.

Gerlach, S. A. (1981). *Marine pollution: diagnosis and therapy.* (Springer, Heidelburg). This is an English translation of a book first published in 1976, with some updating. It is useful for giving the German experience of marine pollution not usually found in English books, but there have been developments in German attitudes and improvements in knowledge since the book was published and it is now a little dated.

Greenpeace (1987). *Coastline: Britain's threatened heritage.* (Kingfisher Books, London). A beautifully illustrated and very readable tour around the British coastline, examining local environmental problems in a balanced way.

Johnson, R. (ed.) (1976). *Marine Pollution.* (Academic Press, London). This is solid reading, but detailed and, despite its age, still authoritative. The chapters on fisheries, oil pollution, metals, and sea birds are particularly good.

Marine Pollution Bulletin (Pergamon, Oxford). This monthly journal contains news and articles about marine pollution around the world. Many of the articles are designed for a non-technical audience.

Newman, P. J. and Agg, A. R. (eds) (1988). *Environmental protection of the North Sea.* (Heinemann, London). This volume includes contributions and discussions at an international conference on the North Sea in the run-up to the Ministerial meeting held in November, 1987. The coverage of subjects and attitudes is comprehensive and authoritative.

Pentreath, R. J. (1980). *Nuclear power, man and the environment.* (Taylor & Francis, London). A useful introduction to radiobiology and radiological protection, although only a small part of it is concerned with the marine environment.

Royal Commission on Environmental Pollution. The reports of the Royal Commission give clear, non-technical accounts of the environmental problems under review, as well as discussing remedies. All the reports are very thorough and authoritative. The following deal, at least in part, with the marine environment. Third report (1972) *Pollution in some British estuaries and coastal waters*. Sixth report (1976) *Nuclear power and the environment*. Eighth report (1981) *Oil pollution of the sea*. Tenth report (1984) *Tackling pollution: experience and prospects*. Twelfth report (1987) *The best practicable environmental option*. (All published by HMSO, London.)

Index